RODEO STORIES II

© Roger Langford

CHIMP ROBERTSON

Rodeo Stories II

NEW FORUMS PRESS INC.

Published in the United States of America
by New Forums Press, Inc. 1018 S. Lewis St.
Stillwater, OK 74074
www.newforums.com

Copyright © 2015 by Chimp Robertson

Cover Photo, Credit JackieJensenPhotography.com (color photo)
Horse, Lunitic Fringe

All rights reserved. No part of this publication may be reproduced or transmitted in any form or by any means, electronic or mechanical, including photocopy, or any information storage or retrieval system, without permission in writing from the publisher.

Library of Congress Cataloging-in-Publication Data Pending

This book may be ordered in bulk quantities at discount from New Forums Press, Inc., P.O. Box 876, Stillwater, OK 74076 [Federal I.D. No. 73 1123239]. Printed in the United States of America.

ISBN 10: 1-58107-283-X
ISBN 13: 978-1-58107-283-9

Because of the dynamic nature of the Internet, any web addresses or links contained in this book may have changed since publication and may no longer be valid. The views expressed in this work are solely those of the contributors and do not necessarily reflect the views of the publisher, and the publisher hereby disclaims any responsibility for them.

CONTENTS

Dedication v
Life's Gamble vii
They Were There. This Is Their Story ix
In Memory Of x
When The Good Times Are Over xi
Preface xiii
Acknowledgements xv
Part I 1
Part II 69
Part III 143
Part IV 213
About the Author 284

Rodeo Stories II

DEDICATION

This book is dedicated to Trey Allen, a cowboy, a cowboy poet and a good friend. For some twenty years now, Jack Trey Allen has been writing and reciting cowboy poetry. He started out gathering intel early in life as a bull rider/bullfighter and graduated to shoeing horses and starting colts. And to those in the know, this should explain a great deal. At the point he began his family however, the conclusion was reached that three meals a week and Copenhagen made less than desirable home conditions and he settled into a real job near the present day metropolis of Hooker, Oklahoma,

While earning a regular paycheck he kept his hand turned at starting colts, shoeing horses, day working, etc. It was during this time he became intimate with a little known group called, "Corporate America." Thirteen years of that and he packed his family up and headed for the mountains of south central Colorado near Canon City and has been a full time cowboy ever since.

Trey has managed some of the biggest ranches in the country including the 60,000 acre Stirrup Ranch west of Pueblo. For nine years Trey has managed the Moyer Ranch in the northern Flint Hills of Kansas, south of Manhattan. When asked about the possibilities of, "Lightin' a shuck," he said, "Pack rats set up shop in my tipi and cut my bedroll up into little tiny pieces. Sure hate to disturb their little enterprise..." Recon he'll stay put.

Trey has performed from the Gulf Coast of Alabama to North Dakota and from Missouri to Utah. He was one of four event winners at the first Cowboy Poetry Rodeo and was fortunate in subsequent National Cowboy Poetry Rodeo events. In 2011,

Kansas hosted the first annual State Cowboy Poetry competition and a win there offered Trey the opportunity to perform for the Gubernatorial Entourage and he considers that a career highlight. Durango and Sierra Vista have been among his favorite gatherings and he plans on visiting a few more gatherings in the future.

Trey has two albums: "Cowpoke" (2002) and "Lowly Cowboy." (2006) He is currently working on an album, "The Remnant Gather," that will be available in 2015. This album will feature a piece with Geff Dawson and Trey's favorite Buckarette musician, his daughter Shandee Allen.

"There will never be any way for me to thank all the people who have touched my life through cowboy poetry. I have been blessed in many ways so I will say the only thing that comes to mind…MUCHO GRACIAS!

Trey Allen
Photo by Brian Schoenfish

LIFE'S GAMBLE
Trey Allen

I sure don't like to gamble, he said.
'Less it's a real shore thing.
But, the way I've lived life I found this to be true
Those are few and a long ways between
They say I got lucky that night down in Ft. Worth
When I hung up to that bad hookin' bull
I walked away from the wreck with a crick in my neck
And this stainless steel plate in my skull.
I bucked the odds that day on the mesa
When lightning gave one final crack
Kilt nine head of heifers and one damn good horse
And three days that I'll never get back
The day that ol' bull ran under my horse
I's perty sure my final bet had been placed
But, I rolled my hole card and called on a friend
And, it turned out I's holdin an ace
Or, the day that colt slipped in the shale
It was lookin' like we'd both rolled craps
But, he caught his feet and blazed a new trail
And, we came through by the skin o' my chaps.
Jack Daniels dealt me a perty sorry hand
Jimmy Beam, he anteed the pot
George Dickle was there the night I went bust
And I still own 'em for what I ain't got.
And, boys as I sit on the edge of my bed every mornin'
My old body it creaks and it groans.
I figger just wakin' up, hell, that's a gamble enough
Kinda like rollin' the bones
But, I do realize that with every sunrise

I get to place one more bet
So I try and stack the odds by givin' thanks to my God
Who's seen to it that I ain't crapped out yet.

treyallen44@gmail.com
785-477-3514
www.trey-allen-amigos.com

They were there. This is their story.

Allen Howard   Andrew Dally   Andy Taylor   Arlene La Mar   Bill Thorpe   Barney Brehmer   Bill Putman   Barry Bunch   Brad Besancan   Bobby Dykes   Bobby Dobbins   Bret Corley   Bruce Ford   Buster Brake   Bobby Cooper   Brad Ewell   Bubba Boyd   Cary Culbertson   Charlie Thompson   Clint Ford   Chimp Robertson   Clay Tom Cooper   Clarence Gipson   Charlie Cook   Charles Case   Curt Brown   Dale Woodard   Danny O'Haco   D. J. Gaudin (Kajun Kid)   David Schlidt   Debbie Garrison   Denny Weir   Dickey Cox   Dennis Luton   Don Mellgren   Don Endsley   Doug Munsell   Dude Smith   Dave Sampsel   Dan Neal   Floyd Trayner   Greg Doering   Janie Liles   Jay Foscalina   Jeana Day   Jerry LaValley   Joe Latona   Jerry Gustafson   Jesse CR Hall   Jim Liles   Jim Sowles   Jon Vick   John J. Sumerlin   Johnny Rivera   Joe Foscalina   Jimmy Blotz   Joe Liles   Kevin Busche   Ken Judge   Lee Jones   Lori Shoulders   Larry Brady   Les Hood   Mark Whitaker   Mickey Young   Mark Trujillo   Monty Penny   Pam Minick   Myles Culbertson   Nick Hite   Red Doyal   Richard Flechsig   Richard Murray   Ronnie Wells   R.j. Preston   Rome Wager   Ron Warr   Ronnie Van Winkle   Roy Barnes   Steve Davis   Sean Baker   Shari Kroft   Scott Fletcher   Sharon Camarillo   Skeebo Norris   Steve Scot   Smokey Brown   Tommy Tarpley   Terry Ward   Troy Vaira   Trey Allen   Terri Abrahamson   Tim Sample   Toni Guirino   Wayne Whitehead   Wes Ward

A Special Thanks to Cowboy Artist, Roger Langford
And, to Rodeo Photographers;
Jackie Jensen   (JackieJensenPhotography.com)
Dudley Barker   (dudley@dudleydoright.com)
Mike Rastelli   (Mrastelli@hotmail.com)

IN MEMORY OF MY DAD AND MY BROTHER

Alton and Jack Robertson

Rest in Peace, cowboys

WHEN THE GOOD TIMES ARE OVER
Chimp Robertson

He was still in his teens the first time he rode
The years went by quickly and a few times was all he got throwed
The crowd always jumped to their feet when he made a ride
And he'd walk back smilin' at spur marks he left on their hide
Yeah, he was a cowboy, the best rider I've ever seen
He rode with the best of 'em all, hard-twisted and lean
The perfect example of how you'd like your son to be
A Champion of Champions and he was a hero to me
But, when the good times are over and boys we all know they will end
It's time to get ready and adjust to the parting of friends
Step out of the spotlight, stay home with the wife and the kids
Sit down by the fireside and talk about things that we did
Yeah, lean back and tell of the wild crazy things that we did.

PREFACE

The start of this book corresponded with the increasing interest in rodeo as a media attraction. People were ready to hear from cowboys and cowgirls twenty to forty years after they'd competed in arenas around the country and **RODEO STORIES II** capitalizes on that popularity.

Their effort is clearly seen because of the authority from which they stake their claim to tell ***RODEO STORIES II.*** They were there.

There were young sunburned faces against old wooden chutes. There was laughter out back of the arena when the competition was over. There was excitement, fun, and humor, and there was blood, sweat, and pain. ***RODEO STORIES II*** provides a voice from the hearts of cowboys and cowgirls who competed in those arenas. These are their stories in their own words.

This is not meant to be a finely tuned effort or intellectual manual. These cowboys and cowgirls tell their stories in starts and stops, spurts and hitches. Memories long stored away are bought to life and written down to be heard, many times for the very first time.

To everyone who shared their memories with me I can't thank you enough. The stories you told are pure gold, and I've put them down just as you told them to me—well, I did touch up the grammar on a couple, otherwise, these are your stories and I'm honored you allowed me to tell about your experiences.

These cowboys and cowgirls do not think of themselves as heroes; they think of themselves as hard-riding, fun-loving, common folks. Well, they are right. That is rodeo. That is the rodeo experience in America. It's all about the memories and the good times.

ACKNOWLEDGEMENTS

This project received help and encouragement from cowboys and cowgirls from California to Florida, from Canada to Texas, from Arizona to New Jersey, and from wives, husbands, and traveling buddies.

And from the people of this book, those cowboys and cowgirls who opened up their hearts and let me carry their memories around for a while.

And in memory of the many cowboys and cowgirls whose stories could not be part of this book, but whose spirit is with us:

To all I have mentioned here, I say, "Thank you."

If mistakes are found I'll take the blame, but if readers will count those mistakes as respect and admiration for the cowboys and cowgirls who sent in their stories, I'll be OK with that…

© Roger Langford

Part I

1. Allen Howard: Duane and Alvin
2. Wes Ward: Lane and I
3. Buster Brake: Cowboy'n Military Style
4. Sean Baker: The Morning the Biscuit Makers Wouldn't Come to Work
5. Dave Sampsel: I Think Salinas Was My Town
6. Red Doyal: Larry Kane Story
7. Janie Liles: After Winning, The Party Is On Janie Liles
8. Jon Vick: Bull Fighter
9. Andy Taylor: The Best Straw Hat I Ever Had
10. Smokey Brown: Bareback and Bulls
11. Charles Case: They Called Me Hippie
12. Richard Flechsig: Watch Him, Dick. He Bites
13. Denny Weir: Rocks and Car Parts in the Arena
14. Larry Brady: Birdell, Arkansas
15. Jerry Gustafson: The Life of a Rodeo Photographer
16. Barry Bunch: Me and Jacky Gibbs
17. Steve Scott: Me and Ellie
18. Clarence Gipson: Summer Of '94
19. Richard Flechsig: The Mount Out
20. Don Mellgren: Panguitc, Utah
21. Les Hood: Les Is More
22. Jim Liles: Swimming With the Snakes
23. Bobby Cooper: A Man of His Word
24. Terry Ward: The Ward Arena
25. D.J. Gaudin: The Kajun Kidd
26. R.J. Preston: Crackin' Out
27. Floyd Traynor: Dad and Uncle Jack

Rodeo Stories II

28. Myles Culbertson
29. Jimmy Blotz: The Big Lie
30. Brad Ewell: Me & Doug
31. Troy Vaira: Borrowed Gear and Rubber Soled Farmers Boots
32. Dan Neal: Hitchin' Rides
33. Ronnie Van Winkle: A Rodeo Cowboy's Testimony
34. Jan Barby Payne: Canton, Kansas
35. Pam Minick: Careful Who You Meet
36. John Sumerlin: Rosser's Camp Pendleton

ALLEN HOWARD
DUANE AND ALVIN

Duane and Alvin Nelson were at the Ride of Champions that was held in Dickinson, North Dakota. They were standing behind the chutes waiting for the draw, to see what horses they had drawn. When the draw was posted Alvin had drawn a horse that really bucked, but the only problem was, this horse had been worked in the harness at a young age.

He was very square shouldered and he was noted for jerking the riders real hard the first jump out of the chute when they tried to mark him out and would buck them off. Alvin was no fool so he just reached down and put his spurs on the opposite feet and went on to make a qualified ride and won the day money on that horse.

Duane was a young man riding bulls in New York and got hung up and hurt pretty bad on one of his bulls. He figured he could tough it out, but the pain got so bad he decided he needed to go to the hospital. He asked around and the guys told him there was a hospital just up the street so Duane, hardly being able to walk, slowly headed up the street and walked in this door.

Coming in from the outside it was dark in there so he took a minute to let his eyes adjust. He could see all the carts lined up in row so he thought he would check one out. There was a name tag on the end of each cart and when he read the card it give the person's name, date, and time off death, and when he lifted up the cover there was a person's feet.

Realizing he was in a morgue and as bad as he was hurt he all but ran out of there, back to the building the rodeo was being held in and said that being in the morgue was enough for him so he never did go to the hospital.

WES WARD
LANE AND I

I remember one story about Lane Frost and I back in 1980. We both competed at the National High School Finals Rodeo in Yakima, Washington. Lane and I, our moms, and Lane's younger brother Cody, all drove a car from Oklahoma to Washington. It was the biggest stage of our young rodeo careers.

Lane won second in the bull riding there and won a buckle and I won the second go in the bare back riding and won a nice plaque. We were two little cowboys on top of the world and that was quite a road trip.

On the way home we stopped by the ProRodeo Hall of Fame in Colorado Springs. The Hall of Fame hadn't been opened very long. The Pikes Peak ProRodeo was also going on and we stayed around and watched the performance that night. I remember after the Rodeo that night we went down behind the chutes. We went down to talk to some of our heroes that were there that night, but we really didn't find anyone who wanted to visit with us kids.

It really seem to bother Lane because on the way home in the backseat he said, "You know, Wes. When we get to be big time rodeo stars we're gonna take time to talk to the kids and sign autographs, aren't we?" I just agreed with him, but it really bothered him.

I look back now and truly believe Lane got Revelation that night from the LORD, on how to be a true Champion. And, now we know the rest of the story don't we? I also remember Jerry La Valley caught a ride with us that night from Colorado Springs back to Oklahoma. That was quite a road trip for us young cowboys. Blessings

BUSTER BRAKE
COWBOY'N MILITARY STYLE

While in the Marine Corps I had two friends that at some point became family. Those two brothers were Jack and Eldon. Eldon was the bull rider of the bunch while Jack and myself both rode bareback horses. We cowboy'd as much as the military powers that be would let us which was kinda difficult at times because we were all in different units. Jack was over on the main side Camp Pendleton while Eldon and I were at Camp San Oro together, but were in different units. This little story is about a couple of those times when our superiors had some unseen reason for Eldon and I to stay off the rodeo trail.

Eldon had just gotten promoted so he had to get a new military ID card. We were gonna go out to the Countryside Bar in Oceanside, California and celebrate his new rank. I was standing outside the NCO quarters wait'n on him when I seen him walk'n my way. I couldn't figure out what the hell he was doing with his hand. Now, I have to tell you this before the story goes any further. Marine Corps ID cards were covered in a soft pliable plastic laminate, but they had recently changed it to a hard crisp plastic covering.

What Eldon was doing with his hand was bending his new ID card between his thumb and fore finger and he kept put'n up to his nose and smell'n it. When he got to me, he said and I quote, "This thing smells funny. Here smell it," and he put it up close to my nose so I sniffed and he flipped one side of it out and since it was laminated with the new hard plastic cover it damn near cut the end of my nose off. He thought it was hilarious, but me, not so much. Needless to say I called him a couple of pet names and not one to let a little blood stop the good time, we went out and done a little party'n.

Well, it was hard for me to forget his funny little prank so I waited about a month in order to set him at ease and to dish out a little pay back. Again, with the powers that be having us stay off the rodeo trail, Eldon and I had planned to meet up after we got off work to go out and do a little party'n. Before he showed up I went down to parking lot and took a sharpie marker and put a bunch of dots on the outside of the passenger side windshield. I wiped them down until they were kinda translucent then I went back to my room and waited on Eldon.

Eldon shows up and we jumped in my green 67 Cadillac and headed to town. Now, it's quite a little drive to main side Camp Pendleton and about the half-way point there is a straight stretch of road that everyone hauls ass on. So, just before we get to this straight away spot I reach over and try rub'n those translucent spots off the windshield.

Of course, they don't come off because they are on the outside. About the time we hit that straight away I asked Eldon what the spots are. I started speed'n up and he reaches up to try and wipe them away. They won't come off so he puts his face closer to get a better look. Now, the brake pedal on a '67 Cadillac is about 8 inches wide and when he got up close for his better look I stomped both feet on that 8 inch wide brake pedal and brought that Caddie to a screetchin' halt.

He ended up with a goose egg on his noggin the size of Texas and couldn't wear his cowboy hat all night which was only fair because I had to wear big white bandage on my nose the night he damn near cut it off. Oh, yeah I almost forgot. He called me a couple pet names too, just about the time the screechin' stopped.

SEAN BAKER
THE MORNING THE BISCUIT MAKERS WOULDN'T COME TO WORK

It was in the summer of 1991, about 4:30 AM, in a Hardees parking lot in Winterset, Iowa. For later reference in this story this is the birthplace of John Duke Wayne. There were three vehicles full of cowboys waiting to get a biscuit and a slab of meat, kicking a hackie sack, chewing snuff, and talking about some of the bad ones they had twisted, along with a few other cowboy things.

Not really for sure now who all was in that parking lot, but Heman, Micah, RC, JT, and myself, were among the cowboys at the biscuit gathering that morning. Suddenly, out of no where one of Winterset's finest came squalling to a stop and began to inquire as to why in the hell all us damn cowboys were gathered in that parking lot.

With a broad smile Heman started to explain how we all had been entered in the rodeo earlier that evening and that the stock had all been feed and bedded down for the night and that we were just waiting on a biscuit. And also, that we were moving on to Somewhere, Indiana for a performance the next afternoon.

The Officer said, "The biscuit makers are the ones who had called and said there was a rowdy looking bunch in the parking lot and that they were too scared to come to work. And, that we needed to move our gathering to some place else, preferably some where outside of town until they were open for business.

Heman said, with that smile still plastered on his face, "Well, I'll be damned. I bet the Duke is rolling over in his grave right about now when a biscuit maker won't come to work just because some cowboys are gathered in the parking lot, especially in the birthplace of the King of the Cowboys."

DAVE SAMPSEL
I THINK SALINAS WAS MY TOWN

It was a cold California night in 2001 at Salinas and I, like a bunch of other guys, made the rookie type mistake thinking California in July would be warm so I forgot a jacket. I drew bull #77 Jam-a-lot, a high horned red bull that was real showy and

93 points later I won the long round and drew a bull in the short go called Red Bull.

I think I was last to go and only Cory Navarre had stayed on in the short round and was scored like 85. I knew I only needed a score because I was ahead of the game by a few points. With a newly purchase sweatshirt under my sponsor shirt to stay warm, I rode him for 91 points and a total of 184 on 2 head and that is a record that still stands

Another unique twist was the PBR screwing my payday again by promoting a so-called challenge. Salinas had $40,000 added money until about a week prior, then at the last minute decided to have a $10,000 challenge between Ty and Adriano. These two guys were already entered and received $5000 each to promote the challenge. They simply got on the bulls they had drawn and with a smokescreen PBR tactic, said it was a "challenge."

Well, neither of them even stayed on, but it did effect my payday especially when I had already won both rounds and the average. 40%. Well, I still won a big chunk and a buckle, but it wasn't the only buckle I was going to win there. I split the win again in 2003, which rather than flip for the buckle I gave it to Jason Bennett since I had one already.

Then, once I went back to rodeoing I won the rodeo in 2007. In 8 yrs of competing in Salinas, I won a round or the average 6 out of 8 yrs. I think Salinas was my town. The Salinas rodeo buckle seems to be everyone's choice and most recognized, second only to a World Champion buckle and I may be the only guy to have both the PBR and PRCA buckles.

RED DOYAL
LARRY KANE STORY

This story was story told to me by Mac McDougal about Larry Kane. They were close friends and Mac spent some time on Larry's and his mother's ranch. According to Mac, Larry and his mother were the only ones at the ranch. One night he and Larry were catching wild horses. Mac said he was on an outcrop in the rough country and he could see Larry chasing a horse.

Just as they were going out of sight both horses fell, turning end over end. Mac headed over where they fell thinking Larry might be dead. It took him a while to find the way over where Larry and the horses were. When he got there the horse Larry was chasing just lay there tied down and Larry was chasing another one.

Later at supper Larry and his mother were talking about when he was getting on some practice horses and didn't show up for supper she would go out looking for him. One night she found Larry still at the practice pen, in the chute, under a horse that had fallen over backward on him. He had been there awhile, but was ok. Larry's mom opened the gate and let the bronc out and they saw this as being very funny.

One summer I was making a run with my son Royd. He was going to a couple of rodeos in Colorado and I thought I'd see some of my old friends. Royd drove all night and I started driving in New Mexico.

When we stopped at Clayton, New Mexico to fill up with gas, Royd was asleep in the back seat. I filled the tank, paid the attendant, got back in and hit the road to Raton. When I asked if he wanted to stop and get something to eat, I realized he wasn't there. He had gotten out to go to the rest room while I was paying for the gas. Heck, he had the highway patrol guys after me. It's a long back track to Clayton from Raton and we missed a performance he was up in Durango, Colorado. Royd never asked me to go with him again!!!!!!

JANIE LILES
AFTER WINNING, THE PARTY IS ON JANIE LILES

In the early 70's everyone in our gang won at the Apache Junction, Arizona rodeo so of course it was party time. We loaded up and headed to the bar. When we got there it was empty so we had the entire place for ourselves. The guys started playing pool and us gals got a drink and proceeded to chat.

Well, one of the guys dropped a glass and broke it so the bartender then chose not to serve any of the guys anymore. Well, no problem because us gals just started buying their drinks. Once the bartender caught on to what we were doing she cut all of us off.

Well, I had had a drinkie poo or two and proceeded up to the bar and I picked up a glass and showed it to the bartender and told her all because of one of these she had cut all of us off? Now, I thought about throwing the glass at her, but thought better of it so I threw it at the back bar.

A bull rider standing next to me looked at Jim and Jim just shrugged his shoulders so the bull rider picked up a bar stool and threw it and cleaned out the entire back bar. The bartender then pulled out a gun and pointed it at us shaking like a leaf. Jim sobered up real quick and started getting everyone out and into the cars and we made it just fine to the next bar.

Oh, forgot, one of our friends had his leg in a cast and was on crutches. He made it to his car just as the police showed up. He fed them some long story and the police just told him that he had best not come back to this bar. He caught up to us and had some choice words for us leaving him. Don't know if the police knew what damage we did to the bar. That's one we got away with. The names have been omitted to protect the not so innocent.

JON VICK
BULL FIGHTER

On Sundays, when I was not away at a rodeo I would drive out to Scrugg's practice arena in Shiloh, Texas, a local stock contractor. A lot of the local bull riders would have jackpots and when I could I would fight bulls there for the boys. There was a sixteen year old cousin to an older bull rider riding that day and we simply called him Billy Bones.

Billy drew a very hot tempered cross bred we called Cross-Eyed Mary. Billy nodded for the gate and as usual the bull spun to the left and as the ride progressed I knew Billy was headed for the well. Instinct proved correct because down he went, his head meeting the bulls and Billy was knocked out cold.

Being the only bull fighter there I freed his hand from the rope and his body dropped lifeless to the arena sand. Cross-Eyed Mary was not done just yet and he charged at Billy who was out cold. All I had time to do was to throw myself on top of Billy's body to shield him.

Old Cross-Eye came over right on top of us and I could feel his hooves, hear his snort, and feel his breath. Then, the first charge was over. I glanced up only to see Cross-Eye coming at us again. I felt his hooves and my body being shook, then the second charge was over.

I looked up and again Cross-Eye was still not done so he made a third charge over the top of us, his head bumping mine and I could feel the hooves. Mike Scrugg's, a good man on a horse, finally roped Old Cross-Eye and pulled him to the catch pen. I stood up to see how many bones I had broken and there was none, not even a scratch. Billy however, was still out cold.

Billy's cousin and a few others placed him in a truck and tore out for Taylor some twenty miles away, the closest medical treatment around. I finished out that day, went home and prayed that night for Billy, still not knowing the medical outcome. Two days passed and on Tuesday at about three o clock in the afternoon there was a knock at the door.

I opened the door and to my utter surprise it was Billy, dripping in sweat and holding a live chicken. I invited him in to cool off and gave him some ice water. I said, "What's going on, Bill?"

He proceeded to tell me that after he came out of the coma he had a severe concussion, and that he was told how I threw my self on top of him to shield him from further harm and that he was bringing me a chicken to repay me for saving his life.

Jon Vick

I told Bill that it wasn't necessary and that I was just glad he was safe, but Billy insisted on the chicken as a gift so I couldn't say no. We visited for about thirty minutes and Billy said he needed to head for home so he could be there by ten. I said, "Why would it take you so long?" Billy said, "Well, I walked all the way over here from Taylor." We lived in Round Rock at that time and Taylor was a good twenty eight to thirty miles away. Billy said he didn't have a license to drive, so needless to say I drove him back home.

On the drive back home by myself I thought there was no amount of money, no gold buckle, nothing any one could do that would ever match that. It made me swell with a pride I've never felt before or since and it took a Billy, a bull, and a chicken, to re mind me of the importance of being a rodeo clown.

ANDY TAYLOR
THE BEST STRAW HAT I EVER HAD

One of the things we'd do every year at the Houston Astrodome Rodeo was go to the American Hat Factory and pick us out a good straw hat for the summer. Bill George, a great rodeo hand from the previous generation was from Canadian, Texas *(where we were from)*, and he'd look me and Mont *(my brother)* up every year we were at the Astrodome. We'd have a beer or two and an enjoyable visit. Bill and his wife owned The American Hat Co. there in Houston.

I was traveling with Russ Baize this particular year and as usual we went out to the factory to pick us out a hat. Oh, and we'd get a heck of a deal on those hats, too. Of course it's been some years since we did that, but we were buying good straw hats for $6 that'll now cost you near $100.00. I picked through about 20 of the Bangora style and found the best straw hat of the bunch. Russ did the same. I creased mine just right and dang it looked good. To this day it was the best straw hat I ever had.

We left Houston to ride in Montgomery, Alabama. Tommy Sheffield, a rodeo clown and bullfighter and good friend had an act back in those days where he'd buy a real cheap little hat of some kind and put it on a committee man. His act was about *'cleaning'* the hat. Of course it was all staged, *(*usually...but not this night!)*. The committee man would act like he was mad and he'd chase Tommy around the arena and finally give up the chase. Then, Tommy would place the hat on his *'hat cleaner';* long story short, he'd push the lever and a huge explosion would blow the hat up.

Well, I thought, "You know, it'd be really, really funny if I could get Russ out there in front of the chutes when Tommy did his act and let Tommy get Russ's new straw hat. I'd already set it up with Tommy. I didn't think I was going to get it done, but just in the nick of time I lured Russ out in front of the chutes as the act started. Coliseum lights were all off and the spotlight was on Tommy, as usual. I'm talking to Russ and his back is turned away from Tommy who is sneaking up on him.

Well, Tommy grabbed Russ's new hat and took off. Now, it's really on. No, I mean it's **REALLY ON**! Russ is not faking and he's as mad as he can possibly be, still in the spotlight chasing Tommy and cussing as loud as he can. All the cowboys are now watching and laughing uncontrollably as well as the five or six thousand spectators.

He finally gave up the chase and just like always, Tommy put the hat on his hat cleaner and just like always, BOOM! Russ's new hat literally hit the ceiling of the Montgomery, Alabama coliseum and then landed back on the arena floor in about 6 pieces. Russ was threatening to whip me, Tommy, and anyone else he could think of and it was one of the funniest things I'd ever seen.

Well, Russ cooled off a little, but not much. We rode that night and headed for San Angelo, Texas, five of us in my Delta 88 Oldsmobile, Russ, myself, Jack Ward, Jess Knight, and John Gloor. We pulled over late in the night to change drivers and took off again.

We'd gotten down the road a few miles and I started looking for my hat, but it was nowhere to be found. I started asking questions only to find out that when we stopped, Russ had put my brand new hat right in front of the back tire and peeled out on it when he took off. Well, now I'm the one that's mad. I'm telling him to pull over because I'm fixin' to whip his butt. We got out, talked a little trash, cussed each other a little bit, then got back in and headed for Angelo and we're still great friends to this day.

SMOKEY BROWN
BAREBACK AND BULLS

I tried my luck at a high school rodeo at bareback riding/first & last time. I got screwed down called for the gate and that gelding blew up and by the third jump I'd lost my grip and went out the back door. As I went out the back door our butts met, which caused me to do a somersault and I landed on my neck with the full weight of my body.

When I came to, the bullfighter was telling the announcer I was talking about a "sunny beach," but in reality I was calling that horse a SOB! The crowd got a big kick out of it and I gathered my senses and walked out on my own power. In my opinion, bareback riders gotta have the strength of a gorilla's arm and the grace of a ballerina.

I was at a Circle 8 rodeo in Aldine, Texas and drew a big bull called 1-T, which stood for One Ton, from Red Williams stock. It took all my rope just to get around him and he was sure power. A big bull and me with my short legs, I got flung off on the wrong side away from my hand and hung up.

He raked me against the fence so I grabbed hold of the fence with my free arm and got stretched out and dislocated my shoulder. A few minutes later I saw Rickey Lindsey climb on him wearing only tennis shoes and smoking a cigarette, He pulled a loose rope and took two jumps then started two-footing that big bull like crazy. I learned a lesson. You ride like it's supposed to feel natural and Rickey made it look easy.

CHARLES CASE
THEY CALLED ME HIPPIE

They Called Me Hippie. I remember the first time I decided to try my luck at riding bulls as a teenager in the 70's. I was raised on a farm and ranch so I was no a stranger to livestock. I was also one of the rebellious types that decided to grow my hair out as long as I could, which had grown long enough to touch the center of my back and could be put in a pony tail – the girls loved it. I would party all the time and just raise hell every chance I got.

In the summer I would let my beard go wild and grow until I had to go back to school the in the fall, which by then grew long enough to make me look like a member of ZZ Top. I didn't have a lot of friends since I lived 23 miles from town, but the crowd that I did run around with would have a hard time telling the difference between a bull and a frog.

One early summer day we decided to go to a small county rodeo near Sterling, Colorado about 90 miles from home to have some fun and maybe chase a few girls. That's when I got a taste of bull riding that I enjoyed for several years afterwards. What started it all was that about 4 or 5 of us were walking around the livestock looking at the horses and the bulls and drinking beer. After about 3 or 4 beers too many I popped off and claimed that I could hop on one of the bulls and show those cowboys how it was done.

It's interesting how brave you can be when you drink too much liquid courage. As we were talking, a couple of cowboys over heard us and started pushing their luck about my appearance and my careless talk. Well, my buddies decided they didn't want any of it so they kind of slipped away leaving me surrounded by about 6 cowboys and at first I though this was going to get real ugly and I would have to fight for my life.

One of the cowboys instead, told me that he would pay my

entry fee if I would show how tough I was and ride one of the bulls for 8 seconds. I figured it would be better to take my chances with the bull then get my butt kicked so I agreed to the challenge. By that time my friends decided to return, with more beer of course, and all of us went over to the office where I lied about my age, registered to ride, got my number, and drew my bull.

Not having a rig, one of the old timers handed me his and asked if I knew what I was getting into. Of course I didn't, as I had only ridden steers in the corral just for fun, but a 2000 lb bull was a whole new experience. When I registered, one of the cowboys jokingly told the official that my nickname was hippie, which is how I was announced and what I went by for a couple years afterwards

I was sitting on the fence when it was my turn to rig up. I'll never forget the look in that bulls eyes as I stood their looking at him and I knew I was going to regret my decision. He was a big Brahma, black as coal and a name that would scare you just to say it. They called him Devils Revenge.

I think that's who originally raised and owned him because that bull was rank. He definitely had a bad attitude and intended to show me just how bad he really was. Two of the cowboys who talked me into this madness assisted me in the chute, getting me situated and ready. That bull wanted nothing to do with me on his back and three times tried to jump out of the chute slamming me into the gate. Needless to say I was desperately thinking of a way to get out of this predicament I had gotten myself into.

That's when the gate swung open and the ride began. That bull shot out of that gate like a rocket. He stood on his head, twisted, kicked up dirt, and bucked like nothing I have ever been on before. I felt like a rag doll being thrown around and felt his tail hit me numerous times in the back of the head and all I could do was hold on. There was no way I was going to wind up in the dirt with this bull on top of me

Once, he stumbled and I thought for sure I was going to be

thrown over his head and get gored. All I had to do was lay back and hold on for eight seconds, eight very long seconds. I guess the adrenaline and the terror held me in place along with my death grip. That buzzer was the most beautiful sound I had ever heard. I kept hearing the bull fighter yelling, "Get off, get off…"

As I jumped off, my hand got hung up and I was tossed all over the place. The next thing I knew I was being helped up off the ground with a bloody nose and took off running for the gate. The look and shock on everyone's face was worth a million, but I did it. I rode my first bull.

Before the weekend was over I rode several more times and walked away with a 3rd place buckle that I still have, plus $50.00. The cowboys that taunted me into riding were excited and I believe, impressed. My friends that were there with me that weekend were in shock. They though for sure I was going to get myself killed and so did I, but they never dared me or doubted me again.

The cowboys shared a bottle of Jack Daniels in celebration, one even gave me an old straw cowboy hat he had in his truck which I wore for years. I may still have that hat somewhere. I was hooked so I tried riding broncs, but never did very well in that event, just ate a lot of dirt. I found there was a bigger challenge in bull riding. For the next couple years I would enter rodeos whenever I had a chance and they always called me Hippie.

RICHARD FLECHSIG
WATCH HIM, DICK. HE BITES

On a September, 1963, Labor Day weekend at a Steiner Rodeo in Columbus, Ohio they had a rain shower. Clark Holden, a saddle bronc rider asked me to give him a pull on his saddle. When I climbed up on the chute, Clark said, "Watch him Dick. He bites."

This particular horse was notorious for biting so they usually bucked him wearing a muzzle, but he was a way better bucking horse without the muzzle and Clark had asked them to leave it off which they did.

I was leaning over the chute pulling on the latigo which was a little hard to pull because it was damp and I had both hands pulling when, Chomp! That big headed sucker bit me right on the love handle. I yelped and jumped down off the chute and Clark asked if he got me and I said, "Damn right he did."

Clark said, "Well, come on. We have to hurry." So, I got back up there behind the chute and started pulling the saddle down and, Chomp! That big sucker got me again. Now, Clark started laughing and I started cussing and just as I started to finish pulling on the latigo the bronc turns his big head like he is going to bite me. I thought, "I'll punch you right upside the head." But, I looked at that big head and my little fist and thought, "Nope. He'd eat my fist."

Thankfully, someone got on the backside of the chute and grabbed his halter and held him so I could finish pulling the latigo. Later that night when I got ready to take a shower I looked at my side and I had two big bite marks almost breaking the skin about the size of small dinner plates and they were getting a beautiful shade of black and blue. Anyone who has ever been bitten by a horse knows the feeling.

DENNY WEIR
ROCKS AND CAR PARTS IN THE ARENA

In 1981 at Middletown, New York, Ron Martin's bull Tinker threw me off and I landed on a big rock and my left free-arm elbow was cracked. I came back to the chutes telling Gary Thorp, Chris Risoli, Darrel Hendon and others to look out for glass, rocks, and car parts in the arena. John Risoli was cussing saying, "We're Professionals and shouldn't have to ride in these kind of conditions."

The rodeo was held on a oval stock car track and the ground

was hard, with rocks scattered around. I rode in an ambulance to the hospital and took a cab back to the arena. The cab driver wanted to drop me off at the entrance gate to the fairgrounds. I didn't want to walk that far so he started cussing me when I requested he take me to the arena. That was a bad experience at the time, but funny now.

In the summer of 1982, Glen McIlvain and I were traveling through Wyoming headed to rodeos in that state. One of the rear wheels came off the car. Glen was driving and handled the situation quite well. We were out in the middle of nowhere so Glen wrote help on a contestant back number and stuck it on a door window. After several hours a car finally showed up and we were given another rental car to continue on. Traveling can be as dangerous as the bull riding.

At the rodeo in Duquoin, Illinois in 1983, I was standing behind the bucking chutes on a flatbed trailer that Bob Barnes carried the arena on for transport. I was helping Monk Dishmon set his rigging on his bareback bronc and was gonna tighten his latigos. The bulls were in a pen right behind the trailer and several of the bulls were chasing and hooking a big Charbray bull, #90 Okie Joe.

Okie Joe decided he had enough and jumped on the trailer, penning me against the chute and the sliding gate bar. His head was pushing against my chest and I had a hold on those big horns with each hand. I thought I was gonna die right there. Monk grabbed under each arm and pulled me up. Okie Joe thrashed around and eventually slid back off the trailer and into the pen. I had a good bull drawn that night, #26 Dittman. I had to visible injury release him because my left arm muscles on the outside of my shoulder were crushed. That was a close call and I eventually drew #26 again at Blue Earth, Minnesota and placed on him.

I witnessed one fatality during my rodeo career. At Mesquite, Texas in 1984, Billy Bob Cleveland was stepped on after making a successful ride on Neal Gay's huge bull, My Buddy. The bull was in front of the let-out gate when the whistle blew, but Billy Bob froze up and didn't make a move to get off. My Buddy threw him off and he fell underneath, getting stepped on and receiving internal injuries.

Billy Bob, who was from Cleburne, Texas, had just started back riding after a two year layoff. He was married with two small children. I split 3/4 with him in the bull riding that weekend. Two weeks later I had drawn My Buddy. He was a very gentle bull, just big, weighing around 2400lbs. When the whistle blew I made sure to get thrown far away from him so I wouldn't get stepped on.

At the Cheyenne Frontier Days in 1983 I had a big Brahma bull that belonged to a North Dakota stock contractor. This bull was supposed to be rank, but he jumped high in the air for about four seconds and then stopped and bullfighter Bob Romer couldn't get him to move. After about twenty or so seconds the bull lunged at Romer and I made my move to get off. Just as I swung my leg over he stopped again. I fell right beside him and he wheeled around and stepped on my right leg calf muscle. I was awarded a re-ride for the third and last section of bull riding. I could hardly walk, the leg was so swollen. I kept ice on it until time to ride my bull. I made a successful ride, winning day money.

That night I was entered at Boulder, Colorado and had drawn Alsbaugh's J9 Fabian. I really was in some pain by then. I laid by my rigging bag with ice on my leg until the bulls were loaded into the chutes. I rode Fabian seven point eight seconds. After the rodeo I caught a ride with rodeo clown Tom Feller, who was from Everman, Texas. Tom drove all night and dropped me off at my brother Jim Weir's home in Amarillo, Texas the next morning. They were at church so I lay on the front porch with my head on my rigging bag. I woke up when they come driving up. They were surprised to see me there and were happy to have me for a few days until I flew on home.

I remember at Ada, Ok in 1982, I had Jim Shoulder's bull 03 Dark Demon and he was a mean son-of-a-gun. Every time anyone walked by the chute he would hook at them. Finally, someone walked on the backside of the chute and Dark Demon caught his right horn under a board and nearly ripped the whole front side out of the wooden chute. The committee members frantically got some boards together and fixed the chute the best they could and I was pretty shook up by then, but I rode #03 and placed third. That chute was not used for the remainder of the rodeo.

My first big check was at Kansas City, Missouri on November of 1981. I had 1978 PRCA bucking bull of the year, #11 Red Lighting of Tommy Steiner. I had had filled my permit during the summer of '81 and was ready to rodeo full time in '82. Kansas City was the first rodeo that counted for points for the next year. Kirk Allmon rode with me to the rodeo and really helped build up my confidence.

Right before it was my time to ride I asked NFR bull rider Art Ray, who had previously ridden #1, if he had any last minute tips. Art looked at me and said very seriously, "Make sure all four feet are on the ground when you nod your head." I won third place and a big jump on the rookie of the year standings. I never really figured out what Art really meant by what he said.

At West Palm Beach, Florida in 1983, Robbie Teel, Kyle Whiting, Chuck Ingraffia and I were at a local club after the rodeo that night and had gotten pretty sauced up when we decided to go back to the motel. We were beside some of our other rodeo friend's car, going down the street by the club and hanging out the windows trying to grab each other. A local police officer was behind us and the lights came on. We pulled over and he wanted to know why we were having a rodeo on his street. Kyle who was driving kept answering, "Yes Sir, and No Sir." We all got straight and told him we just wanted to have some fun and believe it or not he let us go after a good butt chewing.

When I won first place at Phoenix, Arizona in 1982 on Cervi's S20, it was my career best. The Phoenix committee awarded trophy buckles to event winners. There was a catch to getting your buckle. You had to be present to receive it. I rode in the first performance. The rodeo lasted several days and I was up at other rodeos. NFR bronc rider Bobby "Hooter" Brown was there the last performance and was tired of cowboys not getting their buckles. He got a young man to accept the buckle in my place. I was told by another cowboy the next week at a rodeo that Hooter had my Phoenix buckle. Sure enough, he gave me the buckle at a rodeo a couple weeks later. I have always been very grateful to him for doing this for a young rookie he didn't even know.

In 1982, I won the PRCA Rookie of The Year title in bull riding. The awards banquet was to be held at the Stouffer's Denver Inn at Denver, Colorado in January of 1983. The National Western Rodeo was going on at the same time. In the motel lobby, in a glass case were the World Champions and my Rookie of The Year buckle. I was in a dream. Here I was getting my buckle presented to me while Charles Sampson was getting his World Champion bull riding buckle. Hadley Barrett and Larry Mahan were the MC's. Wrangler Western Wear's Mel Parkhurst gave me my buckle and check. Ronnie Rossen, 1961 the year I was born, and the 1966 World Champion bull rider was there. Ronnie was still competing some during that time and was entered at the same rodeos as me. That was a great time in my life.

The first year I competed in the Houston Astrodome I had to ride after the rodeo. The guys who ran the stock into the chutes from the pens had a miss-print on their sheets. My bull was #11 Mean Joe Green of Cervi. On their sheet it looked like a 33. When it got down to the last three bulls to buck I asked them when they were going to run in my bull #11. They looked at their sheet and said, "He don't go out tonight." I said, "He sure does. I have him." They asked Mark Baker the chute boss who confirmed #11 was definitely supposed to go that night. Well, they decided to make me ride after the rodeo and the crowd was gone. The judges, a few cowboys, and bullfighter Miles Hare were there. I bucked off Mean Joe Green and couldn't believe I had to ride after the regular performance at one of the worlds largest rodeos. I was very disappointed because ever since I was a kid I had dreamed of riding there.

I owe a lot of credit to Marvin Paul Shoulders for listening to a fourteen year old kid bug him with questions about all aspects of bull riding. In 1975, my hometown rodeo of Carthage, Texas was a three header in bull riding. They didn't get enough entries because the committee decided not to take permits. Marvin Paul rode all three nights. I stayed by his side every night of the rodeo asking question upon question. He was very patient and answered all my questions. Guys like him are true champions in life. Marvin Paul was then, and still is, one of my heroes today.

When Jim Shoulders produced my hometown rodeo at Carthage, Texas in the mid '70's, I helped with the daily chores of feeding and watering the stock. I got to be around the famous bulls like Andy Capp, Mighty Mouse, Kung Fu, Grim Reaper, Funeral Wagon, God Father, Bat Man, Robin, Cyclone, and Fonzie. Jim had some great bulls during that time. I also worked during the rodeo untying calves and picking up bronc flanks out of the arena.

Jim Shoulders was a great man who sat tall in the saddle. Jim Hill was always one of the bull fighters there every year. Jim would sit by his little horse trailer and show me pictures from his album. He would also tell me about being in the movie, Junior Bonner. I remember, 1975 NFR bull riding qualifier Leander Frey making the first qualified ride on Jim Shoulders' bull Andy Capp at Carthage in '72, scoring 92 points. That kind of score was very rare in those days.

I saw Buddy Lewis become the first man to ever ride Steiners rank bucking bull of the year, S7 Savage Seven. The ride happened at Lufkin, Texas in 1982. It had rained that day and the arena was muddy. I had bull 3X and scored 75pts and placed third. Buddy won first, scoring 87pts. He was the only man to successfully ride S7 that year. Buddy didn't get any recognition like I thought he should have. It might have been muddy, but Savage Seven bucked and Buddy rode him right.

In July of 1981, Darrel Hendon and I set out for the mid west rodeos to fill our permits. At Wyoming, Michigan we met Joe Farrelly, Stanley Thomas, John Harp, Jody Edwards, and Jimmy Lee Walker. Those guys had been the top cowboys for years from the North Eastern Circuit. They encouraged us to follow them up to their part of the country to rodeo. I called home and told my parents I was headed New York and New Jersey. I stayed at Joe Farrellys home in Auburn, New York and Darrel stayed at bareback bronc rider Glen Yeo's home at Staten Island, New York.

We competed at the legendary Painted Pony Ranch Rodeo where I filled my permit at Lake Luzerne, New York. We also rode at the Legendary Cow Town Rodeo in Woodstown, New Jersey. I won first at Woodstown one weekend and it paid $530.00. That was the most the rodeo had ever paid out in any even, at that time. Howard Harris, the owner, had some great bulls that were always sold to other PRCA contractors. After breaking my elbow at Middletown, New York I caught a Grey Hound bus back to Carthage, Texas and that trip took three days.

Denny Weir (Photo by Al Long)

LARRY BRADY
BIRDELL, ARKANSAS

June 1980 we were at a Co-Sanction ARA-IPRA rodeo in Birdell, Arkansas. We arrived early because we had been to Steelville and Fredericksburg, Missouri the last 2 days. We paid up and looked at the draw and I had a little black bull #214 that was called Bullitt of Circle G Rodeo Company.

Well anyway, I was thrilled to have him because he'd been a paycheck every time I'd had him. It had been raining for 2 day's and the pen was sloppy and the mud was deep. When the bull riding started, Harold Lee Underwood the bull fighter came up to the chute as I was adjusting my rope and said, "Larry don't piss him off this time, "because its muddy as hell out there."

He wouldn't really buck unless you spurred him around and got him mad so I started in on him and Harold was yellin', "Don't do that!" But, #24 was slobbering and bawling and wanting to get somebody, namely me. Anyway, he jumped out and cracked it back to the left and stayed hooked up.

It's still raining like hell and Harold Lee was right with him when the buzzer sounded and I stepped off, checked out, and got clear. #24 spotted Harold about 30 feet away and lined him out with blood in his eyes. Harold was almost knee deep in mud and couldn't move very fast so #24 caught him from behind and cow killed him. Then, he ran down the pen and turned around.

The pick up man got between #24 and Harold to try and hold him off of him. So, I got off the fence and got to Harold and #24 had hit him square in the rear end and had chilled him good. I squatted down and was holding his head in my hands and said, "I got you, buddy. You're alright."

Harold said, "Larry, don't leave me," and I said, "Don't worry, Bobby's got him and I'll be here 'till the cows come home." Well, #24 looked under the pick up horse and saw both of us laying out there in the mud and here he comes again, thinking, "I got 'em both this time.

When he gets around the horse and lines out for us, I figure, "Well, I told him I'd be here 'till the cows come home and as far as I was concerned the cows are home so I left, and he got Harold again and I mean got him good. Later we had a big laugh about the cows. Harold said he heard me say I'd be there and then #24 charged again and the next thing he knew his head sunk in the mud because I was gone.

JERRY GUSTAFSON
THE LIFE OF A RODEO PHOTOGRAPHER

I was at the rodeo in Fairbault, Minnesota shortly after I cracked out full time in 1970 after a bareback horse kicked me and broke my ankle while I was on the fence. I sat out a half dozen rides while I packed my ankle in ice and then finished shooting the rodeo. After the performance I drove to East Dubuque, Illinois and slept in my station wagon. I shot the afternoon performance and went to a doctor who informed me that my ankle was indeed broken.

He said he could put a cast on it that wouldn't help the healing process, but would get lots of sympathy from the girls or I could go without and it would heal just as well. I chose not to have the cast and drove home to St. Paul, Minnesota where I was living at the time. I went back to work at 3M for the winter months, then cracked back out In January.

Another time, I was shooting a high school rodeo near Fort Worth and they had so many contestants that we would start at 8pm Friday night and go non-stop until early in the wee hours Sunday morning, take about a 4 hour break, then start again. I was shooting the bull riding Sunday afternoon and knew the next bull would be making a big circle to the left.

I took my photos then climbed up the gate and for whatever

reason I just knew he was going to hit my ankle with his head, but I was so tired I couldn't pop my feet loose and jump. Sure enough, he hit my ankle and broke it again. But, I didn't miss a single ride.

Barney Brehmer (Photo by Jerry Gustafson)

Then in the late 80's I was in Fallon, Nevada for a high school invitational rodeo and was shooting the bull riding when a bull circled back to the left on me. I went to the fence, but wasn't quick enough. He hooked me into the air and I went over the fence and landed on the top of my head on hard-packed dirt. It gave me a concussion and broke the lens on my camera. Fortunately, I carried another lens I could use, but I did miss two rides that time.

During the busy times I would go for months at a time living on 15 hours of sleep a week. I'd be in the darkroom all night processing the film and making prints or driving to the next rodeo. Today's rodeo photographers have no idea how good they have it because of their digital equipment.

BARRY BUNCH
ME AND JACKY GIBBS

Well, Jacky Gibbs and I were traveling down the highway after a rodeo one nice summer night and I was driving so we were traveling at a good fast speed. I had the window rolled down so I could smoke and had the radio up pretty loud. Jacky was in the passenger seat and we were talking about our bull rides that we had just made at a rodeo as we were traveling down the highway with the windows rolled down and the radio on.

Well, we couldn't hear what each other was saying because of the radio being turned up to loud so Jacky says I got to move more closer so I can hear you. So, he moved over to the middle and now we're sittin' side by side. We can hear each other talking now so that's good, plus it's night and the people we're passing going down the highway can't see us because it is dark out.

So, we had been doing this for a few hours and we were getting low on fuel so we pulled into this truck stop to get gas still just sittin' beside each other and talking. So, we pull up to the pumps to get gas not thinking any thing about the fact that we were still sitting side by side in the pickup.

Well, when I start pumping the gas Jacky goes inside and starts reading a magazine. I guess this fella saw us pull in so he starts hittin' on Jacky because he wants in on the action. Jacky comes out to the truck says, "We got to go." So, after we take off, he told me what happened and as he was telling me, we both start laughing and we say to each other, "That fella thought we were a little funny because we'd pulled into that truck stop sittin' together.

STEVE SCOTT
ME AND ELLIE

Me and Ellie Lewis were hauling a load of killer horses out of Oregon. It was snowing and sleeting and I was driving. We were headed downhill and coming from the other direction was a diesel rig pulling a trailer house. Well, I just loved that Jake brake so I figured I needed to slow her down a little because I was picking up too much speed so I flipped on the Jake brake.

You know that it's a compression brake that puts backpressure on the heads and slows the whole drive train down from the motor to the tires. Well, it sounded real good for a second, but then it just went quiet. Ellie was sleeping and he came straight up and hit that Jake break so hard that he broke my pretty toggle switch I had bought and put on it at a truck stop.

Well, those doubles started coming around us crawling across the other lane as it curled around us. The other truck looked like his horn was smoking because of the condensate, but he was set down on that horn.

Ellie hollered, "Don't try to catch it. Pump your brake." Every time I pumped the brake it would straighten those doubles out a little. When we passed that truck my back trailer was still across the line on his two lane road, but somehow he missed me. We got her lined out and Ellie said, "I'll tell you one damned thing. If either one of us would have had one more coat of paint we'd have had a hell of a wreck."

CLARENCE GIPSON
SUMMER OF '94

The story I am offering is very meaningful to me. It came at a time when I, like many cowboys, struggle with faith, family and pretty much life in general.

It was the summer of 1994 and I had entered a Senior Pro Rodeo in Lamar, Colorado, an open rodeo in Aurora (just outside of Denver.) Like most cowboys, we try to juggle faith, family, work, and rodeo. At the time I was living in Pueblo and working in Colorado Springs. It was Friday and I had arranged to get off work early so I could make the performance that night. Well, things were not working out because I had to work late which caused me to leave later than anticipated. Well, I finally get on the road and the rodeo was being simulcast so I was listening to the rodeo as I was driving.

About midway into the trip a voice came to me (later in life I understood it was the Holy Spirit) just as clear as the radio and said, "You are too old and too big to do want you are doing. Only through me, can you do what you are doing. You do right by your child and I will do right by you. And you have to tell someone."

Well, I didn't know what to think. This had never happened before. I was a Christian, maybe not the best, but I believed. I was not really sure what or why it happened so I just continued down the road. I arrived at the rodeo just about time for the bull riding. Bob Blackwood (my spiritual mentor and brother in Christ) met me at my pickup. He helped me get ready very quickly and said a prayer for me and put me on my bull. I got two jumped so I picked up my rope, paid my fees, got back in my pickup, and headed to Aurora.

The next day when I arrived at the rodeo grounds I got to talking to some guys about what had happened to night before. About 6 or 7 of us gathered around a trash barrel and when I told my story they were all inspired by what I had experienced. I was still not sure about what had happened, but I told someone. After I got my fees paid I went behind to the chutes to get ready.

The draw came out and I had a little bull of Dean Drakes, the name escapes me, but I had seen him buck many times. I had just never seen him ridden. Something told me (the Holy Spirit) to get a marker and write, "Expect to win," on my rope pad so

I did just that. Except when I wrote it, I spelled the word two instead of the word to, but it was in magic marker and it was not going to change.

When it came time for the bull riding, mind you, I was the oldest bull rider there. All the kids were watching the old guy. I got on my bull, nodded, and he came out and turned back right in the gate. When the whistle blew, the old guy was winning the bull riding. This was no day off because this bull was a pretty bad cat. But, it was the most effortless ride I had ever experienced. As the bull spun I watched the announcer's booth go past, again and again, then the whistle blew and I jumped off.

The next day a young man rode a really good bull and won the bull riding and I won second. As I was leaving the rodeo grounds the voice came back, "You have been asking me to reveal to you, I Am real. I Am real. I knew you were going to win second and had you write it down." The hair stood up on the back of my neck. For many years I was afraid to share this story, thinking people would think I was crazy. But, it was not until my walk with Christ that lead me to realize fear has no place in Faith. Bob Blackwood would always tell me, "Greater is he that is in you, than he that is in the world." John 4:4. We all are tested and have a Testimony. God Bless Cowboys.

RICHARD FLECHSIG
THE MOUNT OUT

In about 1953 or so, me and a couple of buddies drove to St. Louis, Missouri to attend the Fireman's Rodeo. It was held outdoors back then at the old Walsh Stadium. We snuck in of course and were hanging around behind the chutes when a guy comes by and asks if anyone wanted to mount out a horse for ten bucks.

My buddies got on me and told me to do it, seeing as how I had just started riding bareback horses. I told the guy I'd mount the horse out, but didn't have my rigging so he said, "No problem.

It's a saddle bronc," to which I replied, "Well, I have never been on a saddle bronc so I guess I better pass."

He said, "You'll be OK. I'll get some guys to help you. Go over to the tack wagon and tell Hambone to give you a saddle and bronc rein." So, against my better judgment I went and got the saddle halter and bronc rein. When I came back he had these two guys that were going to teach me everything about bronc riding in ten minutes.

I was introduced to Neal Gay and Dude Smith and they helped me set my stirrups, get me some chaps and spurs and off we go. Tommy Steiner had the stock and he came up and paid me before I got on. Should I have been suspicious? Neal and Dude set the saddle and Tommy said, "Don't get hurt and don't be afraid to grab the apple," referring to the saddle horn that had been hammered down.

I thought, "Well, if I'm going to do this then I'm going to try and ride this sucker." When your seventeen years old you think dumb things on occasion. Dude and Neal helped me measure the rein and I nodded my head and the rest as they say is history. That big white sucker weighed almost 1300 pounds plus and sure did buck. About the third jump he stood me up in the saddle and over the dash I went, but hung my left foot in a stirrup.

Now, I am getting drug, thinking, "Oh, crap. This is not good." The old man who taught me to ride horses always told me if I was getting drug to roll onto my stomach as that would turn my foot over and I'd come loose. Somehow I managed to do it and got loose. I jumped up and ran back to the chutes like something was after me and I'm sure I looked like a doofus.

I couldn't comb the hair on the back of my head for a few days because of a few scabs and I still have a ding in my ear from hitting the ground. Later that year I was reading the Rodeo Sports News and I saw the five best saddle broncs listed and guess what the big white horse was on there? His name was White Eagle. No wonder he was a mount out.

DON MELLGREN
PANGUITC, UTAH

In 1962, Pat Russell and I entered the Panguitch, Utah rodeo. We got to town a few days early so we slept at the rodeo grounds in our sleeping bags and showered at a local motel in rooms that people had checked out of already. They always gave us clean towels and wouldn't take any money for that and were great people. We bucked hay for a local rancher at three cents a bale and had to stack it in a barn.

We were up on Friday night. Pat was sitting second in the bareback riding and I was splitting second and third in the bull riding. So, we waited around until the last performance on Saturday night to pick up any checks we might get. On Saturday as the rodeo was about to start, in drives a red pickup with a plywood camper and out steps a young kid with his very young wife and little baby.

I remember loving the shape of his hat. Funny what I remember. Anyway, this kid was entered in all 3 riding events. He had a big, strong bareback horse named Tipperary and was all over him. He came back to the chutes and I said, "Pretty strong horse." He was mad and said, "Yeah, I really tried him, didn't I?"

I don't remember what he did on his saddle bronc horse, but in the bull riding he spurred the heck out of a really good bull. After that, I was splitting 3rd and 4th. That kid was, Larry Mahan. I remember thinking, "Going down the road with a young wife and little baby, now that is really confidence and chasing his dreams." He became my hero right then and there and he still is.

A local kid named Carl Yardley was in the bull riding. I don't remember what he did on his bull, but he was a nice guy. His folks owned the best steakhouse in town. We got our checks and went straight to the steakhouse. His folks cashed our checks and we had the best steaks money could buy. To this day that is the best steak I have ever had.

I still have those programs. I sure don't know why, but I am glad I do now. Those were some very happy times.

LES HOOD
LES IS MORE
by Wayne Whitehead

As a young kid who could not think of much of anything other than rodeo and wanting to be a cowboy I was fortunate enough to know a guy who became one of my heroes. He was also my cousin. He was born and raised in Central, Texas. He grew up poor, but he and his brothers never knew that they were poor as most everyone they knew were living the same way they were.

His name was Les Hood. He was quite a cowboy from a very young age. He worked every event and was good at all of them. Les was also a horse lover and quite a horseman. He raised some really nice quarter horses and owned several really good studs. Les was a cowboy. He did all kinds of cowboy work until late in his life. He worked in feed yards, caught bad cows and bulls, doctored, and worked cattle, as well as breaking colts for people when most would have considered him past his prime.

As a young kid of about 6 or 7, most of the time we only saw Les at funerals and family reunions. One of my earliest impressions was the trophy buckle that he was wearing at one of the funerals we went to. I thought that was the most beautiful buckle I had ever seen and never forgot it. It was for the All-Around Championship and I remember it as being from Phoenix and the year on the buckle was 1948.

Les had perfected his talents in rodeo as a very young man. He was a member of the Cowboys Turtle Association, The RCA, which later became the PRCA, and had been to rodeos all over the United States. In the early days he got to them any way he could. He hitchhiked, caught rides, and when he had a car or truck, he drove. I know of one incident he even hopped a freight train.

The freight train incident that I know about was quite a tale. He and my dad's older brother decided they wanted to go to Arizona and California to enjoy some warmer weather and enter as many rodeos as they could. They caught a westbound freight train in Central Texas, hopping in an empty boxcar and struck out on the trail.

Les was winning something in one or more of his events everywhere they went and back in those days it did not pay all that well, but sometimes local merchants donated prizes too. One such rodeo was giving a new pair of boots to the champion bull rider. Les needed some new boots badly so he won the bull riding and as soon as the rodeo was over he went to claim those boots.

He said he put them on immediately and was sure proud to have them. He was about to leave and go to the next rodeo when the rodeo secretary asked him if he wanted the money he had won, too. Les said he was so proud of winning the boots that he'd forgotten about the money. My dad's brother did not fare nearly as well as he only entered the bareback riding so he elected to hop him another freight train and go back home.

The train stopped somewhere in New Mexico and he was forced to find another. There were guards in the rail yard watching for people trying to board the empty box cars, but he had to get home because he was out of money. He waited until another eastbound freight was about to leave and jumped up onto what Les called the cow catcher on the locomotive. No one saw him and he made it back to Texas. When the train stopped, someone saw him on the front of the train and approached him and told him to get off of the train. He could not get off because he'd gotten so cold he was frozen to the train after that long ride. They almost had to peel him off.

Les continued on and was successful enough to buy himself a car and drove home after his rodeos were over. Les was also a tough guy. He once broke his riding arm to the point that the bone was separated from itself so Les made himself a brace and kept going to rodeos and competing until it finally healed. He could and did endure a lot of pain and no one else could even tell he was hurt.

Les loved rodeo so much that he would have done it even if there had not been money to win. He truly did it for the love of the sport. The last PRCA Rodeo that I remember seeing him ride at was at Belton, Texas in the old arena down in the bottom by the creek. He was 62 years old that year and only entered the three riding events. They got 3 head in the bronc riding, 2 in the bareback riding, and 1 bull. This was a Steiner rodeo and Les rode 2 of his 3 broncs, both bareback horses, and had YD in the bull riding.

I was there the last performance and saw him ride 1 bareback, 1 bronc, and 1 bull that night. There were a bunch of young guys hanging around Les and they were somewhat his young proteges. This was the first time I ever met Tom Ray from Temple, Texas. He was adjusting the bull rope for Les and I thought he was rosining it up for him.

Years later, I reminded Tom that was where we met and that he was rosining the rope for Les, but he told me I was wrong, that Les didn't use rosin. Tom put the rope on YD and pulled it for Les and he rode YD to the turn back and rode him for about 6 or 7 seconds before YD bucked him off. Les came back to the chutes with his smile in place and stopped next to me and said, "I just wore out." That was pretty impressive for a 62 year old man.

For anyone who ever knew or saw Les, and for some that never had seen him compete, they probably thought he was a crazy old man. He had kind of a trademark when he got on his stock. He put his hat on sideways and pulled her down tight. I have to admit the first time I saw it I thought he might be a little crazy, too.

I asked him why he did it and he said he'd been in a bad slump one time and wasn't placing in any of his events. He said, just before he got on his bull he thought he needed to change something to change his luck so he put that hat on sideways and pulled it down tight and won the bull riding and he always did it from that time forward.

When Les quit going to pro rodeos he was instrumental in helping form several Old Timers Associations. My Dad, Mother, and younger brother went to watch him compete at his last Senior Pro event and he had entered every event and won buckles for first in each event. My Dad asked him what made him decide to call it quits and Les told him that he was 65 years old that year and had won 65 Senior Pro buckles, one for each year he was old.

As I got grown and wanted to rodeo I was able to go to a lot of rodeos all over the country. I never won much, but I was amazed at all the people that either knew or knew of Les Hood. Most all of them had a Les Hood story to share, too. Most all of the older world champions knew him, well. He had many friends and everyone respected him for his toughness, ability, and try. To me, he is a legend and a hero.

JIM LILES
SWIMMING WITH THE SNAKES

In the seventies I flew back to Oklahoma on occasion to work some rodeos and when I did I sometimes stayed with Tommy Crandall. This crazy little guy was one hell of a bull rider, but you had to keep a tight rein if that was even possible.

We were leaving a little town after a rodeo and headed back to Tulsa to catch a plane. Just outside of town we picked up a County Mountie keeping an eye on us. Tommy says, "Jim, put this baggy down in your shorts." You know us Okies. We don't wear none. He continues, "They can't search your shorts here in Oklahoma so you are good to go."

Well, when the belly gut laughing subsided I told Tommy, "You better start eating that stuff because I was born at night, but it weren't last night." He proceeded to stuff that crap down in the seats of that big Cadillac of his and we eased on down the road, yup, on the road in Oklahoma.

We were in between rodeos there outside of Muskogee, hotter than hell and humidity about 90%. Tommy says to everyone, "Hell, lets go down to the creek and go swimming." That sounded like a great idea to all of us sitting around doing nothing so off we go. There was a little creek with the greatest little pond I had ever seen. Just like out of one of those old pictures in Post magazine. Big trees, rope swing, the whole nine yards.

We had been swinging and having a heck of a time for about thirty minutes and I was on the far side of the pond. I started to swim upstream where the creek came into the pond and Tommy Crandall just started screaming at me. I stopped to listen and he says, "No, no, don't go up there. That is where all the Cotton Mouths hang out." Well, that is where I found out that Jesus wasn't the only one that could walk on water and I never went swimming in Oklahoma again.

BOBBY COOPER
3 times World Champion Bareback Rider
A MAN OF HIS WORD

Coming into the last rodeo of the 1984 season, Greenville South Carolina, a Longhorn rodeo production produced by Bruce Luerke and sanctioned by the IPRA, I was 2nd behind Davy Ratchford (better known as Spark Plug, a nickname given by Bobby Cooper and Justin Rowe) in the top 15 IPRA Bareback Riding, but Davy didn't make it to Greenville for personal reasons.

The horse I had was a good one, but I got a re-ride and my re-ride horse was 222 Rodeo News. Most of the bareback riders considered him a bad draw and no one wanted to get on him. I went to look for him in the back pens couldn't find him and come to find out the horse wasn't even at the rodeo because he had been accidentally left behind

Rodeo Stories II

.I thought I would get another horse, but along came Mr. Ken Treadway of the Ken Treadway Rodeo Company and he said, "Bobby if you will let me pull your riggin' you'll win first." I said, "Ken, I don't think the horse is even here," and he said, "Well, let's just go see."

Ken said, "Bobby, your right. He's not here, so what's the next re-ride horse?"

They said, "No, we done sent someone to get him." I said, "Well, where's he at?" and they said, "At the stock yards," which took them over an hour after the rodeo to get back with the horse.

They loaded the big 1275 pound sorrel with flax mane and tail in the buckin' chute and for such a pretty horse he bucked so out of line and changed leads every jump. I strapped my Bobby Cooper custom riggin' that was made by Peter John Hennesy on the back of that wild, raging stampeder, not really lookin forward to the ride.

Ken stepped up said, "Son, if you'll let me set your riggin' I'll guarantee you will win first." I was a bit leary, but said, "OK, Sir. Let's do it." I nodded my head and did what my daddy always said. "Rare back, Son, and throw yourself a fit." KT (Ken Treadway) said, "Go to him, Son." He came out of a left hand delivery and I took it to 'em and spurred him for 85 points to win first and was declared the 1984 IPRA National Bareback Riding Champion. I can say this is a fact. Ken Treadway is a man of his word.

TERRY WARD
THE WARD ARENA

We had an amateur rodeo company at Coalgate, and when Lane and his family moved to Oklahoma, his dad, Clyde, asked my dad if we had a bull that would turn back so Lane could get on a spinning bull. So, you might say Lane got his start at the Ward Arena. I knew his family very well and I remember the day I met Freckles Brown.

But, Lane and I were pretty close and he came to all our high school rodeos. We had a lot of fun at rodeos and he was a chick magnet. By the time he was a senior in high school he could ride everything we had and he'd come over to our arena and practice.

I don't remember the exact night I met him, but he was a freshman in high school. The best I remember, he and my brother Wes were great friends. Later in life they were each other's best man at their weddings and not like the movie.

Lane just rode a lot better than I did. I had to hitchhike to rodeos and sleep wherever I could. I remember one time I had to ride in the horse trailer from Jackson, Mississippi to Dallas, Texas with some barrel racers. Those were some crazy days. I didn't ride as many bulls as I would've like to, but nobody had a better time than I did.

I was at Cheyenne the day Lane got killed and it was a week I will never forget. We were hitch hiking to some rodeos in Kansas and I stuck around for the short go, but missed it by two points. I was entered with Stormy Rinehart, another bull rider from Oklahoma, but he got stepped on at Colby, Kansas and they had to take out a kidney. Then, I hitch hiked back to Cheyenne for my second bull.

The last thing Lane said to me right before his ride was that he forgot his riding glove and I had to go back to his riggin' bag to get it for him. I wish I would've known what was going to happen. I walked out in the arena about the time the paramedics got out there and I was also at the hospital with him.

It was sad as another friend of mine David Barry got hurt that same day and when I asked the nurse if I could go back and see him, she thought I was talking about Lane so she took me back to the room he was in right after they'd pronounced him dead. It was a sad time, but I'm glad I got to see him.

D.J. GAUDIN
The Kajun Kidd (rodeo clown and bullfighter)
KAJUN STORIES
by Todd Gaudin

Member: PRCA Hall of Fame, National Cowboy and Western Heritage Museum, Texas Cowboy Hall of Fame & Texas Rodeo Cowboy Hall of Fame

Dad was known to always drive nice cars. He went through several over the years and many cowboys wanted to hitch a ride to the next rodeo. Now, he wouldn't let just any bull rider ride with him because he felt like some would want to party and tear up his car. He was picky about who rode with him, but one bull rider he let ride often and trusted was Dan Willis.

After the final performance in Louisville, Kentucky, one year, Kajun had told Dan he could ride with him to Texarkana, but he didn't want any others going with him. He said he had filled up a cooler with cold cuts and soft drinks and they could drive straight through as he had to be there the next day.

It was raining when they left Louisville and Dan was starting out driving so Kajun could nap before his turn to drive. They hadn't been on the road too long when they came upon a man hitch hiking in the rain. When Kajun saw it was a service man in uniform he told Dan, "Pull over, pull over. No soldier should have to stand in the rain."

After the introductions they asked him where he was headed and it turned out he was trying to get back to his base in Bowling Green, Kentucky. "Where are you coming from?" they asked, and it turned out he had been back home attending his mother's funeral, but didn't have any money for bus fare so he started out hitch hiking.

It wasn't much further down the road when Kajun again told Dan, "Pull in here." Dan said, "What for?" and Kajun said, "I heard they serve a good steak here." Now, I don't think he knew that, but they stopped and Dad bought the soldier a steak dinner. In the end they ended up driving a 100 miles out of their way to drop him off at the front gate at his base in Bowling Green, Kentucky. Now, I had heard this story from a couple of people and always wondered how true it was. However, I finally heard it from Dan Willis a few years back at a Mesquite Rodeo reunion.

Many a cowboy have told me over the years how my Dad would help some of them pay their entry fees, buy them a meal or bring them home with him between rodeos to help them out. I woke up many Monday mornings to get ready to go to school only to find a cowboy sleeping on the couch, the floor, and one time still sleeping in my Dad's car in the driveway.

In fact, one year after school I went straight to my Cub Scout meeting and when I got home I found my Mom (who was also a Cub Scout Den Mother) had World Champion Benny Reynolds teaching her Scouts how to tie knots. I wasn't too happy about that as he was always one of my favorite cowboys, but I did get some quality one on one instruction later.

After Dad was inducted into the National Cowboy and Western Heritage Museum in Oklahoma City we were having breakfast at the hotel restaurant. My Dad's brother and sister and their families came over from Baton Rouge to see the induction. Dad and I got up to go and pay the check when a cowboy sitting with another at a table stood up and called out, "Kajun. Congratulations on your induction." "Thank you" Dad replied.

The cowboy told Dad about a time when he was about 18 years old and broke. He said he was working a turn out gate at a rodeo that Dad was working and that he had given him $100 to help him get back on his feet. The cowboy then said, "And I'm going to pay you back some day." "Well, how about now," Dad replied. "Oh, no," the cowboy replied. "I can't do it now, but I will someday." he exclaimed. We all had a good laugh and still laugh about that today."

After joining the RCA and going Pro, Dad worked a lot of

rodeos for Bobby Estes. One time Kajun was leaving town after a rodeo and he was pulling his horse trailer. He came upon someone broke down and working in the rain trying to change a flat. As he slowed down he saw it was Bobby Estes and so he honked and kept on going. The next rodeo he worked for Bobby, he came up to Kajun and said, "That's the last time I buy a Cadillac for a clown."

Other tales were told, such as the time Guy Weeks and bulldogger Bernis Johnson marveled endlessly at the new 1962 Chrysler New Yorker that a rodeo clown known as the Kajun Kidd showed up in one evening at the big rodeo in Chicago. Before the evening was out they hid the Kajun Kidd's new Chrysler New Yorker while he was busy in the ring getting spectators to laugh. Later, he spent a dismal hour looking for his car. He found it, but also found that whoever had made off with it had swiped his hubcaps.

Later, Guy and Bernis paid a boy $3 to haul a tow sack into the clown's busy dressing room. The boy was told to offer for sale the very hubcaps the Kajun Kid was searching for. Guy and Bernis were playing cards nearby when the boy began displaying his wares to the Kajun Kid. "Why, you little squirt." The Kajun Kid hollered, "Where'd you get these hubcaps?"

I was sitting in the clown's room one year in Houston visiting with Dad (Kajun Kidd) and Quail Dobbs and a few others. Quail was telling a story about how he told Dad they had a bull out a few nights before that was rank and was going to want to hook something. He told Dad, "You can't run around the barrel on this one as he's too smart for that." Of course, Dad told him, "There ain't no damn bull smarter than me." Now, in those days the producers would let the clowns fight with one or two and it was usually the last one of the night.

The arena in the Astrodome was almost 3 acres in size and they had a dummy they would drop down on a cable from above into the middle of the arena. Well sure enough it was the last bull out and they took the barrel to a corner to play with him a little.

Quail kept telling Kajun to watch it as he would get hooked. "You can't go around it," he kept telling him. Dad decided to fake going around one way and come back around the other side and make a pass in front of him.

As soon as he did his fake move and came around the opposite side the bull was standing there waiting for him. He said all he could do then since he was cut off from the barrel was to make a run for the dummy. "But, there was already another dummy on it," he exclaimed, meaning Wilbur Plaugher, who by this time in his career was playing with his inner tube and the audience, and wasn't getting in the way of any bulls.

Another time in the clown's room in Houston, I had a co-worker and friend Buck Bequette with me. He always wanted me to take him to the rodeo so he could hang out in the clown's room and hear all the rodeo stories. He just loved my Dad and Quail and would just sit around and take it all in until it was time for the bull riding then we would go and watch.

This night Bill Bailey, a local disk jockey for KENR Radio and arena announcer for the calf scramble, stopped in for a while. He and Dad had been friends for a long time and he knew you might be able to find a drink in the clown's room. My Dad usually had a fifth of something in his clown trunk from collecting clowns room dues from cowboys who would want to keep their rigging equipment locked up.

A bottle was pulled out and the custom was that if it were handed to you then you would take a drink and pass it to the next person. Bill was standing next to Dad's clown trunk and the bottle was passed to him. He took a little nip and passed it to Buck who said, "No thanks, I'm drinking beer." So, Bill explained the custom to him and told him to take a drink. Again, he said, "No, thanks.

Now, Buck was easily the largest man in the room standing 6 ft. 5 inches and weighing about 285 lbs. Bill reached down into Dad's clown trunk and pulled out his single action Army Colt 45 and pointed it up at Buck. Now, the gun wasn't loaded and it was used to shoot blanks in one of their clown acts but, Bill pulled back the hammer and said "When I say take a drink, you take a drink." "Yes Sir," he yelled and took a big long pull on the bottle. After a couple of coughs and a shake of his head to clear his mind he whispered, "Thank You." We all had a good laugh about that.

These days Dad has a touch of dementia so he doesn't tell any stories like he always did. But, he hasn't lost his wit and art at being a funnyman all his life. After he retired he loved to play golf although he had quite an unorthodox swing as you might imagine a broken down old rodeo clown would. It always amazed me he could hit a golf ball straight with that old crooked swing he had and it looked like he was chopping wood.

He loved to watch Tiger Woods play as that was his favorite player. He would call me almost every Sunday and ask, "Are you watching, Tiger?" "No", I would tell him. "I'm watching, Phil." I would tell him that just to get a rise out of him. I was over for a visit last summer and asked him if he had been watching the PGA golf tournament. He said he hadn't watched it and asked if it was any good. I told him the last nine was exciting to watch and a great finish. He just stared down at the kitchen table for a minute and then looked up and asked me if I played golf. I said, "Yes. You taught me." He thought for a moment and then said, "Well, you ought to be pretty good then."

And recently I went over to see him and got there about mid-afternoon. Ruth apologized that he was still in bed after taking a nap. She had been trying to get him up to take his medicine, but wasn't having any luck. "Why don't you go see if you can get him up and come in here," she asked. I went to his bedroom and could see he was sleeping soundly.

I didn't want to startle him when I tried to wake him so I gently put my hand on his shoulder and just jostled him ever so lightly. Boy, his head snapped around like a surprised cat and just stared at me. I didn't know if he didn't recognize me or not, so I asked him, "Were you dreaming about some wild bull chasing you?" Without missing a beat he said, "No, it was girls," and rolled over like he was going back to sleep. You just never know what the moment will bring.

R.J. PRESTON
CRACKIN' OUT

When I first cracked out it had been a struggle just to get to go. My dad, who was a three event hand had been paralyzed in a bull riding accident just thirteen days before I was born and he did about as much as he could to discourage me. When he found I would not be discouraged, he and my grandpa Preston did all they could to see I did it the right way.

One of the first rodeos I entered was just down the road and my grand dad took me. He was an old cowboy and had roped calves in the Turtles back in the day. He knew I had the foundation to be a good hand as I could ride a horse bareback like a Comanche. Well, I was nervous as heck and when my time came and when I called for that Angus bull I didn't last much longer than a fart in a whirlwind. I was pretty disgusted with myself, but we stayed and watched the rest of the rodeo as I was in the first section of the Junior bulls and much of the rodeo was left.

On the trip home my granddad was talking about how I wasn't going to make a rodeo hand and that not everyone can be a rodeo hand and that wasn't a bad thing because that was just the way it was and it made me mad as heck. I didn't say a word, but it lit a fire in me to be the best I could after that.

Old Monroe Preston knew how to motivate and in just four years I was at the Prairie Circuit Finals in the bare back riding. I'm sure he looked back at that pickup ride and chuckled a time or two because he had to know I was mad as a wet hen.

I look back at that pickup ride and see it as a turning point in my life. It was when I dedicated myself to my dream of being a rodeo cowboy and I wouldn't trade any of it for anything. Oh, and when he was telling me not everyone was cut out to be a rodeo hand he also told me I'd more than likely make a heck of a farmer. That did the trick with me.

FLOYD TRAYNOR
DAD AND UNCLE JACK

My dad was a team roper. I roped in high school and college, but was never that good.

Dad was jerked off his heading horse one time when the barrier was rigged up the wrong way at the Hurley, New Mexico roping club. The barrier rope wrapped around his neck and he carried the scar for the rest of his life. That was back in the tie hard & fast days.

Don Turner and I must have untied a million calves in that arena. Of course we wanted to chase girls, but our dad's always volunteered us to work the chutes or untie calves.

There was nothing spectacular about my college career that I remember. I went to NMSU in Las Cruces, New Mexico and we all went to a rodeo in Mexico one time and a friend of mine won the prize for rolling across the arena after being thrown from a bareback bronc.

My Great Uncle Jack Traynor is in the Hall of Fame in Oklahoma City. He was the first team roper to heel from the right side. He was also a calf roper and a heeler, but he lost his right hand in a roping wreck while roping a burro. They were drinking, of course, and he decided to rope his neighbor's burro. His horse stumbled just as he reached for his slack and they said that the stump hardly even bled. He wore a white sock over the stump for the rest of his life.

He ran cattle on the San Carlos Apache Reservation in Arizona until he retired then worked at feedlots around Phoenix, Arizona. I have a couple of photos from his rodeo days and also have his spurs. He came to the ranch to help work cattle one spring and Curley Traynor kicked Jack's dog the first morning, so Uncle Jack loaded his dog and mule and they didn't speak to each other for over 30 years.

MYLES CULBERTSON
AY CHIHUAHUA, CARLOS OCHOA

In 2014, an old friend of mine was honored in Mexico for his pioneering leadership in promoting the rodeo sports in that country. The news release credited Carlos Ochoa for his dedicated work over the past 40 plus years inspiring rodeo popularity in a country that always revered ranching and horsemanship, but whose style of competition was very different. In his homeland the Charro was, and is, the historic icon of the competing horseman and "ranchero". Over the years Carlos had a lot to do with bringing another venue to Mexico. As I read the article my memories found their way back to the Chihuahua rodeo of 1965.

Carlos and I became good friends during my first year at New Mexico State University along with a number of other Mexican students mostly from Chihuahua, coming off ranches and farms to attend the College of Agriculture and become proud Aggies. Over the years NMSU became every bit as much Chihuahua's Ag School as our own. Carlos was the consummate Mexican gentleman; self assured, energetic, enthusiastic, able to handle any situation well, whether an academic project, formal public meeting or pugilistic barroom contest.

NMSU was populated by plenty of restless cowboys and Carlos took advantage of the opportunity by inviting a bunch of us to enter the rodeo he was organizing in Chihuahua City. My college roommate Ron Lamb and I decided this sounded like an adventure with our names on it especially with Carlos' offer of fun, hospitality, culture, and roughstock. That was enough for us so several carloads of "hats & boots" college students lit out for a rodeo 300 miles south. None of us had ever been to Chihuahua and few spoke Spanish, but these were minor impediments compared to the notion of roping & riding in an exotic setting.

In those days the highway to Chihuahua was a long narrow two-lane no-shoulder pavement with lots of wide buses and big trucks so there was sure no sleeping in the small caravan of cars on our Friday after-dark trek. We hit town sometime around midnight and spotted a sign with the name of the hotel Carlos told us to look for, checked in, and turned in. Morning light introduced us to a sprawling city of plastered buildings on meandering streets that all seemed to lead to a distant skyline dominated by the twin steeples of a massive old cathedral declaring the city's plaza. Carlos arrived and over breakfast laid out the plan for the rest of the weekend.

The rodeo was going to be just one performance on Sunday afternoon so our Saturday was filled with touring, matched horse races, mariachi music, food, and an abundance of beverage. The local crowds were hospitable, getting a curious kick out of this little band of Aggie vaqueros. That night at the hotel the music didn't end until sometime in the late dark hours with a couple of gringos standing on a table dramatically belting out vocal injustice to a traditional corrida (no, not me).

Finally, the next day we were about to get on with what we had come south for. We arrived late morning at a traditional keyhole shaped arena for the charreada that had been modified to hold an American style rodeo. It was pretty small, at most 30 yards across the round part with some homespun bucking chutes cobbled together on one side and a roping box in the end of the long part of the key. A shaded grandstand surrounded the walled circular area which was already filling with spectators and of course an always-present band of musicians.

Ron, Victor Karnes, and I strolled over to the corrals to get a look at the roughstock. The bucking strings we'd been around in our short careers were typically gentle or at least unafraid of their two-legged opponents, but when we stepped up on the fence these horses fled to the other side of the pen, bunching up in a corner.

The pen of bulls was not so timid. They were mostly crossbred brahmas, but not very big, apparently somebody's range bulls. It was hard to say whether they would have much buck in them, but they were sure showing some snort. We found out later that they were off a couple of area ranches, but the horses were wild, having been trapped in the mountains and brought here for the event. This was going to be interesting.

The atmosphere was festive as the crowd grew, music played and abundant BBQ and beer was consumed. The folks were from all walks; ranchers and cowboys, folks from the city, Mormons, Mennonites, rich, poor; all there to see what this American style rodeo was about. Time didn't mean much and there was no way to know when everything would get started. It didn't really matter other than the longer it took the later we'd be getting back home for class the next day. College wasn't going to wait on us and our plan was to head north as soon as the rodeo was over.

In their own time things started happening. The crowds filled the stands and workers started filling the four hastily built bucking chutes. Instead of drawing for horses we drew chute numbers. As we climbed up with our riggings the horses started trying to climb out. Small by bucking horse standards the horses rattled around and fought the chutes, making pulling the rigging and finally getting set to call for the gate a dangerous exercise in itself. When the gates opened it was a wild show with some running, some bucking, some falling, all hard to score. Each ride was accompanied by the shouts of the spectators and the trumpets of the mariachi. The quality of a high scoring ride

Myles Culbertson

was pretty much lost on this crowd, but the bigger the crash, the more thunderous the applause of the packed grandstand. Among the biggest crowd pleasers was Ron's ride when the chute gate came off its hinges and all three, high spurring rider, wild bucking horse and tumbling pipe chute-gate all piled out together into the center of the tiny arena. Had prizes been paid for the wildest wreck Ron's ride would have been voted the winner.

My first horse wouldn't stop fighting whenever he felt me on his back so I had to take my hand-hold while standing over him and then get set as the gate opened. I was off the rigging a little when we came out and didn't know if I got him marked out. The horse was small and not very stout, but jumped high with head out of sight, twisting all over the place under me.

I spurred over his neck, turning sideways in the rigging just as we hit the wall of the grandstand. Next thing I knew I was on the ground against the wall, scrambling out from under the bronc as he bucked away while the crowd applauded and the mariachis played.

Victor and the other bull riders weren't having much problem making their rides, but had their hands full getting away from these high-horned head slinging brutes that made up for their lack of mass with testosterone driven anger. The same principal of proportional applause-to-wreck applied as one after another found themselves in a race for the fence after their ride.

The calf ropers were using borrowed horses because of the problems they would have had getting their own across the border and then back home. Pat Sedillo caught and tied his calf in the long part of the keyhole-shaped arena and few spectators saw it so the rules were changed on the spot that the roper wasn't allowed to catch until he was in the main part in full view of the crowd. The calves were good, running fast and giving the ropers a good shot at the catch and tie-down.

The riders and ropers were able to get two or three head that afternoon and all came away without serious injury so for all the Aggie cowboys it had been a good run. We piled back in our cars and turned them northward and by the time we pulled off the highway onto the NMSU campus sometime in the dark on Monday morning we were completely spent from a day we couldn't have made much longer.

So went Chihuahua's second annual Carlos Ochoa Rodeo, probably no less wild and exciting as the one a year previous. It wasn't really a rodeo as much as an exhibition and looking back I don't recall if they were even judging the rides, but for Carlos it was a good start as he strove to introduce this new style of competition to Mexico.

Today, almost 50 years later, the American style of rodeo is entrenched in the culture of Mexico thanks to Carlos' early exhibitions, wild and unconventional as they were, and his decades of unremitting support and promotion. Mexican cowboys and cowgirls are now prominent in both their own country and the United States expressing skill and bearing common to the typical world-class rodeo athlete. Some are champions and role models in both countries.

In that single week-end experience a few of us had the privilege to see the early seeding of a nationally recognized sport in Mexico and to have a special appreciation for the dedication of those who brought it into prominence.

Thanks, Carlos. Saludos, y Que le vaya bien…

Myles Culbertson, second from left, with Carlos, shown during his induction into the Mexican Rodeo Federation Hall of Fame.

JIMMY BLOTZ
THE BIG LIE

I was in the 7th grade on my first day back from summer vacation when I noticed a group of guys hanging out by the bike racks waiting on the starting bell. The guys were wearing cowboy boots, Wrangler jeans, big belt buckles and shirts with long sleeves. I liked the way these guys looked and had my mother take me to the Flyin' B Western Wear at the mall and fixed me up with this western garb.

I showed up at school the next day and headed for the bike racks, standing by myself hoping to get noticed. One guy started talking to me and told me that there was a pep rally that day and to set with the other goat ropers. I made my way up the bleachers in the gym to where that rowdy pack was sitting and sat by the guy I'd met before school.

Everyone was talking about a place called the Kowbell so I asked him what was the Kowbell. He said everyone was going to a rodeo Friday night in Mansfield, Texas and then he said, "You do ride bulls, don't you?" I thought for a second, then said, "Ye, ye, yes." We talked a little bit more and he said another buddy that was older was picking him up and if I got a ride to his house, I could go.

I lied to my mom and said I was spending the night with a buddy so she took me to the guy's house and the older guy picked us up and away we went. I wasn't scared at all until we arrived and I saw the bulls, so I watched for a while and found the smallest, mulliest bull I could find.

It was almost my turn when I heard the bull was called Mad Dog. This sent shivers down me, but I was locked in and it was my turn. I got on him and suddenly the chute boss told me to get off that this bull was a jackpot bull and wasn't supposed to be bucked.

Oh, Lord, was I relieved when I was told to get off and to take the next bull. He was a little Jersey-looking, cow-horned, pet and didn't look all that bad. I lowered myself down on him and I know the guys could tell I didn't have a clue how to ride. When the chute gate opened and the bull made a big jump out I think I should have gotten the award of the year for fastest buck off ever, but I was in love.

BRAD EWELL
ME & DOUG

I went to high school with bullfighter Doug Wylie and when we were in school, he was an athlete and also took cosmetology of all things. I was in the rodeo club and was going to high school rodeos so Doug came up to me in the hall at school one day and said, "Hey, what's this bull riding all about? Will you take me and put me on one?" I said, "Of course," thinking one out on one head and he'd bust his ass and be done and we'd all get a big laugh.

Well, after 3 head he and I decided that he wasn't gonna make it as a bull rider. After his last mount out bull, I was in jackpot that night .We were at a Jack Ratjen rodeo in Mansfield, Texas (Kow Bell indoor rodeo) and when the jackpot started I was waiting down in the arena and Doug was standing there beside me.

I'm right handed and my bull was coming out of chute #2 which is a right hand delivery, so I was in the arena. Some kid, about the third guy out of the chutes got hung up real bad to a real nasty Brindle bull with pretty bad clown stabbers. Anyway, the only clown that was there got knocked out and for some reason Doug ran right into the storm and not only got that boy un-hung, but turned the bull back several times just like he'd been doin' it for years.

Nobody even knew who Doug Wylie was, but the kid that got hung up and nearly everybody else goes up to Doug and said, "I'm so and so." I can't remember the kid's name, but he said to

Doug, "How long have you been fighting bulls, anyway?" Doug looked at me and grinned and said, "About 15 minutes," and the rest is rodeo history.

Doug went on to become a well known and well respected bull fighter for 13 years on the PGA circuit. He worked with Leon Coffee, Wick Peth, Rick Chatman and several other great bull fighters. To this day he still says to me, "Brad, I ought to kick your ass for getting me into this…"

Brad Ewell

TROY VAIRA
BORROWED GEAR AND RUBBER SOLED FARMERS BOOTS

I was entered in The Killdeer Mountain Roundup on the 3rd. of July and doubled up in Red Lodge Livingston and Mandan on the 4th. I had planned to play the odds and go to Red Lodge and Livingston on the 4th, figuring two chances are better than one. But, after talking to several cowboys about my draw in Mandan, Bartender, of Dakota Rodeo's I decided I had better go east and get on him. He'd been great and they had been winning a ton of money on him. My traveling partner was up in Belle Fouche

So, I went to the Killdeer Mountain Roundup and rode, not great, but OK. I think I might have split last hole or something even. I was by myself so a bronc rider Ty Manke was going to catch a ride back to Dickinson with me. Without a second glance I helped him load his gear in our van and headed out. I picked up another bronc rider in Dickinson the day of the 4th and headed for Mandan.

We got to the rodeo about an hour before starting time. My bronc rider pulled his gear out first and I reached in to grab mine and found nothing. I had forgotten my riggin' and bag alongside the fence in Killdeer the night before. There wasn't enough time to retrieve it before the performance so I headed behind the chutes in search of gear.

I did have a brand new riggin' under the bed in my van, but it wasn't set up or anything. So, that was it. No glove, chaps, spurs, or nothing. My first lucky strike was coming across two buddies from my circuit that had an extra pair of spurs. The shanks were awful long compared to what I usually ride, but given my current predicament I wasn't choosy.

Next, I ran into a godsend. There was a young Canadian there who rode bare backs, but wasn't entered this particular day, but had his gear along. And can you believe it? He was a lefty.

I went and grabbed that new riggin from under the van bed, tied some latigos on and ran my hand and borrowed glove in it. For never being introduced before it actually felt pretty good. I borrowed his chaps, too. I was pretty nervous the rest of the evening until I nodded my head and we left the chute.

Bartender was great, bucking high and flashy. I made an alright ride on him despite my borrowed gear and my nerves and ended up winning the biggest rodeo of my career thus far. I even got a really great picture out of the deal. My favorite part of the picture is that you can see my rubber soled farmer boots in it.

Troy Vaira (Photo by Jackie Jensen)

DAN NEAL
HITCHIN' RIDES

Back in the 80's, hitchin' a ride was the way to go except if Ricky Lindsey was driving. We all knew better than that. I was needing a ride back to Ft. Worth so I found a ride in Bobby Loug's van, one of those crazy green machines from the 70's. Hell, it even had a stick shift.

There were mostly bronc riders scattered in the back and a couple of bull riders and myself, Allan Jordan Jr. and Joe Winberly as Bobby had gone ahead in trusting the safe homecoming of that pretty that lime green fly van. It sure did good on gas and it didn't cost too much to chip in so the color was worth it.

So, somewhere along the ride leaving Florida and heading to Ft. Worth, Joe Spearman takes the wheel and by the time everybody wakes up we're headed back toward Florida. It looked like we were gonna be late so Allan had us drop him off so he could catch a flight. He didn't trust the slow Texans.

RONNIE VAN WINKLE
A RODEO COWBOY'S TESTIMONY; BE CAREFUL OF WHAT YOU PRAY FOR

I was born on August 25, 1950 and grew up on the northeast side of Houston, graduating from M.B. Smiley High School in 1969 and then Sam Houston State University in 1974. I grew up in a Christian home with my Mother and Dad teaching Sunday school and my Dad a Deacon in a small Southern Baptist Church.

I was the middle child of 3, with my sister Sharon being a year older and brother Billy a year younger. At about the age of 8 one Sunday morning my sister decides to give her life over to the Lord and accept Christ as her Savior and I decided to follow her by walking the isle along with her. I really didn't understand what was happening, but went through the motions. About the age of 11 during a weeklong revival I truly felt the calling and walked the isle that night, giving my life over to the Lord and was baptized at Oak Grove Baptist Church by Brother Bob Baldwin.

I was very active in most school sports and at the age of about 13 I began participating in Junior Rodeo Events. And, at the age of 14 I started competing in the bareback bronc riding at open rodeos while continuing to compete in all events in the Youth or Junior rodeos such as steer wrestling, calf roping, bull riding, and bareback bronc riding. I was pretty good in these events, winning numerous trophy buckles and saddles throughout my high school and college career. I was the 1969 Texas State High School Champion Bareback Rider and represented Texas in bull riding and bareback riding at the National High School Rodeo Association with our team winning the National Championship that year.

I went on to College at Sam Houston State University and was on the rodeo team for four consecutive years and represented Sam Houston State at the National Finals in Bozeman, Montana all four years. It was these years that I started back sliding, a little at first, by not attending church as I should have been. In 1971 I turned Pro and started competing throughout the United States, competing at rodeos such as Houston, San Antonio, Fort Worth, Cheyenne, Orlando, Chicago, etc. I would travel throughout the summer and go to school in the winter and needless to say I was having a blast.

All seem to be going well and it was. I was very disciplined and never touched drugs or alcohol and couldn't stand being around my friends at times when they would go out drinking. Finally, at the age of 21 I gave into Satan and celebrated my birthday while in school at Sam Houston State by going to the local bar and took my first drink and really thought I had a good time. Needless to say, I strayed from my roots and upbringing and continued to back slide further from God.

Even though I felt I had strayed from God, I continued to

pray and He was always there watching over me. It was just that I wasn't always living as a Christian. I knew the world around me needed a change and I would often pray for God to show others around me of His existence in the world. I would pray for Miracles to be performed such as they were back in the days when Christ was in His ministry here on earth, changing the water to wine, healing the lame, causing the blind to see, raising the dead and so on, so that others would come to know and accept Jesus Christ as their Lord and Savior through these miracles. After all, He performed miracles then, so why not now. Did I want proof of Christ for others, I think so, but could I have been looking for answers for myself, or maybe both? Could Satan be working on me?

Anyway, I continued my professional rodeo dream after graduating from Sam Houston in 1974. Shortly thereafter in the summer of 1975 I decided I had had enough traveling around and decided to try finding a job and settle down a little and I did. This put an end to my traveling throughout the states, but I still wanted to rodeo as I was only 24 and still had a lot of good years left. So, I dropped from the professional ranks and started competing at local rodeos, any place I could get to over the weekend and back to work on Monday morning. Life was good and I was easily winning more money at rodeos at the amateur level than I could make at my Monday through Friday job and having lots of fun to boot. Life was good.

In 1977 I bought my first home in Houston and in the spring of 1978 I met and started dating Jo Poorman. Jo was from Katy, Texas had just turned 20, a barrel racer, and I would soon turn 28, but we seemed to hit it off pretty good despite the age difference. All was good, but I continue to stray farther away from God and did not attend church much at all at this time in my life. But, I continued to pray for those Miracles and I knew I needed God in my life and I needed a change, not only for me, but for all my friends around me. I still prayed for the Miracles so others would come to know God and didn't understand why He wouldn't just perform a couple so that all my friends would know that God is real and we would all change our way of living.

Jo and I decided to get married and set a date for September 29, 1978. Things are still going great, or so I thought. I continue working and going to rodeos. Jo competing in the barrel racing at some of the same rodeos I went to which was good as well because I could see and be with her on most weekends. Jo was planning our wedding and I continued as I had been for several years, praying and asking God for those Miracles.

There is a lot in that song by Garth Brooks, "SOMETIMES I THANK GOD FOR UNANSWERED PRAYERS", as my requested miracle that I had been praying for was answered by God in a way that I did not want or expect. One Friday night on August 11, 1978 I had drawn a bucking horse that I had ridden before and won first place on and was sure that I would win again. God had other plans as I crawled down on the horse and nodded my head. The chute gate opened, but the horse stalled and wouldn't come out. After 2 or 3 tries I think someone must have stuck him with a hotshot as the horse jumped into the gate hanging my foot in it and causing the horse to lose its balance and fall on me.

I continued to lie in the dirt, not moving after the horse got off me. I knew my back was broken and at that instant I made a promise to God that if He would just let me walk again that He would not have to watch over me anymore while riding bucking horses and bulls. The Ambulance came in the arena and scooped me up on a board and hauled me to the hospital. Here's the answered prayer by God that I had asked for so many times.

I had completely severed my spine, crushed 3 vertebrates in my back and broke 3 bones in my foot. My severed spine had moved 1 inch to the side and dropped 2 inches, but I was not paralyzed. The doctors could not understand it and said they had never seen or heard of a completely severed spine where the spinal cord wasn't severed as well, much less with no damage to the spinal cord. (The Miracle I had prayed for, the answered prayer that now I wish was an unanswered prayer).

I went through 2 surgeries with the last one being 2 weeks after the accident as they needed that time to prepare the metal plate that would fuse me back together and remain with me for the rest of my life. This took place on my 28th birthday, August 25, 1978. I think it was a month, maybe 6 weeks after the accident that I walked out of the hospital with a cast on my foot, nuts, bolts, and wire in my back, but I walked out. The doctors said that I would likely have to have another fusion in about 10 years, but as of this writing it has now been 36 years without any back problems.

Jo and I had to postpone our wedding a month from September to October 20, 1978, but have been so blessed by God, way beyond our expectations and certainly beyond what we deserve. We married and moved to Waller and joined Waller Baptist Church not long thereafter. We have a daughter and two sons who were all baptized at Waller Baptist Church. We also now have 5 grandkids and looking for more someday soon, we hope. I was ordained as a Deacon in 2007.

Getting back to my commitment and promise I made to God when I had the accident that, "If He would just let me walk again, that He wouldn't have to watch over me anymore while getting on a bucking horse or bull." Although I had several times wanted out of the commitment I kept my promise. I went as far as talking to my Pastor about it, thinking he would offer me a way out. He listened and then told me that my commitment, or covenant, was between myself and God, and not him. Although I never competed again I would often dream of the times when I was young, running the roads, and still getting on those horses and bulls.

The funny thing is that my commitment to God is so strong with me that even in my dreams I have never gotten on either a horse or bull since my accident. I can get to the rodeo, get to the bucking chutes loaded with livestock, but something always goes wrong, usually with my equipment, and I will eventually wake up before the chute gate opens. I've dreamed about rodeos so many times, but I still can't nod my head even in my dreams.

All said and done, I have had a great life with great parents that guided me to Church and Christianity, a wonderful wife and kids that have put up with a lot from me over the years and have been blessed with much more than I deserve. I would not change a thing even the accident, because without it things may not have turned out for me as well as they have.

Rodeos gave me an education, let me travel throughout much of the United States, gave me many lifetime friends, and although I haven't seen many of them in years I can, and do, still call them as my friends. And, it gave me a lifetime partner, my wife, Jo, whom I would not have met without it. Just remember to be careful for what you pray for and be specific as God does answer prayers in His own time and way, and thank God that He is still in the business of performing Miracles."

JAN BARBY PAYNE
CANTON, KANSAS

Daddy was flanking bareback horses and when the horse left the chute, of course, Daddy would pull a bit longer. Just so happened that the other two guys that were standing on that board with him left and the board was not anchored down. The longer he held on the farther he leaned and pretty quickly the board slid out and into the pens. Daddy immediately was shot off the back of the chute and crumpled down into the chute.

The gate man, Keith Cochran, and another one of our hands, Ned Kygar, quickly came do Daddy's aid. Blood was running everywhere and Daddy looked like he'd been in quite a wreck. They were holding him up on either side of him and he kept reaching down. They thought he was passing out and they kept pulling him back up. This went on for a few minutes as pandemonium was all around.

Finally, Dwayne Walker, one of the committee men asked him if he was ok. His reply was, "Yes, but I've been trying to grab my glasses before someone stepped on them. I think I'm too late now." Of course, his glasses were broken, but Mother, being the ever prepared lady she was had his older pair and he was fine. Daddy didn't suffer any injuries a Chiropractor couldn't fix and after that the only telltale sign was a little "divot" of skin off his nose just the exact size of the nose piece on his glasses.

PAM MINICK
CAREFUL WHO YOU MEET

While I was Miss Rodeo America I went to a lot of Cotton Rosser's rodeos in California. He had them in several odd places including a grocery store parking lot in Thousand Oaks and on a football field in Altadena, California. While making my queen introduction lap around the arena at Altadena in early May, my horse slipped broadside and broke my ankle.

I had to continue the next 2 months of my appearances with my foot in a cast and those were the days of the big white plaster casts. In late May I had to go to the rodeo in Fort Smith, Arkansas with my leg in that big old cast. This rodeo was produced by Billy Minick. I remember writing in my weekly column in the Rodeo Sports News, "Thank you for putting me on a horse that took care of me in my cast."

So, 10 years ago I ran into Billy again when I came to Fort Worth to do a TV show. He didn't particularly remember meeting me in Fort Smith and I only remembered because of writing the story about it. But, later we fell in love and the rest is history. So, be careful who you meet because you might end up marrying them on down the road.

Pam Minick heeling and Debbie Garrison heading, team roping.
(Photo credit: dudley@dudleydoright.com)

JOHN SUMERLIN
ROSSER'S CAMP PENDLETON

I was at a rodeo in California and I did not know that much about the bull I was getting on other than he turned back to the left and kicked high, so I was glad to have him. He was one of Cotton Rossers bulls called Camp Pendleton.

I go down right handed. The bull jumped out, turned back to the left and felt good. At the last moment he came to a sudden stop, turned back to the right and welled me. Hooked me in chin, the eye, stepped on my back, and ate my lunch. I kept waiting on the bull fighter, but he was gone to another rodeo down south, I suppose. He damn sure wasn't where I needed him.

Myrtis Dightman was at that rodeo, too, so Myrtis jumped into the arena and got the bull off of me then stayed with me until they got the bull out of the arena and me on a backboard. It was my first ambulance ride. They took me to a nearby hospital and sewed me up. The next day I talked the hospital staff into some Codeine pain killers and they turned me loose. Camp Pendleton damn sure camped on me that day.

© Roger Langford

Part II

1. Andrew Daily: Goin' Down The Road
2. Wayne Whitehead: Spurrin' Contest
3. Cary Culbertson: Four Aces
4. Shari Kroft: Barrel Racing The Rest of The Story
5. David Schildt: Harry Vold's R-111
6. Red Doyal: Punch Time in Houston
7. Janie Liles: Horse Trailer Used for What
8. Ken Judge: Little Oscar
9. Arlene Lamar: From Kansas to Hollywood
10. Steve Davis: Streakin' The Party
11. Charlie Cook: Joe Campos and I
12. Richard Flechsig: His Name Was Garwood
13. Dickey Cox: Cheyenne
14. Lee Jones: Herb Dalton
15. Jerry Gustafsen: Havin' Fun in Houston
16. Bill Putnam: My Final Ride
17. Steve Scott: Traveling With Tombo Jones
18. Clay Tom Cooper: Mardi Gras
19. Richard Flechsig: The Wild Horse Race
20. Doug Munsell: Nfr Stock Sale, 1983
21. Lori Shoulders: One, Used To Be, Cowgirl
22. Jim Sowle: The Ronnie Sowle Story
23. Bobby Dobbins: My Traveling Partner, Jessie James Williams
24. Terri Abrahamson: A Hot Day in OKC
25. Dale Woodard: I'm Not Cold
26. Rome Wager: Marty and Enoch
27. Greg Doering: Life On The Dorering Rodeo Trail; A Peace River Adventure
28. Nick Hite: Texas Cowboy Reunion
29. Joy Foscalina: Chick Magnet

Rodeo Stories II

30. Bret Corley: Team Ropin'
31. Toni Guirino: Black Jack
32. Danny O'haco: Pendleton Roundup
33. Ronnie Wells: A Rodeo Story
34. Jan Barby Payne: Lloyd Barby and The Barby Rodeo Company
35. Red Doyal: Airborne Cowboys
36. Johnny Rivera: My Buddy, Mike White

ANDREW DAILY
GOIN' DOWN THE ROAD

In the summer of 1989, my brother Myron and I were entered in the bronc riding at a TRA Rodeo in Buna, Texas. We lived south of Ft Worth and it was a long haul with no direct route there. We had gotten off work at 2pm and were loaded and ready to go, so down the highway we flew in Myron's '82 Ford Stepside.

We were always ahead of the game and tried to get to every rodeo early because at some of the rodeos they would run the saddle broncs and barebacks together. This time though we barely got there with horses loaded and about to be turned out. After paying the secretary I ran down to see that my brother was already saddled and I was a scrambling.

We both covered our horses, but didn't have the horsepower to draw a check. Now, that sounds kind of an uneventful story to put in a book, but the funny part of this story began after the rodeo. A fellow bronc rider David Terry and bareback rider Mark McGuffin and bull rider Jim Sowle all from Ft Worth had ridden together in Jim's van, with his wife and a mean old blue healer dog.

As we were leaving we saw the van wouldn't start for them so we tried to help, but to no avail. I think the fuel pump went out or something and we couldn't get a new one until the next morning so we decided to stay instead of driving all night back home so that our friends could get what they needed to come back the next day.

My brother's truck had a home made bed liner made out of 2x4's and plywood that was great for storing your gear under, but really bad to give anyone a ride on top of. Jim, his wife, and Myron were in the cab, while me, David, Mark, and that dog rode on top of this thing holding on for dear life and making sure we didn't lose our cowboy hats along with 3 bronc saddles, 5 rigging bags, and whatever clothes bags they had stored underneath the bed liner.

When we were young guys we only had one gear and that was fast so you better hang on. We flew through the night looking for a place to stay. After 20 miles or so we found the only roach motel around for miles. I mean no offense to anyone, but the Middle Eastern gentleman that ran the establishment actually had the audacity to ask Jim's wife, "Do you want it by the hour or for the night?" when she went to get us a couple of rooms. I guess seeing 5 cowboys and 1 woman made him think the party was fixing to commence.

Andy Dally

Jim was a pretty skinny little guy, but he was ready to whip some butt over that comment, but we talked him out of it and went into our low rent palace for the night. Us Dally boys always traveled as cheap as we could so when we walked into that $27.00 showplace of a room we saw why it was so cheap. There was 3" lime green, shag carpet with big holes in it, roaches having their own party until the lights came on, a 12" black and white TV with foil on the rabbit ears, and the beds, well, I won't even go into what that was like. This place looked like we stepped back in time to a cheap 70's porno and we had really outdone ourselves this time.

David, Jim, and Mark, were all IFR qualifiers and really good hands who were older than us and had more experience in the art of rodeo travel. Even this place threw them for a loop. I noticed Mark and David staring at each other then they make a bee line for the bathroom to see who got there first. It made me scratch my head thinking these guys act more like kids than we do, but me and Myron were just tickled to hang out with these guys.

From the bathroom Mark and David are arguing who's getting in the shower first. I thought, "Who cares?" until I finally got my turn. The motel only had 3 nasty stained towels and Mark got the big one, David got the hand towel, Myron got a wash cloth and I got nothing to dry off with when it was finally my turn.

The guy running the place had shut the office down and would not answer so I figured this was what real rodeo traveling was all about. Suck it up! We had the usual after the rodeo beer and talks of, "If I'd had a better draw I'd have placed," or, "So and so didn't even get that horse started," and a lot of war stories from all of us about our exploits.

When it was time to go to sleep I went to get under the covers and found out they stuck together. Of course, McGuffin, and David, just laughed. Between their snoring and the occasional cockroach crawling on me because I wasn't about to get under those covers, I finally got a little sleep.

The next morning I couldn't help but smile thinking this has to be what rodeo is all about. It's the stories, funny maybe only to you, but full of a lifetime of memories. Wow! We must be real cowboys now, we are going home broke in the wallet, but rich in the experience.

After another 20 mile jaunt through the east Texas countryside on top of the bed liner with all the gear and the dog we bought the part at a parts store and went back to the rodeo arena and left Jim and his wife, McGuffin and the dog and headed back to Ft. Worth to drop off David to meet his family.

I've traveled with good cowboys in my short career, some were winners, and most, well, they were just good guys. I've scared IPRA king Dan Dailey half to death with my driving, fixed flats, got stranded, didn't tear up too many hotel rooms, went home hurting, and won a lot of money and hardware for my belt, and through it all I had a blast the whole time.

Traveling with my brother Myron was always a good memory and one I will always cherish. No matter what you do in life or where you go, sometimes it really is all about the journey and not the destination. Some of us made it to the top of our game and some of us got "honorable mention," but not a one of us would trade one minute of experiencing the journey.

WAYNE WHITEHEAD
SPURRIN' CONTEST

Mansfield, Texas, and the Kowbell Arena were an important place to be in the late 60's, 70's and 80's, here in Texas. Jack Ratjen raised bucking bulls and held jackpot bull ridings on Monday and Friday nights as well as having an open rodeo every Saturday night year round. The Kowbell was an indoor arena and weather never affected it.

My dad had a barbershop in Mesquite, Texas, and a lot of the local cowboys or guys passing through, hung out there. Some of the guys I knew growing up and met there were, Freddie Greer, Gene Cummins, David Glover, Frank Rhoades and all of his brothers, R.C. Bales, "Small" Paul Mitchell and many more that I know I am leaving out right now. They knew I wanted to learn to ride bulls and told me about the Kowbell. They let me know that it had practice bulls and was a good place for a kid to start.

In the winter of 1969 I was 17 years old and a senior in high school and started going to the Kowbell to get on practice bulls every Monday and Friday night. I had been on about 10 bulls so a friend of mine thought I was doing pretty well for that amount of bulls and encouraged me to get into the Jackpot. This was a step up from the practice bulls, but I was confident I could do it and it helped that he paid my entry fees to encourage me do it.

In those days especially in the winter there might be 100 bull riders in the jackpot and about half of the current top 15 would be there. It was a tough bull riding. I made the whistle that first time and from that point forward I always entered the jackpot. I did not win anything that night, but that was when I started believing I could. I met a lot of good bull riders there.

I began to make quite a few friends and a lot of them helped me learn more. Being from Mesquite, I was friends with Donnie Gay and he always went to Mansfield and we shared rides over there and back several times. It was easy to get there and for him to be back for high school and me to work the next day. One particular night in the next winter or two particularly stands out in my mind and I want to relate that story to you.

That night was one of the ones where there were tons of bull riders there, so many in fact, that Jack had to run most of the jackpot bulls through twice. Among the regulars that went there, a couple of guys really stood out as very good bull riders. Neither of them ever seemed to buck off and they were the consistent winners. One of those guys was Donnie Gay and the other was Monty Penny.

They both drew one of the best jackpot bulls. His number was 39, and if I remember correctly I believe they called him Flipper. Both of these guys, Donnie and Monty, rode equally as well. With both of them drawing the same bull everyone knew it would come down to a spurring contest for first place. Everyone also knew it was going to be good watching because these guys were good friends, but were also very competitive with each other.

That bull #39 was a black muley, probably an Angus, Brangus cross. He always turned back and made a lot of rounds. If you got him rode you were going to win the bull riding. Donnie had him the first trip out and as soon as he turned back Donnie began to spur him, going very quickly to the neck. It was quite a bull ride and left everyone oohing and aawing. Donnie was naturally winning the bull riding. It took quite a while for them to buck bulls until they brought ole #39 back for Monty Penny. Not a person left because we all knew this would be good watching and that Monty would be trying to match Donnie's spur ride.

When #39 was finally run in for Monty it was on. 39 made the same tracks with Monty as he had for Donnie. Like Donnie, as soon as 39 turned back Monty began giving him the boots and spurs as Donnie had. Monty went to the neck as Donnie had, then an incredible thing happened. Monty went for the top of the neck and spurred this black bull right in the top knot of his head and drug his foot down the middle of the top of his neck, nearly all the way to the handle of his rope. Everyone's mouths just dropped open. Talk about a spurring contest. That was probably the best one I ever saw by both of these guys.

They split the bull riding. Everyone knows who Donnie Gay is and what he accomplished in the sport of bull riding and he is in a class of his own. A lot of people may not know who Monty Penny was and is, but he may be what I believe to be one of the most under rated rank bull riders that I have ever known.

I am proud to say that both of these guys are my friends, both then and now, and just so you know this was not their last spurring contest. It became a regular thing and it got to where you could hear them spurring their bulls from the front door of the Coliseum. Both of these guys and Freddie Greer always helped and encouraged me with my riding more than any other guys did, even though I never won much. I will always remember them for that and will always be thankful to them. Back then people didn't tell you that if you were 6'4," chances are you were not going to be a very good bull rider.

CARY CULBERTSON
FOUR ACES

Although I lived in Las Vegas, New Mexico, I considered The X I T Rodeo and Reunion in Dalhart, Texas as my home town rodeo. My mother, Marie Ellen (Foltz) Culbertson, was the first XIT Cowboy Reunion and Rodeo Queen in 1937. I was born in Dalhart and I had many relatives there. The general offices for W. O. Culbertson and Sons, Inc. cattle ranches were also in Dalhart.

The X I T Rodeo and Reunion was always held the first weekend in August and was a big celebration. The rodeo was hailed as the world's largest amateur rodeo, the stock was tough, and many of the cowboys and cowgirls that entered were as tough as the professional RCA cowboys and cowgirls (Rodeo Cowboys Association changed their name to Professional Rodeo Cowboys in 1975).

It was in the early 1970's and I had entered the saddle bronc riding and was up in the Saturday night performance. I had been in Dalhart all weekend visiting with family and enjoying the festivities. Saturday afternoon I went by the rodeo office to see what I had drawn. The stock was provided by L. D. Ward Rodeo Company, and I had drawn Four Aces. When I saw this a cold chill ran up my back. I had drawn Four Aces three or four times before and he bucked me off each time.

On one occasion I hung up to him with my left foot still in the stirrup and my spur in the cantle of the saddle. He literally kicked the shirt off of my back before my boot was jerked off my foot. Although I went professional for a period of time I did not travel that hard and stayed pretty regional as we had a 64,000 acre cattle ranch to take care of while I was home for the summer from college. During that time I had ridden some RCA national finals qualifying horses, but this stout palomino paint was without a doubt the hardest bucking horse I had ever drawn.

That afternoon I rode him in my mind at least one hundred times. His normal pattern was to buck straight away for 6 or 7 jumps then suck back hard to the left. If he didn't buck off the bronc riders before this, he lost most of the others here. If you got him rode to the whistle there was a very strong chance that you were taking home first place money.

Just before the performance I had gotten my saddle out checked and rechecked my binds, stirrup length, sat in it, and rode and re-rode Four Aces on the ground. The performance started, the grand entry was over, and the bareback riding had begun. I was mentally preparing myself for my ride. The bareback riding was over and the calf roping had begun.

The broncs were being loaded into the chutes. The bronc riders were saddling their horses. I set my saddle down on Aces, making sure the stirrup leathers lay perfectly over the slope of his shoulders. We were cinching the bronc, pulling the latigo slow and deliberate, making sure that the saddle did not slip back. I was careful not to cinch him too tight as to let the front end of the saddle float a little bit through the ride.

I pulled the flank cinch tight in order to keep the saddle in place. I pulled several strands of mane hair off of Aces and measured my rein; fist, thumb and two fingers from behind the swells of the saddle. I tied the strands of mane hair into the rein where I had measured it. All the time, riding and re-riding the bronc in my mind.

The calf roping ended. There were three bronc riders ahead of me and the bronc riding had started. The first two bronc riders had made their rides and the third was fixing to call for his bronc.

With butterflies in my stomach and adrenalin running hard I

was getting settled into the saddle. I had my rein in my left hand, got my right foot into the stirrup sat down into the saddle, reached down put the left stirrup over my foot. It was time to call for the gate. The chute was right hand delivery. I looked into the area to see if it was clear for me to start my ride. I then looked back and focused on Aces ears, lifted on my rein and called for the gate.

The gate swung open and Aces bailed out hard landing on his front feet. I had him marked out with my feet turned out at a 45 degree angle. I held my feet over the break of his shoulders through the second jump and started spurring on the third jump and fell into time with him. Then came the fourth, fifth, sixth jumps and I was thinking to myself, "I have him covered this time." The seventh jump, as predicted, he sucked back hard to the left. I was waiting for him to do this and was prepared for him and I thought to myself, "Well, there is always next time," as I hit the ground."

SHARI KROFT
BARREL RACING, THE REST OF THE STORY

People think barrel racing is just being the fastest around 3 barrels. Being fastest doesn't matter if you can't get there. Traveling is the most challenging thing about barrel racing. I often hear the comment from other cowboy contestants that, "You're driving and I'm flying and you're beating me to the rodeo."

Speaking of flying, towards the end of February, 1980 I was up in slack after the night performance in Monroe, Louisiana. I was driving my 1 ton dually with an 8 1/2 foot camper, pulling a single axle 2 horse trailer with my good horse Geri and back up horse Hawkeye on board.

I was on I-20, just east of Shreveport, Louisiana and had been talking to a friendly trucker on the CB pretty much since Dallas and only 1 1\2 hours to go. It was about 8 pm and we were going about 65 mph. All of sudden he shouts something and I said, "What?" Boom! I hit a railroad tie, sending us up in the air. The 8 tract tapes I had on the dash came flying out, hitting my poor dog.

My front driver's side tire and the inside dual went flat as the railroad tie had ripped the tire and spinal off the trailer and the axle was dragging under it. I grabbed the wheel with both hands and held it straight until we slowed down and I could pull into the center grass media and stop.

The trucker had pulled over and came running back. He said all he saw was sparks and thought maybe when he hit the tie it might have gone through my windshield. I unloaded the horses and they were both just fine and not upset at all. The trucker helped me put the spare tire on the front of my truck.

We left my horses tied to the semi with his partner to babysit while we went to find a phone. I called to turn out my run and the rodeo secretary asked, "Vet release?" I said, "No, horses are OK." So, she said, "Doctor release?" I said, "No, I'm fine. Only a blood blister changing the tire." So, she said, "Ok, we'll give you a hardship release."

Then, the trucker called a friend who had horses who was 50 miles away who knew someone 30 miles away who knew someone else closer and after talking with about 10 people, we found someone 5 miles away who would meet us on I-20 and pick up my horses and keep them for me until I could fix the trailer.

All is good, right? Wrong. On the way back I saw my horse Hawkeye's rear end sticking out of the cab of the semi-truck and the trucker's partner on the CB screaming about a horse in the first east bound lane on 1-20. Hawkeye had gotten untied and the trucker's partner didn't know how to move him.

He was able to hang on to Hawkeye and reach the CB. I felt helpless and thought my horse was going to be hit for sure. I'm headed on the west bound side and can't do anything because the next off ramp is 5 miles further, then 5 miles back. The only thing I could do was beg over the CB radio to not hit my horse.

It was the longest 10 miles, but thankfully he wasn't hurt. Then, the Highway Patrol shows up. His only comment was, "I don't know what you did, but you did it right. This rig should of flipped." Then, he gave me the number of someone who could help get the trailer off I-20.

You would think this is the end, but no. The next morning here comes a 1\2 ton pickup pulling a flatbed trailer and an oil derrick kind of A-frame tow truck thing. Now, my trailer is parked in the unleveled center divider and they manage to get the front of my trailer on the back of the flatbed supported only by the little metal wheel on the jack.

They backed the A-frame rig to the back of my trailer and began trying to lift the rest of my trailer on to the flatbed. Unfortunately, not being level my trailer kept tilting. So, now they decide to move to the right side shoulder of I-20 because it is more level. I stood there holding my breath while the flatbed was driving forward and the A-frame was backing and my trailer titling between them, moved to the other side of I-20.

I look up and here comes 2 semi trucks headed straight for us. Well, they made it across safely, but the trailer wouldn't fit on the flatbed. It rested on the back of the trailer making the truck very light in the rear. Driving 15 mph we made it the 20 miles to the shop, but he can't back into the driveway because it was uphill and he had no traction.

He tells his son who's driving the 1\2 ton to go down the road and turn around so he can back down into the driveway. We wait and wait, but, no son, and no trailer. I, half jokingly said, "With my luck, he probably wrecked." Pretty soon here comes a guy who tells us that the trailer and the son had jack knifed and we need to go down and pull it out of the mud.

So, we get in the A-frame rig and go down the hilly two-lane road and at the bottom of these two was the truck and trailer in the mud. We managed to pull the truck and trailer out, but we're facing the wrong direction in the road and just as the son drives off I look up and coming down one hill is a little pickup traveling in his proper lane, but coming from the other direction down the hill was a 3 ton logging truck headed straight for us.

He had to either hit the little truck head on, the A-frame head on, or drive off into the mud where we had just pulled out the trailer. Well, I had to jump behind the A-frame to keep from being hit and the 3 ton hit the mud and slowly rolled over on to it's side. The tow truck guy says, "Oh, that's old Joe. His brakes never work." I look over and here comes this guy climbing out the driver's side window. He says, "It'll take about 20 minutes to unload the truck. You can come back and upright me then."

We get back in the A-frame and go back to the shop and everything went pretty smooth after that. The trailer needed a fender welded back on, a new skid bar on back, a new spring, and a friend , Steve Davis brought me a new axle from Dallas, Texas. 6 new tires later I was good to go. I learned that my horses could survive a wreck in this tough little trailer. I believe to this day that it kept us from rolling and getting seriously hurt that night. Many times people tell me I should buy a new trailer, but I still own the old 76' single axle McQuerry I bought from World Champion Byron Walker and his dad, and I believe I always will

DAVID SCHILDT
HARRY VOLD'S R-111

In 1976, I was working as a recreation specialist for the Billings Indian Center one year after becoming, and realizing my dream, of being a bull riding champion at the 1975 GPIRA Bull Riding Championship in the Indian Cowboy Circuit which included Montana, North, and South Dakota. I had to hitchhike and ride busses and trains all those years which kept me pretty broke. I was 16 when I started and 21 when I won the big one and my very own saddle.

For me this was special since in my childhood I had to fight my older brother over the only saddle our family had every time I wanted to go riding on the Blackfeet Indian Reservation at the base of the Northern Rocky Mountains in Montana.

After the win in 1975, I chose to enjoy the title and attend college at Eastern MT in Billings and go after a college degree. I only competed in rodeo in college for fun that year.

In August of 1976 Harry Vold brought his bulls and broncs to the Crow Fair Rodeo which he produced at Crow Agency. I was helping put up a hot dog stand for the Indian center at the powwow grounds on a hot Wednesday afternoon. I had called the rodeo call back number and was told I was up on Thursday. I finished my work and dressed in a billed sun visor, tank top t-shirt, Nike shoes, and jogging shorts, I went to watch the rodeo to get an idea of how the stock might pitch in this 100 degree heat.

As I was grand standing and sifting my way through the rodeo program I checked the bulls, which was the next event. When I came across my name by Vold's bull R-111 I thought, "What heck was I doing up on Wednesday"? I was told I was up on Thursday. I headed down to the rodeo secretaries office and found the secretary. Ken told me they decided to move me in order to get someone on this feature bull that they had just won the short go on at the Cheyenne Frontier Days. I thought, "Well maybe this is a blessing in disguise," so I just thanked him and went behind the chutes to try and borrow some rodeo gear.

It was a challenge, but I eventually borrowed an old ragged looking rope, and attire from boots to hat. It was not what I had been used to considering what I had been riding for the last 7 yrs. But, what the heck, I was confident in my ability and thought it would be great to ride this little Brahmer. As the bulls rolled in I got a look at this little 1100 pound bull R-111.

The bulls came in what seemed kind of quick that day as usually a Crow Fair Indian Rodeo would last 7-9 hours so they can sell a lot of Indian Tacos. I stuck my borrowed rag rope on R-111 and got on. As I was heating my rosin the bull fighter walked up to my chute and said, "Be ready. They just won Cheyenne on this little bull and he's gonna set and turn back lightning fast right in the gate."

I thanked him and smiled, telling him that bulls that turn back away from my hand were just what the doctor ordered. As I pulled my rope I noticed R-111's body get rock hard, like he was getting mad as I pulled my rope.

Well, the bull fighter was right. R-111 bailed out of there and cranked it back to the right so fast all I saw was his nose come up and his ears flop. The next thing I knew was I could hear a nurse saying, "He's waking up." The man's voice, who I thought was a doctor said, "Give him another dose," which must have been sleeping gas because I woke up on the table a while later with 38 brand new stitches in my head.

I guess he was faster than I thought and he managed to step on my head in the process. One of my rodeo buddies said, "Poor bull. Did he hurt his foot?" I can laugh about this today, but I guess God wanted to keep me around for a while. How they stripped me of all the borrowed gear I don't know. Only an Indian can steal that fast.

The next time that I got on a bull I remembered one thing. Never say, "This bull is just what the doctor ordered."

Being a cowboy musician I wrote this song about my trip:

Vold's R-111

Dave Redboy Schildt © 7/22/13

I woke up this morning at the Crow Fair Rodeo
A perfumed scarf round my neck from where I don't know
Splashed water on my face from a livestock trough
Found coffee to kill the morning chill off.
Tomorrow evening it's bull ridin' fame
I have R-111 and he's known to cause pain
I ride the Brahmas, nothing beats that
Not Olathe Boots or American Hats
I'm reading the day sheet for this afternoon

Havin beer, makin jokes, and singing a cowboy tune
Living it large and getting' some air
Like a real Bird bronc down at the Crow Fair
Then, I start a cussin' and questionin' 7's.
My name is right beside R-111
I ran to the judge and said, "This is wrong"
He must've believed me standing there in my thongs
He said, "If you want this bull rider's gold
Git rid of that thong and get R-111 rode."
I borrowed it all from boots to a hat
Bull rope and rosin, spurs and old chaps
Borrowed entry fee money, I should've stayed home
R-111, he's best left alone
The scarf around my neck I tied to the fence
I should have borrowed some good common sense
With a whiff of her perfume I yelled for the gate
My minds at the dance hall, still on Cattle Kate
The chute gate swung wide and out came the beast
And R-111 dove off to the East
His Brahma ears flopped, his eyes were red.
Bull snot was flyin' all over my head
When I came to, I heard a nurse say
"Give him more gas," then she faded away.

RED DOYAL
PUNCH TIME IN HOUSTON

I'll need to start this off by saying no one in the world can spend a story as well as Gary Leffew and he was telling me about the first time he came to rodeos in Texas. He and another rider had made it to Texas and I think that rider was Jerry Hixson, a bronc rider from around Modesto. They ended up with Bo Ashhorn in Houston, all broke and trying to get by.

Bo got up early one morning and left and when he got back

around lunch time he said, "You guys about ready to go eat?" They were all excited as Bo had borrowed some money from someone so they all went to a small cafe and sat down. When the waitress came over to take the order they sat and waited for Bo to order so they would know how much money he had borrowed.

Bo said, "Chicken fried steak and all the trimmings," so all the guys followed the lead and ordered the same. They finished eating then waited for Bo to take care of the bill, but he looked at them and said, "How are we going to pay for this"? Gary said they ordered extra tea to kill a little time and after a while four younger guys came in and sat down fairly close to them.

Bo looked at his buddies and said, "All will be ok," then got up and walked over by the other guys at their table. Gary thought he knew them and was going to borrow some money from them, but suddenly one guys jumped up and hit Bo and a big fight followed.

Gary said he didn't know why, but he ended up with a salt shaker in one hand and a pepper shaker in the other and held them up like guns and shouted, "Everyone stop." The guys stopped fighting, but the owner was shouting, "Get out of my café." Gary, Bo, and Jerry, backed out the door and made a very fast exit. So this is how to get a free meal on Bo Ashhorn.

JANIE LILES
HORSE TRAILER USED FOR WHAT

After Jim quit bareback riding he just couldn't stand not going to a rodeo. However, as he approached the time to quit, the big 40, things started to change. I saw an ad in the Gilbert Newspaper which said a group was getting together to save Gilbert Days. Keep in mind at this time there wasn't even a stop light in town. I told Jim he should go and see if they were going to put on a rodeo. He went to the meeting and the group said they knew nothing about putting on a rodeo. Jim said he did and they should do it. All agreed and the fun started.

We founded the first rodeo in Gilbert, Arizona and it later became one of the best IPRA rodeos in the west. To put it together the first time we had to tear down friends corrals and borrow bucking chutes. We told everyone in town that we wrote checks to, not to cash them until after the rodeo. The first rodeo was out in a field. We had a rain storm the day before the first performance. Committee members who had heavy equipment came in with buckets and got all the mud out of the area and dumped it out in the field. They worked most of the night to get it done.

The next morning we had to water the arena because after the committee members hauled in new dirt it was dry and dusty. Mary Cravens, the rodeo secretary who had been rodeo secretary all over the country at IPRA Rodeos said she had never seen a committee do what ours did. We went on to have our own rodeo grounds, arena, concession stands, soccer field for the kids, and lots more. Over the years I became one of the first woman rodeo Chairman in the country.

Anyway, in preparation for the rodeo all us lady members of the committee decided we would cook for the concession stands. Of course, the men said they would help. They helped the way men usually do when cooking and that is to have a few beers. That was probably best because then they stayed out of the way. What better to cook, but Mexican food. We did everything from scratch, cooking the pinto beans, making refried beans, shredding the beef, roasting the green chilies and so on. Much to our amazement we sold out in a couple of hours the first day so we had to go the grocery stores and buy stuff for hamburgers and hot dogs. We also had to roundup BBQ's to cook on.

Back to the story I really wanted to tell on Jim, the parking lot wasn't the smoothest one. My friend Jeri Lilly, a great trick rider, and I, saw Jim going into the horse trailer to do what every cowboy and cowgirl has done. I'll let you figure that one out. So

Jeri and I looked at each other with a gleam in our eyes and a smile on our face. We made a bee line for the truck. Got in, put the keys in, and slammed on the gas. The trailer gates were waving in the wind and we couldn't really hear what Jim was yelling, but I probably couldn't put the words here anyway. Jeri and I were laughing until tears flowed. When we circled the trailer and went back to park, it is needless to say that Jeri & I locked the truck doors until Jim went back to the arena.

KEN JUDGE
LITTLE OSCAR

As athletes, we all know the meaning and power of home field advantage. Well, I considered this pen just that. When you have confidence in yourself, having confidence of the venue is merely a bonus. During the course of my career I had a lot of success at this pen in McGregor, Texas, actually my home town for 12 years.

I was fortunate to have been crowned bull riding champion there seven times and had one of my most memorable rides there on a legendary bull of L. J. Huffmans, Little Oscar. It was and remained my highest score of 91 points and that was in a time when the low 70's would be enough to win it. I was very blessed and will cherish the memories for as long as I live.

Little Oscar was not linked to the famed Oscar, however he resembled him so much that he was dubbed Little Oscar. The night I rode him was one of those times where I just knew there was no way I was gonna buck off. It was a sultry, summer night in June of 1979 and I had been riding for seven years and had gained a lot of confidence in my ability.

Myself and my traveling buddies and good friends as well, Pogo Scroggins and Billy Keith Crawford, were entered that night and either of them could take the money on any given night. Pogo had drawn Skippy, which was a mean, black bull that was hard to twist and also had a reputation of getting' in your britches. Billy Keith had drawn Red Wasp, a chute fighting Santa Gertrudis bull that was definitely a bucker.

The excitement filled the air as the announcer was building the crowd for our task at hand. The Stock Producer L. J. Huffman hauled some of the rankest bull around at that time and normally they only got one or two rode and sometimes three, but not too often when he brought the A string.

Well, it soon came time for the bull ridin and like always we gave each other pats on the back and a little pump up. When the the bulls were loaded they saved us three for last. The announcer did a great job working the crowd as we were local favorites. There were ten riders up that night and they had bucked seven bulls with nobody making the whistle.

Pogo was next on Skippy and I knew the first bull ride of the night was about to happen. Pogo was handy for sure and had a ridin style a lot like Larry Mahan. My prediction was right as I heard the buzzer and the crowd cheering, but I didn't see the ride as I was preparing for my own. Nevertheless, Pogo did his job and was the first guy to get a score with two riders remaining.

Then, on to my other buddy Billy Keith on Red Wasp. Wasp was a rank dude that didn't get ridden very often, but my buddy was capable of getting it done. By this time the crowd was hungry for more, but judging by their reaction my friend didn't make the buzzer. I had to stay focused as it was now me and Little Oscar, the matchup the crowd had been waiting for.

My good friend Marty Honey was also there and he pulled my rope. Actually, he had helped me on my very first bull when I was about fifteen. Marty had a way of keepin the nerves in check so when he pulled my rope I took my wrap, eased up on Little Oscar and said to the gate men, "Let's go, boy's," Then, it was just me and Little Oscar.

When the gate opened Little Oscar bailed out, standin on his nose like he usually did and had a reputation for slamming you to the ground pretty quick. But, I had a good seat and was zoned in as he kicked hard for two more jumps then turned back to the right which was into my hand. I knew if I could make it around that first turn in good shape I was gonna get him rode.

Well, I did, so I got more aggressive and turned loose with my outside foot. I was in full control when I heard the buzzer and didn't waist any time gettin off. I landed on my feet and the crowd roared. The judges relayed the score to the announcer and when he yelled out 91 points the crowd jumped to their feet as I tipped my hat. I was overwhelmed as my buddies ran out to congratulate me and it was definitely a moment that will stay with me for as long as I live.

ARLENE LAMAR
FROM KANSAS TO HOLLYWOOD

"My life began on a small farm around Kingsdown, Ford County, Kansas." Arlene says. "I was the youngest of eleven children and I started riding when I was five years old." If it had four legs Arlene, as well as her sister Cretia, was on it. A bull calf made a fine mount for a while. Later, a horse named Babe helped Arlene become a trick rider. "I dropped out of school before the eighth grade and helped on the farm with the chores," she said.

She was taken to her first rodeo and was dazzled by the trick riders. A quick learner, she would go home and make the straps that she had seen on the saddle. Up on Babe she practiced the tricks she had seen. All alone out in a back pasture with a barbed wire fence to keep Babe going straight, Arlene, barefoot, was up in the Hippodrome stand, off on the fender drag and generally throwing herself all over Babes neck, rump and back. "I was always a dare devil," she said. "I kept going to the rodeos and I kept practicing and even got myself a trick saddle."

I bought a Western Horseman Magazine often and in one issue I responded to an ad from Mr. and Mrs. Joe Stoddard of

Nampa, California asking for girl riders. I sent them a letter and in return they wanted me to join them. I left home and went to their small ranch." Ernie Kirkpatrick of Bradford, Pa, who had ridden with the White Horse Ranch Troupe, taught Arlene Roman Riding. Later, Donna Rosium from South Dakota who had also ridden for the White Horse Ranch joined the Stoddards and became a close friend to Arlene.

"We trained for three months before going on the road. Our first show was a fair at Jordan Valley, Oregon then on to Winnemucca, Nevada showing at their fair. I will not forget that I was on the race track doing my one foot stand in the saddle when a piece of paper blew in front of my horse Silver. She shied and I landed on the track. They helped me off the track and I walked around a little and went back riding."

After Winnemucca they were on the road again. "Donna and I drove Stoddard's car behind them in the truck full of horses. At one point we were going so slow up a mountain that I left our car and jumped on the running board of the front truck to ask a question. Mrs. Stoddard didn't expect me and got so scared she told me not to do that anymore.

We were on our way to Napa, California showing at the Santa Rosa Fair. When we showed at the Napa Mental Hospital some of the patients climbed the fence and scared the horses so much that we thought we would need to leave the horses in the Mental Hospital. Then we went to the Veterans Administrative Hospita and finally on to the Stockton State Fair."
"I met the movie star Bill Elliot who was the Grand Marshall of the rodeo. Elliot starred as Wild Bill Hicock in the movies. After we did our riding we were on the race track with our horses and Bill Elliot had his horse Stormy Night tied to the railing at the track. I mentioned to Donna that I was going to ask Bill if I could ride Stormy Night, but she said he would not allow that. After he was through talking to a fellow I went over an asked him he said, "Sure."

Arlene Lamar

"He gave me a leg up as the stirrups were too long and he was six four. Anyway, in that process he about threw me on the other side of Stormy Night." "That was very nice." Donna said, as she was surprised he let me. I said, "All you have to do is ask," and she said, "I don't have the nerve you do." We showed at Sacramento State Fair in California and we stayed in Napa around six weeks.

"We went on to San Francisco and on our white horses we rode in the 4th of July parade down Market Street to City Hall. "My horse Frosty jumped every white line at the intersections. That was exciting and the people on the street would clap. They thought it was a stunt so I just waved back at them like it was."

"Then we went to Palm Springs, California where we rode in the Desert Circus Parade, finally wintering at the Lazy C Ranch in Palm Springs. We had a show at 1000 Oaks in the Mojave Desert. At that show the Stoddard's had a beautiful Albino stallion that

I rode bareback and jumped a five foot hurdle with. When I rode in to the jump I would put the reins under my leg and throw my hands in the air as we went over the jump. I needed to get the reins back in my hands as soon as hit the other side as he liked to buck after a jump, but I liked jumping him."

While the Stoddards and their show were at the Banning, California fair grounds they met Frank and Lois Hall who had a son and daughter. The daughter wanted to learn how to Roman ride and the Stoddards wanted to sell out so the Halls bought the show. The new show was named "The Valkeries and Their Flying White Horses."

The Valkeries moved to the Broken Arrow Ranch on Sherman Drive in North Hollywood and started doing benefit and live TV shows. The ranch had a nice arena and every Sunday they would have practice and jackpot roping with quite a few PRC, Professional Rodeo Cowboys attending. Those were really great times.

Their new trainer was Merle Christenson who was a double for Roy Rogers. "The Valkeries were chosen to be in a movie at Republic Studios, 'The Heart of the Rockies.' Arlene said, "We were on the set four days for our part in the movie. In the movie we did a square dance on our white horses and Roy Rogers called the dance. Donna and I had to ride under a gate and stop, turn our heads towards the camera and smile. Donna jumped the five horses in the movie."

During a publicity photo shoot with the famous cinematographer Sid Hickock, the girls and their horses posed for several photos with Roy and Trigger. They did a photo of all of them standing on their white horses with Roy, and then Sid Hickock said, "Roy, how about you sit on Trigger and one of the girls can stand behind you with the other six horses three on each side?" Roy agreed and said to Arlene, "You'll do," and she hopped on over onto Trigger's broad back behind Roy. She remembers that

Mr. Rogers was a real nice guy. The movie was released in 1951 and is still a western classic.

In 1950 at the Los Angeles Coliseum Roy Rogers was the Grand Marshall of the Sheriff's Rodeo. The Valkeries and Their Flying White Horses were showing at this rodeo in front of an audience of 102,000. Arlene said, "We were in the Grand Entry of the rodeo and we did our square dance with Roy Rogers calling the dance. Donna jumped the five horses and Sydney and I had a three horse Roman race. There were a lot of Marines in the audience. As I rode by styling, the Marines were whistling and waving and I won the race." Photo # 25—Arlene LaMar

STEVE DAVIS
STREAKIN' THE PARTY

I can't remember the year, but it was at San Angelo, Texas and Bo Ashorn always had a big party. Well, as night got late and lots of beer got drank a certain bull rider decided he'd streak the party. He went to the bathroom and came out in only his hat and as I recall, he made a lap around the tables then back to the bathroom only to find his clothes gone.

He had to borrow a girl's long coat to get back to his room, but there was no sign of his clothes. Well, the next day at the Sunday afternoon performance the big talk was not about his streaking, but what happened to his clothes.

However, all questions were answered after the barrel race that day when they brought the clown's dummy into the arena. It was dressed in this bull rider's duds, shirt, pants, buckle, and all the way down to his exotic skin boots. A rodeo photographer took a picture of the dummy and it made the front page of the sports news. It was great.

CHARLIE COOK
JOE CAMPOS AND I

Joe Campos and I had entered an open rodeo in the winter of 1993 at Edinburg, Texas and when the bulls were drawn we were told by the stock contractor Lance Young that we had two identical looking bulls, black muleys. Since they were new and not branded we were relying upon Lance or his dad to get us on the right bull.

As the bulls were being loaded in the chutes, one of the black muleys was the third bull loaded. I asked Mr. Young if that was my bull and he told me it was. I put my rope on the bull and Joe pulled it for me and I nodded for the gate.

That black bull came out and immediately turned back to the left away from my hand. I rode him and the judges marked me high enough to be in first place. By the time I retrieved my bull rope and got back behind the chutes the other bull that we assumed was Joe's was loaded. When I got to Joe he was already getting down on the bull and Lloyd Koerth was helping him.

As Joe was warming up his rope the question arose that I might have actually gotten on Joe's draw and that he was sitting on my bull. As the judges began to question what might have happened and could be done to correct it Lloyd immediately told Joe to pull his rope, take a wrap, and get out of the chutes.

Joe did just that before there could be any more discussion. Joe nodded for the gate and he made an excellent ride on his black spinner. The judges marked the ride high enough to place him third. Of course all kinds of hell broke loose from one bull rider at the finish, complaining that Joe and I had gotten on the wrong bulls and that we were taking away most of the money.

He wanted the bulls run back in and for us to ride the bulls that were had actually drawn. Since they were young bulls Lance didn't want to buck them a second time and the judges decided that the scores would stay as marked. Needless to say, Joe and I got our money and got out of there ASAP.

Thank goodness for Lloyd's quick thinking to get Joe out on his bull before anyone really figured out that Joe and I had ridden one another's bulls. To the complainer, I told him that the only difference in the outcome is that Joe would have won first and I would have taken third and that he still would have kept his fourth place finish.

RICHARD FLECHSIG
HIS NAME WAS GARWOOD

In 1963, Jack Fettig called me and asked if I could come out and fight bulls at the Montana High School Rodeo Finals in Glendive and as an added incentive, work Killdeer the following week. I said I would go and left Illinois at about midnight on a Wednesday and arrived in Glendive on Friday morning about 10:00am. I was a tired puppy and talked to the rodeo secretary and told her I was going to get some rest and would see her that evening.

Have you ever been so tired you couldn't sleep? Well, that was me and I tossed and turned and just finally got up about 4:30, cleaned up and went out to the rodeo grounds. I talked to Jack and he said we were going to buck fifteen bulls in the performance and about fifteen after. I was the only bullfighter and Jack had a black kid that worked for him called Snowball that was going to work the barrel. If any of you that were ever at the old Glendive arena you know it was big.

I got along OK in the performance and did find out that Snowball wasn't the most mobile barrel man out there. In the slack they bucked a little red bull that probably weighed 1100 pounds with kind of nub horns and fast as greased lighting. His name was Garwood and he caught me away from the barrel after the rider had bucked off and ran me down and did wear me out.

I made it through the rest of the rodeo OK and thought, now I can go shower and sleep late. Jack told me before I left that they had a rodeo parade Saturday morning at 9:30am and they wanted me to ride my mule in it, so no rest for the wicked.

By the time we got finished with the parade I decided to just leave my makeup on and nap at the arena and I don't do well napping.

That afternoon we bucked fifteen more and had more slack and guess what. That little red sucker was a long way from the barrel when he got the rider off and I turned him a time or two, but he nailed me again and this was getting old. All told, Garwood hit me three times in four performances and there was just no way by myself, I could get away from him without running to the fence and that wasn't in my play book.

When I got to Killdeer on Monday evening the announcer and I had to go to Bismark to be on a radio show. When I met him at the rodeo office I asked the secretary how many bull riders she had entered and she said only seven. Remember, this was long before Procom so you had to call in directly and she was there until about 9:00 pm when the books closed. I had my bull riding bag with me so I told her to put me in if she didn't get ten entered

When we got back from Bismark we stopped at the office and asked the secretary how many bull riders she had and she told me ten. I said, "Good, then I'm out." I really didn't like riding when I was working, but she said, "No. You're number ten."

The next day before I got ready I went over to see what I had drawn in the bull riding and guess what, I drew that little hooking sucker Garwood. Damn, not good. I always had them hold my bull until after the performance to give me a chance to put on my jeans and get ready and a chance to catch my breath.

I took my rope over to the chutes and put it on Garwood and got on and one of the guys asked if I needed pull, but I said, "Nope, I'll pull it myself." He looked at me like I had lost it. I explained how this little bull had ate my lunch three times in three days and now without a bullfighter I was just going to step off and live to fight another day and that's what I did.

When I called for him I took hold of the chute gate and said, "See ya." It wasn't the best deal for sure, but I had other contract obligations to fulfill so I had to look at the big picture. I didn't draw Garwood in the second performance and got bucked off my second bull, but that little red hooking machine had made an impression on me for sure, along with a few bumps and bruises.

DICKEY COX
CHEYENNE

We were living in Meridian, Texas and had a meat processing plant that kept us very busy. Judy suggested we take a vacation and go to Cheyenne to the rodeo and visit our good friends Kenny and Ginger Stanton who were living in Colorado Springs.

Back then, Cheyenne started the rodeo with a junior bareback riding and Judy wanted our son Kenneth Lee to enter it since it would be the last year he would be eligible. He had won it twice before. I said, "Well, if we're going to Cheyenne then I'm going to enter, too."

Mind you, I had retired two and a half years earlier. Judy said, "Are you crazy?" I said, "No, but if we're going then I'm entering." Well, when the books opened I entered and started going up to the high school athletic department and working out. Every day Judy would say, "Have you drawn out?" and again I'd say, "If we're going then I'm going to get on," and that went on until we got in the car to leave.

We stopped and spent a couple of days with our friends and they decided to go up with us. I rode my first bull and didn't place, but came back and won third place in the second round. Then, I rode my bull in the short round and won first place. When all was said and done I had won the average and our son Kenneth Lee had won his event, the junior bareback riding.

It was such a great win because I think every cowboy wants to win Cheyenne, the Daddy of them All, and especially that buckle with the diamond in it. That was 1974 and I won a little over three thousand dollars and it really helped as we were just getting ready to build a house.

I remember as were leaving the arena Donnie Gay said, "OK, old man. You've had your fun. Now, go on home so us kids can make a living," and that's exactly what I did. We returned home with two buckles and lots of great memories.

LEE JONES
HERB DALTON

Herb Dalton was an all around hand in his younger days. He was a direct descendant of the famous Dalton Gang of old time outlaws and on his tombstone is a picture of him riding a really famous bull. Herb was not an old fellow you wanted to mess with. He wasn't very big, but he was tough as they come.

He picked up for Steiner's and hauled a good bulldogging team. He had an old green pickup with a sleeper and pulled an old, beat up 2 horse trailer. He always started a day early to the rodeo because he was not going to drive very fast.

On one trip he got in front of a line of trucks on a narrow, curvy road and they had to follow him at 40 MPH for miles. This was back when every one had a CB and they were giving Herb a real cussing. He told them there was a truck stop about a mile up ahead and that he would like to pull over and straighten out the guy who was calling him bad names.

When they get to the truck stop Herb pulled over and took his sawed off pool cue and stepped out of his truck. The truckers were all mad and pouring out of their trucks and one ran ahead to get to Herb first. Herb hit him right between the eyes with the pool cue and said it sounded like a pistol shot. The trucker went down like a pole axed steer.

One of the truckers heard it and said, "The crazy old S.O.B shot him, run for your lives," and they headed back to their trucks. The funny part of the whole deal was Herb pulled out in front of them again and they still had to follow him, but he said no one was cussed him on the CB that time.

JERRY GUSTAFSEN
HAVIN' FUN IN HOUSTON

While at the Astrodome in Houston for the rodeo in 1973, legendary rodeo photographer Al Long came over to me at half-time during the first performance and said, "Jerry, I've got a picture of every rodeo photographer I've ever worked with except you. Remind me to get a picture of you before the end of the rodeo." At the time my wife Emmy was back in South Dakota at her parents, waiting to give birth to our first son Shawn.

Every day Al would come by and say, "Don't let me forget to get that picture of you." Finally, the last Saturday he comes over and says, "Jerry, the steer wrestling is about to start. We've got to go. Stop by my display and I'll get that picture."

I grabbed my camera and went to his display and Al grabs his camera and says, "Back up a little bit." So, I did and Al said, "Back up a little more." So, again I did. Al said, "Back up a little more." So, once more, I did. Then Al said, "That's perfect. At which point the most notorious camp follower in rodeo wraps herself around me and Al takes the picture. He then makes an 8x10 print and titled it Having Fun in Houston and mailed it off to my very pregnant wife.

Emmy got a big kick out of it, as she was used to the practical jokes we used to pull. However, all of our mail went to my mother who in turn forwarded it on to wherever we were. To this day I don't think my mother believes I was innocent.

BILL PUTNAM
MY FINAL RIDE

Twenty-six years, that's how long I was blessed to do what I loved doing and that was riding bulls. I started my rough stock riding career in 1967 at thirteen years of age riding steers at Hill's Arena in Oak Hill, Texas. In 1968 it was more steers with some little junior bulls added to the training sessions. The first rodeos that I entered were in '68 as well.

In 1969 I began riding the big bulls and from high school and junior rodeos on up through the open and professional ranks, riding bulls was my passion. I entered my hometown rodeo Austin, Texas every year from 1969 to 1993 except for 1973 when I was out of competition for part of that year with an injury. As the old saying went on ABC's Wide World of Sports, I experienced both the thrill of victory and the agony of defeat.

Fast forward to the 1993 season. I was approaching my 40th birthday and I knew I was in the twilight of my bull riding days. I gave a lot of thought and prayed long and hard about how I wanted to retire from the game and what I truly wanted my last trip out of the chutes to look like. My dream and prayer was to have my last ride be a successful.

8 second winning ride. I played that scenario over and over in my mind until I could see it happening just that way.

Then, that day came. I could feel it when I woke up that particular morning and that feeling stayed with me throughout the day and evening. It was July 4th 1993 and I was entered in the bull riding that night at the Wimberley, Texas Rodeo. As an interesting side note I wore the same white shirt to the rodeo that I married my wife Tammi in.

I loved that shirt.

Rodeo Stories II

Bill Putnam

I arrived at the rodeo and found out that I had drawn a good looking black and white spotted bull that was a good one to get on. I felt really good and everything fell right into place from my preparation to the nod for the chute gate and the ride itself. I knew as I picked up my bull rope and was walking back to the chutes that I had just made my final ride. Certainly not the rankest bull I ever rode, but he had a good trip and I placed on him.

Looking back at the way it all happened I would have to say it was one of the best rides of my career. Oh, not because of the actual mechanics of the ride or even the bull, but the feeling I get when I think about that ride and the significance of it. You know, it's not often in life that you have your eyes wide open to an actual ending, a chance to say goodbye to something.

I think that ride meant so much to me because even though it was bittersweet it allowed me to tip my hat to a chunk of my life in which I got to do what I loved so much. In a sport as dangerous and unpredictable as bull riding, so many unfortunately don't get to choose how their career is going to end. I feel blessed that mine came to a conclusion that night in Wimberley the way it did. Glory to God.

STEVE SCOTT
TRAVELING WITH TOMBO JONES

I had been traveling and rodeoing and came home for the winter in 1976. My home town was Angleton, Texas. There weren't many winter rodeos in those days because there weren't as many indoor stadiums as there are now, but there began to be a lot more in the next few years.

I looked up an old buddy of mine Tombo Jones. You just had to know ol' Tombo. Anyone who knew him will immediately be able to see his crazy grin as they read this. Tombo just enjoyed his life. He was always laughing. He talked slow and dipped snuff. He was a heck of a cowboy, too. Oh, sure he rodeoed. He rode bulls and broncs. But, Tombo Jones was a hand when it came to real cowboying like gathering and working cattle, breaking a colt, feeding out, just real cowboying.

If you never worked wild, crossbred, rangy Brahmer cattle on the Texas salt grass prairies, well, you just missed a real party which included a few rattlesnakes and mosquitoes that could turn your dog tags over to see what your blood type was.

And, when we say gathering and working cattle you can believe me that a set of working pens was a luxury. Tombo was a cowboy, not just in the rodeo sense of the word cowboy, but in the sense that when it got right down to the snuff dipping, nut cutting, Tombo Jones was a cowboy.

I mentioned to Tombo that I was going to be heading out in my motor home, pulling my clown car, heading out for the West coast. Tombo got that big ol' crazy grin on his face and he wiped the snuff where it was running out of the corner of his mouth and he said, real slow, "Hell (sounded like 'haaayul'), I'm going with you." I said, "Damned straight, you are."

I was pulling a 1926 Ford Standard Sedan. It had a dodge slant six motor in it and I was working up a bucking Ford act in it. It had a hole cut in the roof where I could put my clowning barrel down inside the car to haul it. Well, when we hooked up the drawbar on the trailer ball neither one of us thought about tightening down the trailer ball and the nut on the shank of the ball was just hand tight.

So, we got stop lights on it that worked real good and I think that since it was grounded through the ball we both just thought it was all right and never put a wrench on it to tighten it. So, we lit out for the left coast, me and Tombo and Willie Nelson on a Craig eight-track. I also had a Queensland heeler pup named Patches.

We were going through San Antonio on the Interstate in the middle of the night when the nut vibrated off the ball. It came loose and we parted ways with the 1926 Standard Sedan in the middle of the Interstate at about sixty five miles per hour. Tombo looked in the rear view mirror on his side and said, "Haaayul, somebody's having a wreck." I looked in the mirror and all I could see was fire flying from the bolt on the trailer ball where the drawbar had dropped down and the thing was grinding steel down the interstate, two o'clock in the morning. I said, "Yeah, I think that's us."

I jumped over to the left lane and hit my brake so we could see what was happening, not that I had any real plan yet. As I did that, the thing passed us up on our right side, fire still flying. It looked like a Fourth of July celebration down the Interstate at sixty five miles an hour with no indication that it was ever going to slow down.

Of all things to say Tombo says, "Looks like them running lights are still working." I never did understand that. Well, the thing ran off the Interstate finally and jumped real high in the air when it hit the median. At the same time both of us said, "Daayum." This was right in the middle of San Antonio.

We went on up and turned around and come back down the Eastbound lane till we could get back over in the Westbound and get back to the wreck. The whole trailer ball and hitch was glowing. We got it pushed back on the side of the Interstate and got the stump of the bolt on the ball stuck back in the hitch and wired her down with bailing wire. Here we go, "On The Road Again," me, Tombo, Willie, and Patches.

We made it to Kerrville and pulled into a station just off the highway. The driveway up to the station sloped uphill. We pulled up to the gas pump and got gas. The station attendant told us of a truck stop down the road a ways where we could probably buy a trailer ball. As we headed out downhill to get back on the Interstate the right front tire from the bucking Ford came bouncing past us and out across the road and under the underpass and kept going, threading it's way through the cars and thank the good Lord it didn't hit anybody.

When it went by bouncing at least ten feet in the air Tombo said, "Daayum, somebody lost a tire." I said, "I think that would be us." We got out and saw that we had a three legged Ford. We hot footed it across the way and retrieved the tire. The bearing on that wheel had seized up when it came off in San Antonio and hit and bounced so high, I guess. Anyhow, all the way to Kerrville it was mostly just bouncing on that wheel and it ate the bolt holes out untill the wheel just broke off.

The guy at the gas station took us to his brother's junk yard to try to find a tire. While we were there we got chased by a junk yard dog that bit the gas station guy, but me and Tombo jumped up on the bed of a wrecked truck. Tombo looked at me and grinned, and both of us said, "Daayum." We never found a tire and I sold the bucking Ford to the guy for $150.00. We took the clowning barrel out of it and turned it horizontal and ran a rope through the back windows of the motor home, through the barrel, and just strapped it on the back bumper like we were packing a mule.

Onward we pushed, me, Tombo, and Willie. My pup Patches was still with us, but I think he was thinking about quitting. We made it to West Texas and stopped to use a phone at an old store. We both had kind of long hair and were kind of scruffy looking, old dirty felt hat and cow manure boots and we went in the store to ask if we could borrow a phone. Naturally, Patches followed us in. The lady got a disgusted look on her face and said, "We don't allow no long haired hippies in here and we damned sure don't allow no dogs."

So, we left and went across the street to a garage and as we walked up, we heard the guy's phone ring. He picked it up and said, "Yeah, I see 'em." We asked if we could use his phone and he said it was a business phone, not for personal use. Tombo looked at me and said, "These are about some friendly &#(&^$." I said, "Yeah, 'bout as friendly as a rattlesnake."

When we got to California I pulled in to see my ex-wife on her mother's horse ranch. Her mother locked the gate on me and pulled a gun on me and Tombo and said something about me owing her a pretty good sum of money, about a hundred dollars. She said she'd shoot the tires out on my motor home so we crashed the gate which tore most of the fiberglass off the front of the motor home.

We were going down the road, fiberglass flapping, Willie blaring, Patches the pup hiding as far toward the back as he could get and Tombo looked at me and said, "I think I might ought to go back home." He said something about helping Doc Stanger or Doc Venhaus work cows or something like that. I talked him into hanging on a while and just give her a try. He did and we had a blast. I have to tell you, I loved ol' Tombo like a brother.

Years later his brother who was also my friend, Terry Jones, got killed in an explosion at Dow Chemical Company where I was working at the time. I was there that night. A few years ago Tombo died from some disease, but he smiled that crooked, crazy smile, to the end. Tombo, we'll see you again some day, pard. Tombo Jones was a cowboy right to the end and I miss him.

CLAY TOM COOPER
MARDI GRAS

We were on our way from Arcadia, Florida to the Houston Astrodome Rodeo and I had reservations at the Marriot Hotel in New Orleans. So, when we got there Marshal Backing dropped me and Brad Gjermundson off on Bourbon Street and said he'd take care of my horse. So, he did. He took him up the service elevator to our room, run the tub full of water and put a bed against the wall. It had been raining a little and the muddy hoof prints across the lawn and on and off the elevator sold us out.

We got back to the room about 5:00 A.M. and about 6:00 A.M. the hotel manager, a maid, and a cop were banging on the door. We got kicked out of Mardi Gras and the cop escorted us out of town. After a ways he pulled us over and said, "Boys, come back anytime, but please leave that horse at home."

RICHARD FLECHSIG
THE WILD HORSE RACE

Hillsboro, Missouri had a fair and rodeo every summer and one year I talked two of my buddies into entering the wild horse race. I would ride and they would mug and hold the rope. Now, these two were bulldoggers so I had some beef on my side. My mugger was a good friend Joe Courtney and Joe was a hand.

In this wild horse race you could either use a bareback riggin or a saddle so we decided to use my bareback riggin. A little secret about wild horse racing, rather than getting your head kicked off reaching under some of these broncs for your cinch, I would straighten a coat hanger and wrap one end around the cinch loop to the other loop then tie it off and bend it in a slight "U" shape so that way the cinch sticks up under the horse and is easy to grab.

I never worried about my horse in a wild horse race. I know where he's at and it's those other horses that I watched out for. They drew a line across the end of the arena farthest from the chutes and you had to ride across that line to win.

Our horse was pretty salty and once he kicked the rigging out of my hand. Joe, my mugger was biting the horse's ear. PETA wasn't around back then and I'm scrambling, trying to get my rigging on and Joe through clinched teeth told me to hurry up. I said, "I am hurrying so what's the problem?" He yelled through his clinched teeth, "My dental bridgework is about to fall out," so now I'm laughing.

I got my cinch pulled up and just ran it through the handhold of my riggin and jumped on and Jim my holder turned the old bronc loose. We had gotten drug way down the arena to where after I got on and I only had to stay on about five jumps and we won the darn thing. We split a big check of $110.00 three ways and that came to about $36.00 and some change each, but I had $36.00 worth of fun.

DOUG MUNSELL
NFR STOCK SALE, 1983

Monte Berger, Bobby's nephew, Donnie Bell, Raymond Wessel, Todd Teggerstrom, Sam Minnick, and I were entered at the NFR sale in 1983 in Oklahoma City. A couple of them got antsy so we left around midnight the night before. We got to Oklahoma City at about five in the morning and tried to sleep in the van of the times, you know the ones with the shag carpet all over in it. I don't know if it was the cold or the excitement, but none of us could sleep.

We had to confirm our entries by 8 a.m. so we had pulled an all nighter for a 5 hour trip and we started getting on our bulls a little after noon that day. We got to meet lots of the NFR guys and lots of legends that day, but a lot of the guys we had already met at rodeos we had entered in on our permits.

Monte Berger's hero at the time was Kenny (Wilco) Wilcox. I can remember pulling Monte's rope and telling him to ride like Wilco and Kenny was standing right behind me just by coincidence. They just chute drew the stock and thank God, I did not have the bull Harry Vold brought that everybody knows as K3.

He was a big Brahmer that could be an eliminating mean son-of-a-gun. I ended up with a little black muley bull, just what everybody wanted or so I thought. I think he might have come from Growney's.

Anyway, I am in there pulling my rope and this little booger tries to flip over sideways. He was literally standing on one hind leg with his shoulders basically against the back of the chute. Jim Shoulders rides up and says, "Son, are you ever gonna nod your head?" I just calmly said, "As soon as he stands on two feet, sir."

About that time Jim McClain jumps over in the chute and sits on this little blacks head and the bull is jumping up and around and I nod my head before McClain can get out there, but he did somehow. The little black bull jumps out there and digs a hole into my hand and he gets a pretty good spur bath. I might have been in the low 70's, but it did not matter as I did not win anything.

I got off on my feet and ran for the fence because the little muley was mean and you never would live it down if a little black smokes you. Jim Shoulders rode over to me and stuck his hand out and said, "Son, that is what being a cowboy is all about. Nice ride, and way to make a hand in the box." That meant more to me than any check or buckle I ever one. Jim Shoulders was not only a legendary rodeo Champion, he was a Champion man, too

LORI SHOULDERS
ONE, USED TO BE, COWGIRL

It's a good thing my mother Georgiane Pridey Primrose always had a job with good insurance because I was an accident prone kid growing up and used it often. I grew up on a ranch west of Tucumcari, New Mexico with two older sisters LeDawn and Loell. My dad should have had 3 boys like his brother Presley had instead of three girls.

He worked us hard and made ranch hands and cowgirls out of us. All three of us went through college on Rodeo Scholarships. I grew up as Pete and often still have people call me that.

I was at an ENMJRA rodeo in Belen, New Mexico and hit a barrel and it put a hole in my left knee. They put a butterfly bandage on it to hold it together until I got back home and Dr. Evetts sewed it up. About two weeks later I was practicing my goat tying and the goat hooked my knee and busted the stitches open. I didn't go back to the doctor and ended up with Gangrene in my leg and had to spend two weeks in a contraption with my leg up in it, hoping to get the blood count down so they wouldn't have to amputate my left leg from the knee down.

I was helping my dad hold up a mare's tail while he unsutchured her and the blood caused me to pass out and I hit my head and got a bad concussion and a cracked skull. When I got out of the hospital I was at a 4-H meeting and went outside afterwards because I wasn't feeling well and stepped through the plate glass window next to the door and almost cut my right foot off. It cut all my ligaments and tendons in that foot from the ankle down.

I had to use a different dismount in the goat tying from then on and land on both feet instead of just one. I healed from both of those accidents and went on to win the Tri-State all-around, the National High School all-around, and four other national rodeo titles, including two in the goat tying.

My last two accidents were off of the last colt I kept of my dad's before he passed away, in memory of. I broke my wrist at a barrel race and shattered my shoulder team roping on him.

I am just a trail rider now and don't much get out of a trot, but am blessed to still have both feet to walk up and down the aisles waiting on people in the air as a flight attendant for American Airlines for the past twenty nine years.

JIM SOWLE
THE RONNIE SOWLE STORY

We were headed to a Mid-States Rodeo Association, MSRA, in Indiana I believe. Don Goofy Gettinger was driving and Ronnie Sowle was riding shotgun. Tom and Steve Pooley, Mike Ery, myself, and Frank Branch were in the camper. As we got on the Ohio Turnpike I noticed a car was pacing along side of us and Goofy was yelling back and forth with the guys in that car.

We weren't sure of what was being said or why, but the four of us in the camper all tried to fit our heads into the cab of the truck to see what was going on. Our guard started to rise as we slowed down and started to pull over. The other car was now behind us and the boys in the back still weren't sure what was happening. Ronnie said he was going to go back and buy some TV's from those guys and for us to stay in the camper. Several puzzled faces pondered this while he was gone. Within a few minutes we opened the camper door to see Ronnie running back with two plastic wrapped TVs and he handed them off to us. As the two cars sped away, happy with the transaction, I started to look at these AC/DC TV's with remote that were such a great bargain and the clear plastic wrap was holding what appeared to be magazine pages covering the TV. What was underneath those pages were two junk TV's that were fit for the trash. We'd been had. The sting of that $200 lesson remained with us though we did laugh it off fairly quickly and just figured it was good motivation to win it back at the rodeo later that night.

A few years later we ran into Goofy who was judging one of J-J's rodeo's and he could hardly contain himself as he asked Ronnie to guess who he saw at the bar the other night in Toledo. Goofy said he spotted the guy in the bar and knew right away he was one of the Turnpike TV guys. He watched him for a bit then followed him outside when the guy left.

Goofy said he acted like he knew the guy and chatted him up for a minute, but the guy kept saying he didn't know him. Goofy asked him, "Well, if I was driving a red Ford truck with a white camper and a brown horse trailer behind it on the Ohio Turnpike, would you recognize me?" At that point the guy's eyes got real big and Goofy knew he had him. One punch put the guy down and revenge was had. We all felt better knowing the story didn't end one afternoon on the Ohio Turnpike.

BOBBY DOBBINS
MY TRAVELING PARTNER, JESSIE JAMES WILLIAMS

Jessie was like Steve Martin, a wild and crazy guy. We were headed to a J.C. Ward Rodeo one afternoon when all of a sudden he said, "I've got a problem. Sunday, my cousin threw my hat on the bed." I said, "You are in trouble." Just as we pulled into the town where the rodeo was we met an ambulance all lit up making an emergency run. I said, "I hope he makes it back in time for the bull riding."

When we got to the arena and checked the draw and Jessie had the pick of the herd, Old One and a Half. Jessie was always one to scoot and wriggle around taking a long time getting out on one, especially so that night. Finally he said, "Judges ready, photographer ready, am-bu-lance ready? Outside!" and won first place.

We were making a three rodeo run in Southeast Oklahoma one week in 1967, ending up at Chandler on Saturday night. I rode a big red Brahmer and when I stepped off I hung my spur in his hump and I popped my head pretty hard on the ground. When we got ready to start home I told Jessie he would have to drive. He said, "I'm not sure how to get to Durant," and I said, "Just go south every chance you get." I took a couple of Aspirin and lay down in the back seat of my rodeo rig, a 1964 '98 Olds. Sedan.

In a little while my head ache eased and I fell asleep. Sometime later I woke up and the car was stopped, the engine was running and we're facing west at a T-Intersection and Jessie was leaned over the steering wheel sound asleep. I said, "Jessie, what's wrong?" And he said, "I ran out of road." I guess he didn't know which way south was.

Jim Shoulders was the producer of the Crockett, Texas RCA Rodeo, in 1965. Jessie entered the bull riding and his secondary event, the saddle bronc riding. There were only six bronc riders entered so they each got a horse every performance. In the first go-round, Jessie drew one that had a history of taking a long run at you before he broke. So, Jim, thinking he could shorten the old bronc up some and make him start bucking sooner, stood in the arena with a pair of chaps.

When Jessie and the horse cleared the end of the gate, Jim threw those chaps at the horse's front legs and he exploded, launching Jessie higher than the arena flags. The next morning at the coffee shop, Randall Stevens asked Jim if he was going to "chap" Jessie's horse the next performance and Jim said, "Hell no. I don't want him falling on me again."

For the 1968, July 4th run Jessie and I were on the rodeo trail. July 1st we were up at Sulphur Springs, Texas and July 2nd at Mangum, Oklahoma and on Sunday the 3rd we were headed to the Benjamin Stables Arena in Kansas City. We were traveling in Jessie's 1960 Pontiac and somewhere on the Kansas Turnpike I began to hear a strange noise coming from the front of the car.

With no air condition and the windows rolled down I could hear a rattle that sounded serious.

I told Jessie it sounded like a fender was about to fall off so he shut it down on the side of the highway and raised the hood. The fan was sitting at an angle and when I shook it a little it fell off and hit the ground. So, what do we do now? It's Sunday, three in the afternoon, July 3rd and it is 103 degrees and we have no fan. We sure couldn't fix it and there was no way to find a mechanic until Tuesday and we had to be back in Wright City, Oklahoma on July 4th.

I said, "What are we going to do, Jessie?" and he said, "Just drive it until it quits. It only cost me $600.00 bucks." So, he fired it up and took off and the faster we drove the cooler it ran. When we got to Kansas City we caught a couple of red lights and while we were stopped, the engine began to heat. We discussed the matter and Jessie said he had the solution. We ran every red light between there and the Benjamin Stables Arena.

At the arena we were explaining our troublesome situation to George Taylor the clown and funnyman and he offered us some money, but what we needed was a mechanic. We talked to one cowboy who was a mechanic and he said, "That model Pontiac is equipped with a clutch that disengaged the fan at 35 mph and it was basically air-cooled after that." Jessie said, "We travel at night from now on."

We left Kansas City around midnight on our way to Wright City, Oklahoma for the big 4th of July Celebration and an hour or so later we pulled into a full service gas station, the only kind they had in those days as self-service didn't take over until the late 70's. It was just a shack with two pumps, Regular or Ethyl, and a single 60 watt light bulb hanging over them.

Bobby Dobbins

An old man in overalls came out with a flashlight that looked like it held nine batteries. Jessie said, "Fill it up and check the oil. And, by the way, while you're under the hood, check my fan. It's been making a lot of noise." The old gentleman raised the hood, shined his light in from the left side and took a long look. Then, he walked slowly around to the right side of the car and did the same thing. He came back around to the driver side window, shined that bright light in Jessie's face and said, "Sonny Boy, you ain't got no damn fan."

We were in St. Jo, Texas at an Adrain Parker Production Rodeo and Jessie is wriggling and scooting around in the chute, pulling his had down and taking a lot of time, which was his usual procedure. Losing patience, Adrain, chewing on his cigar, rode right up against the bucking chute on his big, grey horse and yelled, "Talk to me, Jessie!" Jessie jerked his hand out of the rope, crossed his arms on top of the chute gate and looking at Adrain, eye to eye said, "Been getting any rain, Adrain?"

By 1975, I had hung up my bull spurs and was an auctioneer at five weekly cattle auctions. I hadn't seen Jessie in a couple of years when I ran into him at Hoyt Winnett's place, one Wednesday night. He said he was shoeing horses for a living so I made a deal with him to shoe three head for me the next day, but he never showed up. The next time I saw him was 17years later in 1992. He had joined the army and made a career of it.

And, while stationed in Germany he had won the title of European All-Around Champion Cowboy.

Photo #17...Bobby Dobbins...Credit Bill Dobbins, Tulsa

TERRI ABRAHAMSON
A HOT DAY IN OKC

Here is a story from a photographer's point of view. It was at the OKC State Fair Rodeo and Benny Buetler had the stock. It was a great performance, a hot day and lots of good rides and photos. During the bull riding I asked Donnie Gay about a bull that was up next and he said that I could get pretty close because the bull always went around to the right and bucked real good.

So, with my camera ready I get off a shot and then the bull came around to the left and knocked me down. He came back at me and had me in the dirt. His head was on my neck and I could see his horns on each side of my head. Leon Coffee and Rick

Chatman got him off of me, but that this isn't the end of this story.

I never knew what the competitors ran into when they got frapped. The ambulance men were so concerned even though I told them I was OK, but that I needed to check my camera to see if it was OK. Then, they tried to take my temperature. Gees, it was a hot day and I had just photographed a whole performance so I assured him I was warmer than 98 degrees.

They finally let me back in the arena to finish photographing the rest of the bull riding and after the performance Clint Johnson and John McDonald offered to take my sister and I to dinner for having such an experience. They took us to the nearby McDonald's and Clint suggested that we could get a Big Mac since we were with little Mac. It was so fun and they were fun and very nice. It was a good night and I was glad that bull didn't hurt me or my camera.

DALE WOODARD
(1992 NFR Barrel man)
I'M NOT COLD

As a kid I always liked animals. I was interested in building my cowboy skills and being a rodeo clown never entered my mind. I just wanted to ride my horse and be a cowboy. But, once I started going to amateur rodeos my team-roping partner got us a job fighting bulls at a weekly jack-pot bull riding. My clowning career grew out of that, but I still continued to compete in calf roping and team roping, sometimes in my clown costume.

After I joined the PRCA in 1975 I traveled to rodeos with a friend Rolie Wilson. Rolie rode bareback broncs and bull dogged and I roped calves. Rolie made the NFR one year in the bareback riding, but this story took place before that happened.

I lived in the little town of French Camp, California where I had grown up. Rolie was also living in California and was working on construction jobs, but he was originally from Kalispell,

Rodeo Stories II

Montana. When we would drive to rodeos on weekends he loved to tell me stories about Montana and he used to say, "In Montana, you can do whatever you're big enough to do."

On this particular weekend we were going to a rodeo in Long Beach, California. Rolie had a little motor home and we hooked my horse trailer to that motor home, loaded my roping horse and away we went. We got the Long Beach at about nine o'clock on Friday night and it was raining, but it didn't matter to us because it was an indoor rodeo. I told Rolie I was going to take my horse over to the building and get him a pen for the night and Rolie said, "Fine, I'm going to bed."

As I led my horse across the parking lot it was pouring down rain. Going past the front of the building I saw a young man standing on about the third step. I looked his way, but kept on going toward the back of the building. After I had gotten my horse settled in a stall I headed back for our motor home.

The rain had let up and now it was just a light sprinkle, but this young cowboy was still standing on that same step. He had on a cowboy hat, a white shirt with the top button all buttoned up, jeans, and cowboy boots and his shirt stuck to his body like a wet T-shirt. He looked like he was waiting for someone.

I said, "Hey, buddy. The building is open. You don't have to stand out here in the rain. You can go inside and look out those big glass doors." He sort of bowed up and said, "I'm not cold. I'm from Sweetgrass, Montana." I said, "OK. Suit yourself," and went on my way.

When I stepped inside the motor home Rolie was in bed at the back, so I made my bed on the couch. After I had gotten in bed I just lay there thinking about that kid standing out there in the rain. About that time Rolie spoke up and asked if I'd found a pen for my horse.

I told him I had and then I mentioned the kid on the steps and that I'd told him the building was open and that he didn't have to stand out there in the rain, but that he'd said he wasn't cold because he was from Sweetgrass, Montana. Rolie's reply was simply, "He's probably telling you the truth."

I asked Rolie if he'd ever been to Sweetgrass and he said, "Yeah. There's a border crossing there into Canada and it is a big, wide open country and the cold wind blows down off the Artic Circle right through there and the only thing to stop that wind is a four strand barb wire fence and you can imagine how much help that gives you."

To this day whenever I offer a coat or blanket so someone who looks like they are cold and they answer, "No, thanks. I'm not cold." I finish their sentence with, "I'm from Sweetgrass, Montana."

ROME WAGER
MARTY AND ENOCH

In 1972 I was 17 years old and had been entering RCA rodeos for a couple months. I was at Rapid City, SD and had a Korkow horse named Eagle Butte drawn. I asked around about the rein length to use and Dan Corr said, "Go X-3," so I gave him some more, but he was a little bigger than the chutes and it had been raining straight down right up till I got on.

The 3rd jump out he swallowed his head and threw me over his head and I landed on my belly, elbow deep in that watery sand. I started crawling and when I looked back I saw a big platter foot as he squished me into the mud and I came up going the other way and he stepped square on my head. They said I went under the mud as he stepped on my knee and left my mouth packed with sand.

The paramedics were holding my hands down, but I was trying to get the mud that was packed in my mouth so I couldn't breath. Finally, I got one hand free and they said it looked like I was pulling a big chew out of my top and bottom lips. They said, "Does your head hurt?" I answered, "No." "Does your neck hurt?" I said, "No." "Does your back hurt?" I said, "No." So, they said,

"Well where does it hurt?" and I replied, "Do you really want to know?" They said they did so I replied, "Well, my little finger really hurts."

The style of buck reins that were popular at that time were those big, fat, hard, reins, and when he snatched me down over his head it dislocated my little finger. Everyone cackled after a wreck like that, a 112 lb. bronc rider hurt his little finger. I had been riding broncs for 3 or 4 years and I had never been bucked off a total of more than 30 head out of over 400 broncs.

But, for the past two months I had been bucked off everything I got on and I was discouraged and ready to hang my bronc saddle up. I was an extremely shy kid, right off the Reservation. When I noticed Marty Wood and Enoch Walker had come out to stand by me, I said, "Mr. Walker. Mr. Woods. You've been to every one I've been to for the last two months. I've never had trouble riding broncs, but I can't ride nothing. I don't know if you've watched me or not, but if there's something I need to do or quit doing, please tell me"

Marty and Enoch smiled, then Marty said, "Kid, we have been watching you and you have nothing to worry about. This ole bronc riding comes and this ole bronc riding goes so just getting on and one day it's gonna come and stay a long time because you have what it takes." They shook my hand and smiled at a very beat up, happy little Indian cowboy off the Reservation who for 7 more months bucked off everything, but every time I hit the ground I heard Marty's words and remembered the looks in those old champions eyes.

Well, over 3,000 more broncs and 35 more years of riding I still think of that day and even though I didn't know my neck was broke I smile because good days and good fellas still make a difference in the plan of God for a man's life.

GREG DOERING
LIFE ON THE DORERING RODEO TRAIL; A PEACE RIVER ADVENTURE

In the 60's and 70's my dad Karl Doering clowned and fought bulls at many rodeos across the border in Canada. We traveled as a family throughout British Columbia, Alberta, Saskatchewan and Manitoba. Often at times we felt more at home with our Canadian friends. We knew all about the border crossing, veterinarians, and the best times to cross.

In the 70's we were quite the menagerie with our turquoise Dodge one ton truck with a horse van pulling a travel trailer. I followed with my Ford pickup with canopy pulling dad's red Model A Ford bucking clown car. We always had the clown mule Homer and later, Jasper. My mom usually had a barrel horse and occasionally my sister would be packing another horse for competition. Of course we usually had three dogs. One was a small lap dog Peri and a couple Blue Healers named Killer and Grumpy that became well known on the rodeo trail as protectors of our camp.

Not to get side tracked too far, but these two dogs also entertained a young up and coming bull rider Jordie Thompson one afternoon at one of the far northern Alberta rodeos. Jordie and a buddy sat in our trailer with the window open during the rodeo. My dog Grumpy was chained up to the trailer. She laid under it in the shade until she heard Jordie shout, "Watch out for the Dog." She would lunge from under the trailer and nail the passing, unsuspecting hippy. She made her escape back under the trailer before they knew what happened. She provided great entertainment and kept the hippies away.

Of course, no clown truck would be complete without a pet skunk. Blossom traveled the rodeo trail for many years, both scaring and entertaining rodeo crowds and making appearances at schools and pre-rodeo festivities.

Karl was well liked and respected by the rodeo community and especially the bull riding fraternity. At the very first Canadian Finals Rodeo in Edmonton in 1974 he was selected by the competitors as the sole bull fighter to protect the riders. Now they have 3.

Some of the jobs came directly from the rodeo committees like the Calgary & Williams Lake Stampedes. At others, the clowning contracts were with the stock contractor producing the rodeo. Dad worked for Perry & Hook, Grasslands Rodeo-Ted Vayro, Malcolm Jones & C.N. Woodward, Verne Franklin, plus Harry and Wayne Vold. A good portion of rodeos were Reg and Greg Kesler's.

Dad had a temperament that often matched Reg's and they got along great for many years working rodeos for them on both sides of the border. When you worked for Reg you didn't just show up at the rodeo, ride in the parade, help promote the rodeo, and perform during the performances. No, there was a far bigger commitment. The whole family got involved.

My mom Kay would carry the Colors in both the Parade and Grand Entry and usually be one of the official timers while still trying to be competitive in the barrel racing. She was always the, go for, when Reg needed an extra hand.

At Bassano, Alberta Reg volunteered mom to ride a rank thoroughbred horse in the Bassano Derby when the intended jockey got hurt in a previous race. It was the feature race of the day, a mile and a half race on a bush track loaded with rocks and prairie dog holes. About halfway through the race a couple of the jockeys tried to intimidate her and box her horse in. She cussed them out and they let her through. By the end, her legs were wobbly and she feared of falling off and being trampled by the horses back in the pack. She held on for the win and made the owner of the horse happy.

My sister was a little younger and didn't get to help out as much. KK would be flag girl and help mom with extra projects.

I was always on the labor list, helping care, feed, and doctor the live stock. And of course sorting prior to the rodeo performance was expected. I would also assist dad getting the mule saddled and the props ready for the upcoming performance.

I usually helped out in the clown acts. For years I was the old heifer girl-friend Sally Clapsaddle in dad's clown car act. I had to crank and push the car to help get it running. In the process I'd lose my skirt, exposing my beautiful hairy legs. I would get thrown in the back of the car and be the ballast so the car can rear and spin around.

Early on I participated in the cow ridings and junior bull ridings. When I turned 18, I began riding bulls at the rodeos. Reg would occasionally do me a favor and enter me in the bare back riding at his rodeos when he was short of contestants. One of these times was a three head riding at Medicine Hat, Alberta. I had the privilege of getting on 3 of Reg's top horses, all previous horse of the year in either bare back or saddle bronc riding. I made Creamo Moon Shine and Red Top all look good. I thrilled the crowd and gave Reg a good laugh or two.

Despite his rough appearance Reg had a big heart as he helped me with one of my best bull rides of my rodeo career. One year at Kalispell there was a two head bull riding. Montana's favorite son and former All Around Champ of the World Benny Reynolds got a re-ride in the first go on a bull that lopes off down the arena. I ride a short time later and get another mediocre bull that follows the same tracks as Benny's, but no re-ride for the kid from Oregon. I am the last rider out on Sunday and I have drawn his NFR bull Ivory Lightening.

The bull had thrown me very quickly at the Salmon, Idaho, rodeo the year before. As I am getting ready to mount up Reg pokes his finger in my chest and says, "All right you round ass kid. You have been bitching and moaning all week about the bulls not bucking and today we are going to see if you are a bull rider."

That got me pumped up and I rode his bull for first place in the go round and even slipped into the average. Reg, with a big grin and laugh was the first to shake my hand and congratulate me.

While we all helped out as needed, it was dad that got the blunt of the work load. It seemed that Reg was always short at least one hand. One fond memory was when dad was called to ride one of the ranch horses to gather bucking horses off the Indian Reservation outside of Bassano, Alberta. He looked at the unshod horse with untrimmed feet and questioned its usefulness. The comeback was, "You will be glad for the big feet when you are flying across the plains filled with prairie dog holes." It was quite the adventure which ended by bringing the herd of wild horse directly through the local golf course into the rodeo grounds. In the States the golf course superintendent probably would have shot that group of cowboys.

Reg knew every short cut road that ever existed on either side of the border. Some were only passable in dry weather and most weren't recommended for semis. More than once road construction delayed the short cut and once a farmer had to use his tractor to pull a stock truck through a mud hole. We knew this, all because often Reg was short one truck driver and dad got volunteered to drive one of the semis and mom and I would follow in our two rigs.

One of these fun adventures led us to the Peace River Country. Reg often had a couple rodeos going on either side of the border. He headed to Montana and left dad to lead the caravan from, Southern Alberta up north to Edison, Grimshaw and High Prairie. All were 200 miles plus north of Edmonton where the Northern Lights shined brightly and the mosquitoes were Texas sized.

I was always more of a lover than a fighte, and did not really look for a fight. On the contrary, my dad Karl was a feisty 6ft. 145 pound scrappy guy that was always on the side of justice. He didn't like hippies, men that were abusive to their families, loud mouths, or those who used foul language. He would go out of his way to make sure justice was served no matter how big the opponent. I would have to step out of my comfort zone twice over the next 48 hours.

The first encounter was a late night adventure with a couple truck stop yokels in Edmonton. They were bitching about having to fill 5 vehicles with fuel late at night. They were taking their own sweet time all the while cussing about the *#*#* cowboys. Dad had about enough and was sizing up one of them when I came around the corner just in time to see the second one sneaking up to blind side Karl. It was time to step up. I spun him around and got his attention and helped avoid a real nasty brawl. We finally regrouped and wound our way north.

We arrived late at night and got things unloaded and turned out on the infield to graze. The next day is busy acquiring feed, water troughs, and a water truck to bring water to the dry grounds. After the all night run and a long day we are exhausted and ready for a good night's rest so we would be ready for the first performance next day.

Well, about midnight we were awakened by some drunken carneys starting their own rodeo. They had got their carnival set up and decided to ride a couple of the pick up horses and to turn out the livestock on to the streets of the town. Well, it was just me and dad there to stop their fun. We ran off a couple of the less brave and jerked another off a horse. I leave dad to tend to a couple of them and I go chasing after another one, hopping over 3 or 4 fences of the corrals before I catch up with him.

I put a choke hold on the guy and he his grasping for air and I am out of breath and can't talk. Dad hollers,"Are you okay?" Well, I haven't yet caught my breath yet so I can't call back. He gets a little concerned because he hears the choking and fires a couple rounds from his 38 special into air.

125

Rodeo Stories II

Greg & Carl Doering Clowns

The fun is over now and the carneys quickly retreat. We secure the livestock just about the time the Royal Canadian Mounties showed up. Normally that would be a blessing, but being a Yankee and having a hand gun in Canada is not a good thing. Fortunately, they must have been rodeo fans and were glad that we helped them out because not a word was said about the gun fire. Life on the rodeo trail was full of adventures, good times, and good friends. I wouldn't trade the memories for anything.

NICK HITE
TEXAS COWBOY REUNION

Back in 1982 I was entered in the bull riding at the Texas Cowboy Reunion in Stanford Texas during the 4th of July weekend. I was up on July 3rd which was my Fathers Birthday and he was driving me to the Rodeo. I was sleeping on way and as always I was dreaming of me riding a black horned bull that turned back to the left and bucked like hell and in that dream I went 90 points on him.

Nick Hite
Photo Credit, dudley@dudleydoright.com...

When we got to Stanford my dad woke me up so we could something to eat at the DQ and my dad was giving me heck about my snoring during the drive. So, I proceeded to tell him about my dream and he laughed and said, "That would be nice."

We got down to the rodeo grounds and I went to pay my entry fees and looked at what I had drawn and sure enough, it was a black horned bull that Terry Walls leased from B-J. The bull was F7 and I found out that he would go both ways. I got Jess Gorley to pull my rope for me and sure enough, I made the best ride of my life and scored 90 points just like in my dream and won it all.

I still hold the Arena record in the bull riding and out of all the buckles that I have won, this one I still wear every day because that was the best birthday present that I could give my dad. After that, I rode a lot of rank bulls like #105 of Del Halls and #5 of Del Halls that my dad got to see me ride, but none of them made him as happy as when I went 90 points on his birthday.

JOY FOSCALINA
CHICK MAGNET

The rodeo is the Sydney/Melbourne World Cup in 1982. Jeff Jones, my traveling partner and I were up in the first performance in Melbourne. Our friend Pat Speedy was the bullfighter and Quail Dobbs was in the barrel and doing the comedy acts with Pat. Because Quail Dobbs is from America, he wasn't able to bring his animal acts so Pat supplied the animals for Quail's acts.

There was a bag of snakes and a small whiptail (A baby kangaroo) among the animals. Unfortunately, Pat Speedy took a hooking and was hospitalized so he was unable to care for his animals during the remainder of the rodeo. This is where Jeff and I came into the story. We became nursemaids for Pat's animals.

The animals all stayed in our hotel room and then we would take them to the rodeo and turn them over to Quail Dobbs. The little Whiptail Wallaby needed to be bottle fed throughout the day so Jeff would carry the Whiptail inside his shirt and his little head would be sticking out his unbuttoned shirt.

When you walk around the rodeo grounds with a baby kangaroo in your shirt you attract plenty of attention. We got to meet nearly every girl in Sydney and Melborne thanks to this little whiptail chick magnet.

Apparently, somebody else wanted a chick magnet too, so they stole the Whiptail and the bag of snakes in Sydney. I'm not sure what kind of girls the snakes attracted, but the little Wallaby was the best magnet ever.

BRET CORLEY
TEAM ROPIN'

Back in the mid 90's I hired on with a small rodeo company from north Alabama to announce for them. I worked a few shows for them and they asked me if I would finish out the season for them. Of course I said I would as they were a fun bunch and easy to get along with.

They told me to be in Wedowee, Alabama the next weekend, but I'd never even heard of Wedowee let alone know where it was. I finally found it on the map and was set up and ready to emcee at showtime. Now, if you've ever been to Wedowee, Alabama then you know there aint much to do on Saturday while waiting for the performance to start so they penned some steers and had a little team roping practice.

I just sat on the panels watching when the boss man rode up and said, "Come and rope one." I told him I'd only roped the dummy from the ground, but never a steer from a horse. He said I could use his horse, so I said. "OK, I'll try it."

I backed in the heeling box, nodded and away we went. My header missed so I kept my steer running while he rebuilt his loop. We lined him up and my partner caught the head and turned him. I took 2 rounds and caught the heels and that was the first loop I'd ever thrown from a horse.

The bossman said, "Do it again," so we backed in the box and once again my header missed so I rode past him made 2 rounds with my rope and caught both horns, dallied, and hollered, "Come catch these heels."

Those fellows couldn't believe that was my first time team roping. They told me to enter in the rodeo that night, but I said, "I believe I'll quit while I'm ahead.......and heels."

TONI GUIRINO
BLACK JACK

My Dad, Labe Guirino, came to me said, "Toni, you wanna make the finals?" I said, "Yes sir, with all my heart!" He said, "Well, I found you the horse." So we loaded up headed west to Ft Smith, Arkansas from Dayton, Ohio. The horse was a 13 year old solid black Quarter Horse owned by Dude Crane. He had told my that dad his daughter Kris Crane didn't get along with him, but if I could ride him I could win.

When we met his ranch manager at the Ft. Smith Futurity, he came walking up leading a wild-eyed, big stout black horse and I looked at dad and he said, "Saddle him." I got him saddled and the man handed me the reins so I ask my dad, "Should I trot him around the pattern?" and he said, "No, make him run."

Now, here we are at the big Ft Smith Futurity with all those top barrel racing people I knew from home and at rodeos so I start to head down the long alley and I mean he took off like no other horse I had ever ridden. He made the three turns so quick and when he ran out of the alley my dad said my eyes were as big as silver dollars and yelled, "He's the one!" People came up to me and wanted to know if he was entered in the futurity and I said, "No, I'm just trying him out," so they wanted to buy him.

But, we bought him and left from there headed to an open rodeo in Barsndale, Oklahoma where I won 3rd place. We headed back to Ohio with my new horse Black Jack and I entered the first IPRA in Goshen, Indiana. It was the first weekend of June and was put on by J-J Rodeo Company. I was up on Sunday afternoon and I won first by a half second.

I made the finals that year although I had not won anything until June I and was in tenth place going into IFR15. I hit a barrel in the first round and hit another one in the second round, but still won it. Then, in the third round during the Saturday afternoon performance I won first place, plus I ran the fastest time of IFR 15 and then topped that off by placing second in the fourth round and third in the fifth. Black Jack was one of best horses I ever rode and the next year he took me to IFR16 in third place where I ended up runner-up to the World Champion that year.

DANNY O'HACO
PENDLETON ROUNDUP

In 1983, the rodeo season was in full swing from June in Reno, to September in Pendleton and I was road weary when I arrived in Oregon, ready to join the competition ahead and all its festivities to follow.

The Letter Buck Room is located under the stadium where a beer or a cocktail is a welcome sight to a broke bareback rider after the rodeo. Among the re-ride stories in this hot and smoke filled saloon I was content to lean on a bar stool and share a cold one with friends.

Two women struggled through the crowd unable to make it up to the bar to order so I offered to buy them a drink and they were appreciative of my offer. After several hours of visiting and drinking I was wanting out of the crowded heat of the Letter Buck Room.

It had been a fun afternoon, but I was tired from traveling. Duffs place was full and without a room for the night or a car to crash in I searched for a place to share. I asked the friendly woman from Portland if she would like to join me outside for some air and Dee Dee, but I called her Double D, accepted with a smile and we stepped out into a beautiful evening to breathe the cool night.

Still, without shelter for the evening, DD explained she had a sleeping bag in her friend's car and went off to retrieve it. I knew Pendleton had a grassy infield so we headed to the middle of the arena and sprawled out under the stars. It seemed like a perfect place to camp for the night.

September mornings are meant for lovers and the smell of pancakes and coffee drifted from the teepee village. My competition was over and DD and I had slept soundly in the grassy Pendleton arena. As I lay there dreaming of last night's events a stranger reached down and tapped me on the head. A calm and soothing voice drew close to my ear and spoke the words, "Y'all better get out of the arena. The slack has started."

With socks and Tony Lama's scattered and my Resistol lying at my feet, I wondered if this would be the first stadium streakers to ever attend the Pendleton round up? Only a crowd of about one hundred contestants would ever know.

RONNIE WELLS
A RODEO STORY

It was summer of 1970 and me, Duke Gayle, and Cody Gupton were out in Baytown S.R.A. Rodeo on Thursday Night. Duke and Cody got a check and I got thrown off of a big red bull with some sure enough honkers of L.L.Reeds, and he flipped over backwards on me in the bucking chute.

Friday night we went to Aldine and I won first place and got a little check. Saturday night we went to Simonton and I drew a big Brindle that they ran up in the number one bucking chute which was pretty close to fence. He jumped out there and turned back to right which it was into my hand and I thought, "Yeah your ass is mine now."

Needless to say, he had other plans and he threw me over his head and hung a horn between my legs and completely threw me out of the pen where I landed on the first row of the stands. That was the second wreck of the weekend. Well, on the way home we decided that Sunday we were going to Brazoria to Dodger Park to an S.N.C.A.Rodeo which was the Colored Association.

Duke said he's come and pick me up, so Sunday morning arrived and we had to be there at noon to get entered. About 11:00

o'clock I heard a beep, beep, and when I came out of the house, there sat Duke Gayle on a Honda 90 Scrambler Motorcycle. I said, "What in the hell are you doing?" He said, "Come on. It'll be fun," so I got on behind him and had 2 riggin bags, one on each shoulder. I was thinking, "Lord, just let me live through this."

Well, we took off and got on the highway and both of our hats where flipped up in the front like we were in a stampede. When we got into Brazoria and turned into the rodeo pen, he hit the brake and slid sideways and threw me off and knocked all the air out of me because I landed flat on my back. He asked if I was alright and I said, when I finally got enough air to talk, "Hell no, I ain't alright." I finally got my senses back and went and entered.

Well, I drew Black 6 of Frank Harris' and the only person I'd ever seen ride him was Bubba Goudeoux. Well, when I called for him, he kicked open the slide behind him and JP22, and JP22 followed us out and I did not know it. Needless to say, it was a wreck. Black 6 jerked me down on his head and knocked me out and JP22 hooked the hell out of me, also.

Then, after the bull riding was over, Duke asked if I was ready to go. I said, "Duke, ole buddy, after the weekend I've had I ain't getting back on that damn motorcycle," so we loaded it up in, I believe it was Steve Scotts truck, and went home. The moral is, I lived and I wouldn't trade that experience for the world.

JAN BARBY PAYNE
LLOYD BARBY AND THE BARBY RODEO COMPANY

Back at the ranch the cowboys would sit around a table telling these short 8 second burst of events they cherish. These stories are of 8 second rides, laughs with Lloyd and Ruth, just cowboys stuff told by Gary Cates and Roy Chockley, pickup men and truck drivers for Lloyd during the rodeo season, as well as Bob Cates, family friend and rodeo man.

Lloyd got big laughs every time we would run horses in the chute and nod for the gate and hit the dirt. Gary bought JC Bonine and Pat Howey to Lloyd's one time to get on some broncs. On arrival JC asked Gary, "How many broncs did you tell Lloyd we wanted to ride?"

Gary told him he has said something like a few, but Lloyd had run in the whole remuda. JC wanted to get on Cutter Buck and when that horse burst out the chute Bonine was in for ride of his life. He went on to ride Bar Y, and Pat Howie got on Medicine Hat. The funny part of this story is Gary had asked Lloyd if he and 2 others could come out to get on a few horses, but Lloyd had gotten the word out and there were cars everywhere. Gary asked Lloyd, "Why are all these people here?" and Lloyd replied, "They came to watch a rodeo!"

After this visit JC and Pat would return, get good meals, sometime ride practice horses, help with feeding and ranch chores and then they would start stopping by with whomever they were hauling with at the time. Lloyd and Ruth's house became a handy stopping off place between Denver, Ft Worth, and Amarillo winter Stock Show Rodeos.

This was a highlight of the winter for them all. Many good friends were made and lots of cowboys spent time at the ranch. The list was numerous and many will be left out, but there was JC Bonine, Bud Monroe, Cody Bill Smith, Rick Smith, Joe Alexander, Ivan Daines, Jimmy Dix, Ace Berry, Mel Hyland, Wilf Hyland and Clint Johnson just to name a few. Lloyd never knew how many would show up in the night, but Ruth always had floor space if necessary and plenty of good home cooking for them.

He would put on a rodeo, but if he wasn't doing that he was going to a rodeo because he loved it. He thought a rodeo could and should be put together in two hours. He'd turn out bucking horses, meanwhile pickup men are trying to clear the arena, but Lloyd would get so anxious to keep the action going he'd turn out a rider too quickly a few times.

Cutter Buck was a bucking horse and boy could he buck. Lloyd kept this horse and turned him out at many a rodeo. Lloyd sure knew how to pick em. Blackie Williams and Donnie Eccles were telling Lloyd of a horse that he should buy to be used for a pickup horse. When they saddled him up and were pulling the back cinch the horse bowed up

Well, Lloyd decided to run him in the chute and told Gary to get on him just to see what he would do. Lloyd was there with the flank, Ruth got her whistle and stop watch and was standing beside him, Blackie was in the arena to pick up and I think Donnie was pulling the gate. When Gary called for him the horse bailed out of there and reared and snorted and bucked Gary off in one jump. Gary picks himself up and turns around to look at Lloyd and he and Ruth were bent over with laughter.

Lloyd went to Elk City, Oklahoma to the Beutler Bros Arena to purchase more broncs. He bought 2 or 3 that were used in the Wild Horse Race. These horses were branded KTY from the Born to Buck program and were were pretty wild. Lloyd premiered them at one of the ranch jackpots. Gary tried to ride one, but the horse was so crazy wild bucking that Gary threw his elbow out of socket.

Lloyd hauled Doc Calhoon the local doctor and family friend to the end of the arena and they set his elbow back and never missed a lick. As the rodeo just kept on going. Lloyd loved the action and being able to supply the stock no matter the weather. He would buck them in fog and mist and you could see a horse buck 2 jumps then lose sight of him, but he said, "The show must go on."

The only time the show didn't go on (or was interrupted a bit) was at Watonga, Oklahoma. It was raining and lightning and the committee were rebuilding the pens and bucking chutes. Everything was done, but the announcer's stand and there was no cover, only the pipe and some boards for the floor and a makeshift place for the sound system.

The rodeo started and the lightning was around, but things were going pretty good until one lightning bolt got near enough that it came through the sound system. Did they call the rodeo? Nope, Lloyd just paused for a moment while all the sound system was moved to a vehicle and the rodeo went on.

At Dumas, Texas saddle bronc rider Steve Crowder heard a bragger going on and on about how good he was, how tough a rider he was, and that there wasn't nothing in Barby's pen he couldn't spur the hair off of. Well, Steve went to Lloyd and asked him to run in Memphis Blue for an extra rider.

The bragging cowboy then started backing up and making excuses like I don't have a saddle, etc. Steve gladly took care of that and proceeded to put his saddle on the horse. That ole bragger got thrown off so hard the ambulance crew came to help him out of the arena. Lloyd told him, "Come back anytime and you can try to ride some more of my broncs." Lloyd gathered himself and went on with the rodeo.

Lloyd & Ruth were both very loving and caring people. Lloyd always made sure his help was treated right. Ruth fed everyone like they were her own. She would put out a spread in the motel room every night after the rodeo for all the crew. Sandwiches, fresh fruit and watermelon always tasted so good when you'd been on the road eating fast food all the time. Sometimes, she would even bring other appliances and fix roast and potatoes in motel room.

RED DOYAL
AIRBORNE COWBOYS

My flying to rodeos began in the Fall of 1966. I had filed for my permit in May and rodeos at home had gotten very bad so in June I got my RCA card. I had a very good summer run and was in the top twenty by the end of August. Larry Mahan offered to let me fly with him so I jumped in the plane and we were on our way to the Pendleton Roundup.

Things went very well until the Pendleton Roundup. We had gone to Larry's home in Brooks, Oregon while waiting for Pendleton to start. I was up the first day in the first section which is what they started the Roundup with in those days. I had #4 bull of Harry Volds, a very good bull. We got in the plane and when we started flying through the mountains we got into some fog about half way.

We flew back to the airport and checked the mileage to drive it was too far for us to get there in time so we decided try again, only to have to return. We checked commercial flights, but no go, so we headed out one more time. Larry said we needed to go back, but we hit a clearing and went on.

We called ahead and asked them to hold my bull for last. I put my spurs and chaps on in the taxi going to the rodeo. I jumped out and ran to the chutes and got on #4 and that was the last I remembered because #4 hit me under the chin and knocked me out. The bull and I had two or three more head on collisions before it was over and I ended up with a split and broken nose, shattered cheek bone, and a concussion.

I was unconscious for two days, and in five days I was headed home. After returning home I went to my doctor and found out that one-half of my face was paralyzed. The doctor said that it would take five to six weeks for all the feeling to come back in my face. I didn't rodeo during that time and just stayed home and tried to get prepared to ride again.

I went to the Cow Palace after six weeks at home and split second and third in first go, bucked off second bull, and went home and waited for Chicago to start. I believe the best thing was that I didn't remember anything from Pendleton. I didn't ride real good in 1967, but won enough to stay on the road. In 1968 I hit them for a good lick in Denver and didn't buck off of a bull until after Houston, but only split a fifth and sixth at Fort Worth. We all had stretches where the draw gets you.

In 1967, when we were at Forth Worth, Bobby Mayo and I were talking about what we would do if we were flying and something happened to the pilot. I knew Mahan had his first plane stored at a small airport outside Fort Worth so we asked

Mahan about allowing us to use his plane for lessons. Of course, he OK'd the deal and Bobby and I started taking flying lessons and learned how to take off and land.

During the Houston Rodeo, George Paul told me that his grandfather had told him to win the world if he could because after that he was going to have to take over the job of running their ranch in Mexico. George asked me if I would go with him for the rest of the year. He told me if it was just the two of us he wanted six cents per mile, but if the plane was full it wouldn't cost me anything. He knew I had taken some lessons and could help with the flying so no way could I refuse a deal like that.

We almost lived in the airplane that year. One, two, and three rodeos per day because of the time zone changes and it was possible to work two or three rodeos the same day and all being in different states. Sounds crazy, but we have done this many times during our rodeo days. For example, Central Time, Western North Dakota, Mountain Time, Montana, Pacific Time, Eastern Oregon, three rodeos, same time, same day.

Two things that stick in my mind about that year was being a run from Seattle to a rodeo in Prince George, BC. The first thing was, we were flying through the mountains because at Seattle, Shawn Davis had been bucked off and kicked by Christensen Brother's bull, Missoula. That caused him to have fluid in his inner ear so we could only fly so high and we had to follow a river through the Mountains to get to Prince George.

Things went well on the way up there and the next morning we headed back to the States, following the same river. George and Shawn were in the front seats and Bo Ashorn and I were asleep in the back of the plane. We hit a down draft and have no idea how far the plane dropped straight down, but everything hit the top of the airplane and this being a Comanche 250, the door wraps over the top of the airplane. Shawn hit the door and knocked it open, but George calmly nosed it up, reached over and closed the door, and just flew on. Underneath us was a raging, rocky river. Needless to say, Bo and I got no more sleep on this trip.

The second thing was, it was close to the end of the year and since George was so far ahead in the bull riding he could not be beaten for the title so we decided to stay home for a few days. George called the next day and told me he had a chance to break the all time winning record and asked if I would like to go with him up north to make a few more rodeos.

He picked me up the next day and we were entered in five rodeos in three days, the last two being Anaheim, California for one night, and Raleigh, North Carolina for the next afternoon. That is going from the Pacific Ocean to the Atlantic Ocean overnight. We fueled up at 3 AM and on to the rodeo in Carolina, then back home and George did break the money winning record that year.

One year, either '67 or '69, I was up in the first performance at Cheyenne and when I got to the arena someone told me that the day before, an Air Force drill team was practicing for a fly over for the first day rodeo when one plane stalled and crashed.

The pilot ejected, but his chute didn't open and he landed on the concession stand and it looked like a bomb had torn it all to heck, scattering pieces all over the place and the plane crashed in one of the big, turnout pens for the animals. There was only one bull killed, a bull from a small producer, and the very best one he owned. Sometimes you're lucky and sometimes not.

JOHNNY RIVERA
MY BUDDY, MIKE WHITE

I was at my home town rodeo in DeKalb, Texas, one of Gerald Smiths. After I got off my bull, the clown had backed in the chute and he pulled me in there with him, but at the head end of the chute. The bull came in there to get me, but I'm all the way up in the corner so he turns to go back out into the arena.

As he is bucking and kicking out of there he falls on me, smashing my ribs against the pipes. Mike White grabs me and pulls me out of the chute. I lay around out back for awhile trying to catch my breath when they finally decide I might need to go to the hospital. Mike puts me in his new Dodge dually, but first makes sure he has a towel to place on his seats.

He drove 100 miles an hour which sounds like he was concerned for my well being, but with over 50 speeding tickets I realized it was just his MO. When he got me to the hospital and they were doing my blood work they wanted to know if I was diabetic. I said, "No, but I had a glass of Hanna's sweet tea before we left for the rodeo." We called it diabetic tea from then on.

They put me in a room, but I couldn't get comfortable so I was kneeling on the floor with my head on the bed. Shortly, I feel them putting something around my neck and I'm thinking it doesn't hurt and that they are just probably taking precautions to make sure I'm stable

Then, it's starts to get real tight around my neck and it was getting harder to breath. I turn around and it's Mike with the blood pressure cuff and he's pumping it up and grinning. .

One time he asked me if I wanted to go to Lake Charles with him. I told him I was broke, but he said there wasn't any entry fees so I threw in with him and we left after I got off work.

We drove all night to get there and as I hung my rope on the fence I heard the announcer say to get up there and pay your entry fees. I went and found Mike and said, "You told me there were no any entry fees." He said, "There isn't. I paid yours." I ended up winning two buckles there, a go-round and a reserve average…My buddy, Mike White.

© Roger Langford

Part III

1. Andy Taylor: Booger Bryant
2. Sharon Camarillo: Rodeo Reminices'
3. Cary Culbertson: Navajo Code Talkers
4. Red Doyal: Stories Clyde Vamvoras Sharred With Me On The Road
5. Debbie Garrison: The Lost Finger
6. Kevin Busche: It's A Small World
7. Jay Foscalina 1: Labor Day Weekend Show
8. Barney Brehmer: Pendleton; Cowboy Justice
9. Steve Scott: Freckles Brown Outside The Rodeo Arena
10. Charlie Thompson: An Escape Story
11. Richard Flechsig: Just A Little Help
12. Don Endsley: Inducted Into Texas Rodeo Cowboy Hall of Fame
13. Lee Jones: San Antonio Holiday Inn
14. Jerry La Valley: The Trophy Buckle
15. Bill Thorpe: The Broke Leg
16. Steve Scott: Workin' On My Contest/Contract Card
17. Clint Ford: Me And Big Al
18. Richard Flechsig: What Happened To The Dirt
19. Dude Smith: My Rodeo Story
20. Mark Trujillo: Texas vs Oklahoma Shootout
21. Jimmy Blotz: Girlfriend's Horse
22. Bobby Dykes: Ol' Pete
23. Tommy Tarpley: A Bad Night In Louisana
24. Dale Woodard: That's All I Need
25. Ron Chockley: Barby Rodeo Company
26. Jan Barby Payne: Albuquerque
27. Mickey Young: Rodeo Days
28. Joe Latona: That's Bullridin'
29. Bruce Ford: Bare Backin' A Bull

30. Wayne Whitehead: Old Murphy And Me
31. Danny O'haco: Flyin' To San Francisco
32. Roy Dell: Yogi Bear
33. Jan Barby Payne: Mangum, Oklahoma
34. Red Doyal: Cowboy Hazards
35. Johnny Rivera: Tough As They Come
36. Jan Barby Payne: R. J. Preston

ANDY TAYLOR
BOOGER BRYANT

Well for starters, just the name ***Booger*** gets your attention, right? Booger Bryant could be described in a lot of ways; cowboy, bull rider, bull rope maker, believer.....A man's-man! Booger lived in Hagerman, New Mexico not far from Roswell. He was probably 8-10 years older than me when I started my professional rodeo career at 18.

Back in those days when you were a *rookie* and just starting out most of the older, seasoned cowboys wouldn't talk to you until you had *paid your dues* and had proven yourself. But, Booger wasn't that way at all, at least with me. There's no telling how tough Booger really was, but he didn't try to push that persona. But, you could obviously tell that he wouldn't be pushed around by anyone.

In the mid to late '70's there was a surge of Christianity through professional rodeo. And, as it often happens with people who first experience salvation, there was a lot more zeal than common sense displayed by a lot of these rodeo people. Many of them were in-your-face with it. They meant well, but to be honest it turned me off and I avoided most of them the best I could. I'd gotten saved in a countywide crusade in Wheeler, Texas in 1974, but I pretty much kept it to myself and wasn't doing a very good job of living it out.

But, Booger Bryant was different than the others. I knew he was a Christian, but it was different. I wanted to be around him. We had quite a few visits about the Lord, but he hardly ever initiated them as it was mostly me. I knew he'd be 'straight-up' with me and I knew he wouldn't be pushy about it. He didn't have some subtle agenda like the rest of them. I knew I could trust him. He knew I wasn't doing a good job of walking it out, but he never mentioned it. He stood his ground between the over-zealous believers and the hard-ass, old-school cowboys who didn't want any of it and would dang sure tell you about it if they needed to,

He got cancer, but never complained about it. He's just say he was trusting the Lord, with it. He fought the good fight for sure, but finally went to his reward. He left behind his wife Bonnie and a little boy, Blu. He made my bull ropes for several years and was always a trusted friend, kinda like the big brother I didn't have. But most of all, he showed me how a real Christian ought to be like and his impact on my life was deep, even though I didn't know it at the time.

I never got the chance to talk to Booger after my life had really made the turn in 1984 because he was already gone. But, I did get the chance in the mid-'90's to tell his son, Blu, who was leading the world bull riding standings at the time how much I admired him and how much of an impact his dad had on my life. It felt pretty good. I'll forever be grateful to Booger Bryant for helping to show me the way.

SHARON CAMARILLO
RODEO REMINICES'

Looking back over my introduction to rodeo and inevitably the career it provided, little snippets and memories come back to me, usually always invoking a smile.

Like the experience in the seventies when Wrangler sent a troupe of it's endorsees to South America for a match between United States and Argentina. Jim Shoulders and Howard Harris ram-rodded the crew of cowboys and champions including, in part, Donnie and Pete Gay, Hawkeye Henson, Leo, John and Lisa Davis to rope, ride, and run barrels against the Argentinean Team. It was a politically volatile time for Argentina and armed guards and bulletproof vans often escorted us.

On arrival into Buenos Aires, Jim and Howard got all of us together and made sure we knew how important it was to stay together, be safe and keep our passports with us at all times. Respectfully we listened, but the ego/confidence level was greater than our naivety and within a few hours Jim and Howard were called to the police station to persuade the authorities to release two of our rambunctious, rowdy cowboys arrested for having too much fun. The major problem was, they had also misplaced their passports so the next few days were spent in and out of the American consulate replacing Rob and Pete's, I won't mention last names, passports.

I'm sure, remembering back over our rowdy crew, not to mention adapting polo ponies to barrel horses, Argentine stock to bucking horses and roping steers, this was only one of the many challenges Jim and Howard and Den Mothers Sharon and Irene had to suffer thorough during our adventures. Good news, Wrangler/America won the Team Challenge. Recognizing the American flag and listening to our National Anthem in a foreign stadium in a distant country is another one of those memorable moments one doesn't forget.

There was the time Leo and I pulled into the Oklahoma City fairgrounds for the National Finals Rodeo, my first qualification and another one of many for Leo. We walked in the coliseum and there were no banners, no pomp and circumstance, only concrete floors and tractors carrying in dirt, still a few days away from opening ceremonies. I'm not sure what I expected, but when I voiced my disappointment following a long year of anticipation, Leo barked, "What did you expect. The National Anthem?" Nobody ever said Leo was tactful and often I look back on his sarcastic humor usually with a smile. However, I was well rewarded and the thrill of riding in that first Grand Entry behind the California flag and my husband, acknowledging our families proudly watching from the grandstands, was yet another memorable moment in my career

I remember some of the lessons Leo taught me as a newbie to professional rodeo competition, especially the fact that most of the year the road was our home and it was important to gain home court advantage by making the next rodeo arena our new back yard. I always loved arriving at a rodeo ground, unloading my horses, finding their stalls, bedding and fresh water, completing the preparation necessary for comfortable surroundings, and the managed competition. Leo had a game he played that I didn't much appreciate or tolerate and certainly may have been one of the reasons for the eventual decline of our marriage.

Sharon Camarillo...

He worked to keep the intimidation card over his peers and fellow competitors, which always started with the poor volunteer gate man. After long drives between rodeos it was nice to pull into the rodeo grounds for the duration of a stay, whether for the day or week. Leo began his competition with the gate attendant. If he could make him mad it seemed to boost his ego and prepare him for his upcoming competition.

I thought this was totally out of line and unnecessary, not to mention rude, particularly because these were often local committee volunteers who in part provided our rodeo opportunity. Of course at that time in my life, though I had the thought of not having to have the last word I must not have had the ability, so the encounter usually extended much further past the gate and on into the day between Leo and me. Our personal challenges always made me ride a little harder as I unconsciously focused my competitive edge on proving to Leo, one didn't have to be mean to be competitive. At the time I didn't realize how he unconsciously helped me develop my winning edge and competitive fierceness, another lesson learned.

So often, opportunities are just perceptions, for an example, attending the Presidential Rodeo during the Reagan Presidency. I certainly don't know for sure, however, I perceive the rodeo was inspired by both President Reagan and Secretary of Commerce Malcolm Baldridge to give rodeo champions, supporting ranchers, agriculturalists, and western artists including men like Louis L'Amour an opportunity to visit Washington DC during their term.

Honored with an invitation I made sure to arrive in DC early and stay late, unlike some of our cowboy celebrities who were juggling rodeo competitions. My priority was to utilize the opportunity and experience each moment. I saw the lights go on at the Whitehouse's East Lawn in preparation for the Western themed barbeque, enjoyed moving though the Whitehouse with many of the rooms open to us, seeing books owned by Lincoln, dishes used by Washington, all a finger away with no glass or restrictions. What an honor. I look back on that experience and wish I had been a little more apt with a camera. Today's digital resources and a selfie stick would have provided much clearer memories.

Rodeo Stories II

I look back and feel I took a lot of my experience for granted. There is an ignorance of youth which one often uses to advantage, that without it could turn into a state of intimidation. I always felt confidant in the arena, on the grounds, and in situations where contestants were invited. I felt each experience was a stepping-stone to the next and continue to feel that same way today. It was just what we did even though there wasn't much money in our pockets, the win resume seemed to make up for what we didn't have in the bank. It was life as we dreamed it before we let the responsibilities of real LIFE get in the way.

Grateful for the experience, opportunities, and life long friendships, though I honor and admire the contestants of today, I'm so glad I don't have to do it over again. I work with about 500 horses and riders per year in my Horsemanship for Better Barrel Racing programs. Inevitably, students ask me if I miss competition. Even when I see the opportunities presented at events like the National Finals, Rodeo Houston, Calgary Stampede, and The American, all prestigious facilities, television exposure, and large purse money pay outs I understand the efforts and sacrifices it takes to make successful outcomes no matter what the era.

That was my life then, but today the effort and commitment necessary to gain rewards from competition is no longer my passion. The facts are, the road isn't any shorter and the preparations just as grueling. No, I don't miss competition, however I can't help but wonder what it would have been like to have experienced the same rodeo opportunities.

Two of our biggest competitions back in the day were the Copenhagen Skoal Match in Ft. Worth and the Winston sponsored Tournament Rodeo. Both events, I can proudly say I was apart of. As far as rodeos, I loved competing at Cheyenne, but my favorite remains Rodeo Houston. I will never forget walking down into the Astrodome for the first time as a competitor, nor in later years ,my 16-year stint as one of Rodeo Houston's rodeo announcers alongside Bob Tallman, Boyd Polhamus, and Bill Bailey, both at the Astrodome then moving to Reliant/NRG Stadium.

I never lost the awe factor of entering those arenas. My annual salary as an announcer far outweighed what I made running barrels at Houston. Truly another totally rewarding and exciting highlight of my career, and again, directly related to my experience as a professional rodeo competitor.

All things come to pass. I enjoy a wonderful life with enumerable opportunities earned through my past rodeo experience, success, and contacts. I truly live the life I had envisioned for myself and appreciate the fact that my life still revolves around horses and the Western lifestyle they generate. I do have to say, when I have reunions with fellow competitors who's friendships have endured over the years it is great fun to laugh and reminisce about our lives then, but most rewarding to talk about our lives today that have been influenced and enriched by our mutual experiences.

CARY CULBERTSON
NAVAJO CODE TALKERS

In June of 1974 a couple of friends and I had entered the saddle bronc riding in the Gallup, New Mexico rodeo. We were up in the Saturday afternoon performance and we had gotten to Gallup early so we went to the arena to see what we drew.

The performance was at 2:00 PM so we had some time on our hands and decided to take in the parade. While watching the bands, floats, and horses passing by, we were visiting and cutting up a little when I felt a tap on my leg. I looked down and there was a Navajo boy about seven or eight years old. He put his forefinger to his lips and said, "Shhhh," then pointed towards toward the parade and said under his breath, "Code Talkers."

I looked up and there was a float carrying a number of the Navajo Code Talkers. As they were passing by everyone who was able, men, women and children, stood at attention, removed their hats and saluted. There was not a word spoken or a sound made until the Code Talkers had passed by.

That was a very moving and touching moment that left me with a profound sense of patriotism and filled me with pride that I was an American. I thought about the freedoms we share and enjoy, thanks in part to these Native American heroes who through their service in the Pacific as U. S. Marines during World War II saved countless American soldiers lives and helped to bring about the defeat of Japan and the end of the war.

The U. S. Marines used the Navajo language which was an unwritten language as the basis for the code that confused and confounded the Japanese. This code was the only code that was never broken by the Japanese. Not one of the Navajo Code Talkers was captured by the Japanese.

It is rumored that the Marines were ordered to kill a Code Talker in the event he was being captured as depicted in the movie, Windtalkers. I have not found anything to support this claim as the Code Talkers were very well protected by their brother Marines.

The Navajo Code Talkers were participants in every assault the U.S. Marines.

conducted in the Pacific from 1942 to 1945. At Iwo Jima, Major Howard Conner, 5th Marine Division Signal Officer declared, "Were it not for the Navajos, the Marines would never have taken Iwo Jima."

"By the end of World War II there were between 300 and 400 Navajo Code Talkers in the Pacific, some who may be still alive at the time of this writing. There were other tribes, Comanche's, Lakota's and others using their native languages that were Code Talkers in Europe, but the Navajos were the first and most notable.

I was very impressed and moved as to how the Navajo Nation honored their Heroes. Maybe the rest of the country could take a lesson from this. At parades I see so many people not stand up, remove their hats, salute, place their right hand over their hearts or otherwise acknowledge the Stars and Stripes as it passes by that so many men and women have died protecting.

After the parade was over we returned to the arena for the performance where I picked up a third place in the saddle bronc contest. I wanted to ride as hard as I could in honor and tribute to these National Heroes who were seated in the audience.

Chester Nez, the last of the original 29 Navajo Code Talkers passed away June 5,th 2014 at the age of 93. July 26th 2001 Chester Nez and the other four surviving members of the original 29 Navajo Code Talkers were awarded the Congressional Medal of Honor by President George W. Bush. Instead of shaking the Presidents hand after receiving their medals they stood at attention and saluted.

RED DOYAL
STORIES CLYDE VAMVORAS SHARRED WITH ME ON THE ROAD

Clyde told me this story about the night he and some of his cowboy buddies left a rodeo heading back to the hotel and decided to stop in and have a beer and play a little pool.

They were up north in a college town, either Billing or Bozeman and this place ended up being the drinking hole for the college football players. As time went on and after a few more beers and feeling no pain one of the football players started giving them hell and started bragging about how tough the football players were.

Well, the first to get sucked into the conflict was Jim Smith, better known to the cowboys as Kickapoo. He was about 5'9' tall and weighed about 150 pounds and needless to say that was a pretty short battle.

And, as the night went on another one fell into the trap, John Edwards whom they called, Hey Tex. Clyde told me he thought Hey Tex might possibly be able to handle the football player, but he was wrong. Clyde said they got all squared up and the football player punched Hey Tex and it was over.

That was it and back into the bar once more. These players got really high on themselves about how tough they were and kept laughing and talking about how they could take on anyone who wanted a piece of them.

The rodeo guys weren't happy at all and the more Clyde listened to the football players brag on themselves the more confident he felt that he had to give them what they didn't want. So, Clyde decided to step up to the plate and here they go outside. After a little fighting, Clyde finally got the player up against the wall with his hand on his throat and after choking him for a while, the player began to slide down the wall.

Clyde was able to lay him out and finish the fight. They went back into the bar and were sitting at a table when the football player came walking toward him. Clyde was thinking, "Oh, hell. Not again."

The football player stopped at the table and asked if they wanted a beer. He brought the round and then said to the boys, "I only made one mistake." Then, he looked at Clyde and said, "I should have started with you first." Everyone had some more beer, had some more pool, laughed about the fights and had a good night.

Clyde and C.R. Boucher bought a small ranch in Oklahoma across the river from Burkburnett, Texas and it became the layover for passing cowboys. One time a car load of us were staying there a couple of days and Clyde's mother was visiting from Louisiana. She was a small Cajun lady, always happy and laughing.

When you cross the river the first road that went west had a bar on the corner and this was the daytime hangout. The ranch was about two miles on down the road. One day we spent the day at the watering hole and Clyde's mother came along with us. We started home for supper time driving along the road and she started shouting for us to stop.

She jumped out of the car and ran back up the road. Hell, none of us had any idea what was going on. Then, here she comes walking back with a big turtle in her hand. She said, "Boys, we will have turtle soup tomorrow." It was delicious.

DEBBIE GARRISON
THE LOST FINGER

It was about 1990 or 1991 when I was attending a Bud Light Team Roping at an indoor arena in Benbrook, Texas. The arena was cut down to accommodate the roping and the cattle were running pretty hard. I was heading for my husband at the time and we drew a runner. I roped the steer and when I went to the horn the steer ducked right and my horse ducked left. I felt a burning sensation when I dallied and turned loose of the rope.

Thinking I had just burned my fingers I took my glove off and noticed that the top half of my index finger was gone. So, I pulled up and stepped off my horse and held my hand up in the air, pinching off the blood flow thinking that would keep it from hurting so bad, kind of like you do when you smash it with a hammer.

When I did that Walt rode up and asked, "What's wrong?" I said, "It's gone!" and he says, "What's gone?" and I reply, "My finger!" Then everyone starts coming up and people are yelling, "Get ice, call 911, take her horse," and all I could think to do was to go out of the arena and wait for the ambulance.

I go outside and sit down on a trailer, waiting, when a fellow roper who was a paramedic comes up and says, "Let me look at you finger, Debbie." So, I let him take a look. He has some saline solution and pours it on the finger and asks, "Where's the tip of your finger?" I replied, "Oh, it's gotta be in my glove," and he says, "Where's your glove?" Then I paniced, thinking that it's been dropped somewhere or it's in the arena.

About that time Walt is walking up from tying up the horses

and I tell him to go find my glove. He says he has it and he pulls it out of his pocket. Then, the roper/paramedic tells him that my finger is in there and to get it out for him so he can see how damaged it is. The look on Walt's face was priceless. He gets this deer in the headlights look on his face as he looks at the glove he just retrieved out of his pocket and stands there for it seemed like hours.

You could tell he just realized what he had been carrying in his pocket and that now this guy wants him to reach in there and pull out the severed digit. About this time Walt shoves the glove at the roper/paramedic and says, "Here, you get it out, you're the F*$%#&^G paramedic."

So, while all this is going on, inside the arena another calamity is going on with my fellow Women's Champion Team Roper Friend Cindy Waters. She's running to the concession stand to get ice for me. For those who don't know Cindy, she's a top notch roper who's only about 5ft tall and running long distances isn't necessarily her specialty.

Anyway, she runs all the way to the concession stand to get ice and is running down the arena to go outside to where I am when she passes another Women's Champion Roper Jeana Brooks who is one tough Cowgirl and competitor. Jeana stops her and asks what's going on. Cindy tells her that I have cut off my finger and she's getting me ice.

About that time Jeana has a minute to let that answer sink in and she passes clean out hearing the news and falls off her horse on the ground in front of Cindy. So, Cindy looks at Jeana on the ground, then looks at the cup of ice and makes the decision to throw the ice on Jeana to bring her around. Then, Cindy is off to the concession stand again to get more ice for me. By the time Cindy gets to me she is about to pass out and is begging the paramedic for oxygen.

So, I'm sitting outside waiting for the ambulance when Billy Minick, former NFR bull rider, stock contractor, and part owner of Billy Bob's Texas, and Doyle Blagg, famous horse shoer and all around good guy walks up and asks me about 100 times if I am OK. The more they look at me & my severed finger the more their color turns from tan, to green, to grey and then they are holding each other up and are slowly sinking to the ground. So, I send them away to recover about the time the ambulance arrives.

The ambulance arrives and the paramedics jump out and start asking all the questions. About that time I realize that Walt isn't looking so great either. He looks kinda nervous and his breathing is fast. The paramedics get us in the ambulance and they start trying to get me stabilized for the trip to Harris Hospital in Fort Worth.

I tell the paramedic that I'm OK, but I was worried about Walt having a heart attack. The paramedic tells me that by law he has to get me taken care of first and then they will check on Walt. I'm laying there thinking that he had played in all those football games, 2 Super Bowls, played with broken bones, etc., and he would leave this world from a heart attack over me cutting off my index finger. At least this was all a great diversion tactic to take my mind off of my missing finger.

Anyway, we make it to Harris and they get me in the ER and a nurse gets with Walt to ask all the pertinent questions about the accident and to also very slyly, check his blood pressure. By then, everyone knows that Walt Garrison's wife has cut her finger off and he is at Harris Hospital with me.

The helicopter care flight crew came in to see me. They were flying in from Mineral Wells, my home town, back to Harris when they heard about my accident. Several of the crew knew me and since Benbrook was on the way to Ft. Worth they had landed at the arena to pick me up. After landing they learned that the ambulance beat them so they came on to check on me. So, that helped me get the extra attention in addition to my Dallas Cowboy husband being in the house. It looked like we were having a party in the ER.

I had to wait for the hospital to contact Dr. Walter Gracia and get him to the hospital to do the surgery so they put me in a nice room to wait with my finger wrapped in saline soaked gauze on the tray beside the bed. It took about 5 hours, but we had plenty of attention from nurses coming in checking on me and making small talk with Walt.

While I was laying there at about hour 4, a cute young nurse comes in to check me and as she walks by I guess she figures that the wad of gauze on the tray is trash and in one fast sweep pushes it off into the trash can. I look at Walt, knowing he didn't realize what just happened and that he wasn't going to reach in there and dig it out so I tell him to get the nurse back in there to retrieve my finger again.

Anyway, after a long successful surgery I finally got my finger back where it belonged and even though it's a little shorter it's mine and I hope to not loose it again. Most of the people there that day still remember that exciting team roping and continue to relive it with me when they see me.

Debbie Garrison and Pam Minick team roping.
Credit-dudley@dudleydoright.com

KEVIN BUSCHE
IT'S A SMALL WORLD

I began my 18 years of rodeoing in the fall of 1975 when I joined the Fort St. John high school rodeo club. We spent several nights each week practicing riding bulls and a few bareback horses whenever there were any to be tried out. Much of my childhood and teenage summers were spent on my step-grandfather's ranch and he rodeo'd in the 1920s and 30s in central Alberta in the Pete Knight era. I think it was his stories of those days that made me want to pursue rodeo.

For several years I competed in all three riding events, as well as steer wrestling. I soon realized that bareback riding was not my strong suit and gave it up and competed in three events until 1984 when I took a real good hooking in a two head bull riding and hung up my bull rope as well, but kept on riding broncs until the end of the 1993 season. My wife Moe had given birth to our oldest daughter in 1990, followed by twin girls in 1992 and it was then that I started to realize that suddenly I had a lot of people depending on me. After 18 years of competing with minimal injuries and none that were extremely bad, that it was a matter of time before the odds would be stacked too high. So, at age 33 I hung up my bronc saddle too, while the decision was mine to make rather than wait 'til it was made for me.

Over the years I competed in the (NRA) Northwest Rodeo Association of Canada, the (IRA) Interior Rodeo Association which later became the British Columbia Rodeo Association and for several years in the (C.P.R.A.) Canadian Professional Rodeo Association on a permit. In the late 1970s an organization called N.A.R.C., the North American Rodeo Commission was formed and consisted of most of the Amateur Associations in the U.S., Canada, and Australia.

Each year they held the "North American Finals Rodeo" which started in Spokane, then moved to El Paso, then to Denver which is where it was when I qualified my first of five times in 1981.

They took the top three year-end finishers in each event from each association, so contestant-wise at the time it was the largest rodeo in the world. They had a pretty healthy payout and it was the start of giving Dodge trucks to event champions. It was a big deal, but for us boys from way up north it was the bright lights, beer in the grand stands and more people under one roof than we had ever seen. It was almost intimidating and hard to focus on riding broncs.

It was a two header with the top ten going to the short round and riding for the money, the huge buckle, and the truck. There were so many contestants that everybody had to get on one in the slack and one in the performance. We had a huge party in our room the night before I had to get on my first one and I woke up in the morning to a hell of a mess, a killer hangover, and a cowboy sleeping on the other bed that I had no idea who he was. It turned out to be a young guy from Nebraska who was also a bronc rider and he was winning the first round on a horse called "Top Deck" who coincidentally I had drawn for my second horse. His name was Skeeter Thurston. Yep, the Skeeter who went on to qualify for the NFR and he now has two sons going down the road.

The youngest one, Zeke, just won the bronc riding at Houston last month and I believe around $50,000 dollars. Skeeter ended up marrying a Canadian gal and her sister is married to a guy that I rodeo'd with up here for many years... it's a small world! So anyhow, the area that I am from is well-known for producing great bucking horses for many years. Canadian Finals, NFR, and Calgary Stampede horses came from here originally, Holly-Warrior and Oot Pik are just a few that come to mind. So, with horses like that in our back yard it's made for some pretty tough bronc riders.

My first horse that hungover morning in the slack was a

little buckskin horse called Billy Jack. Now, we had a buckskin up here with the same name and he was the pick of the litter and I had won at least four firsts on him so I was tickled to hope this American horse with the same name might be as good. I was asking around behind the chutes and nobody seemed to know this horse. There were at least 15 or 20 stock contractors that had stock there. Finally, a skinny little guy with glasses on and still about half drunk from the night before claimed ownership. He told me what a great horse he was and he said over and over, "You sit up and ride this horse and we're both gonna make some money."

They had a $500 cash bonus to the contractors for the highest marked horses and bull in each round and he wanted that real bad. They loaded the chutes which were still the old tall wooden ones in the Denver Coliseum with very narrow spacing on the slats so it was hard to hook your latigo and back cinch, and equally as hard to lean on your stomach over the top of the gate to pull your saddle. Especially on this skinny little buckskin because he couldn't have been 14 hands high and 750 pounds with a skinny little neck and hardly any shoulders. Those little horses are not fun or easy to ride. But he was mine so I'd take him and hope for the best.

The old boy that owned him (whose name I don't recall) was coaching me from the side and telling me the rein measurement, trying to be helpful, but the whiskey fumes off him weren't helping my hangover at all. Because of the large number of contestants, time was of the essence to keep things rolling on schedule. So, when the pickup men returned from the catch pen and assumed their positions in the arena, they blew a whistle and you had fifteen seconds to be ready and nod your head then they would open the gate, ready or not. The only exception was if you had a chute fighter.

Now I never was one to sit in there and fidget and mess around, but this little buckskin was leaned back and against the back side of the chute. He was far from being in a good place to nod, but the chute boss was giving me the warning so I called for him rather than hold up the show. He shot out of there straight sideways and flat and I tried hard to spur him out but it was a weak one and he took off on the dead run. The first rule of thumb is to hold it in 'em 'til they break. I was behind from the get go and he was picking up speed so I went to the guts and tried to bear down.

About 2/3 of the way across the arena with him on the dead run like he thought he was a triple A rated horse off the track, he turned a 180 degree right turn and launched me out the front door like a missile. Up and outta control I came down like a lawn dart, right on top of my head with my feet straight up in the air. I could feel a crunching sound in my neck and things went dark for a moment, then it was seeing stars as they say. It was like welding flash, just dark with all these intermittent flashes of light. I couldn't even find my way back to the chutes. Finally somebody came and took me by the arm and led me back behind the chutes. I was scared as hell because I couldn't see a thing and in the back of my mind I was thinking, "I can't end up in the hospital here. I don't have any insurance."

A lot of things were running through my mind at that moment, then I could hear a girl's voice yelling, "George. George." I looked up toward the sound coming from the chute, but I couldn't see anyone or anything. Man I was scared. About 45 minutes later my vision slowly started to return and in a couple hours everything was back to normal except for a headache and my neck making the same clicking sound as a ratchet when I turned my head.

My thoughts returned to the voice calling me George. I wondered who that might have been and why as the only people I knew in Denver were my fellow cowboys and cowgirls from Canada who were also competing there. Back at home in Fort St. John, I had a good friend named George who people sometimes mistook me for. I never really understood why as he is quite a bit taller than me. Our hair was the same reddish color, but that was the only similarity as far as I could tell. I kept thinking this far from home that it was pretty strange.

I recall one time several years later George called me from the bar one night and said, "There's some guy in here that thinks I'm you and he's been buying me drinks for two hours non stop." I said, "Well ride it for all it's worth." Neither of us ever found out who that guy was. The next day my neck was bothering me so myself and several of my buddies hopped in a cab and went to downtown Denver to a sports place where they played racquetball and stuff. The cab driver told us it was a good place to get a massage. We went into the building and were advised to take the elevator to the 4th or 5th floor to the masseuses, which we did. When we stepped out of the elevator the girl behind the desk stood up and said, "Oh my God! I saw you at the rodeo yesterday and I was calling you. I thought you were George." What?? Well, now what were the chances, of all the places in Denver to walk into of that happening? We talked for a few minutes and I told her that I had lost my vision for awhile and couldn't see who was calling out that name. After a few more minutes I discovered that she had a cousin in Fort St. John that she had been visiting a couple years before and during that visit she had actually dated my friend George, who she'd mistaken me for at the rodeo. We were supposed to go out after the rodeo the following night, but she stood me up. It's a small world...

On a footnote, Skeeter Thurston did win the first go on that big black horse named Top Deck. I rolled off him at about the seven second mark in the second go and threw away a bunch of go round money as I was tapped off and making a good ride. I think it was too much partying and not enough paying attention to business. Twenty some years later I was at the Dawson Creek Stampede, which is now one of the top ten rodeos in Canada. It was intermission time and I was going down to the chutes to visit a couple of my friends that were judging the rodeo, Terry Cook and Eugene Auclair (both men had finished judging the Houston rodeo in 2015 and are the first and only Canadians to have been invited to that prestigious event). Just as I got to the chutes the announcer was introducing the trick riding act, The Thurstons. I asked Eugene who these Thurston kids were and he said, "Those are Skeeter's kids."

Now, I knew that Skeeter had moved to Canada and married a Canadian gal, but I had not seen or spoken to him since in left Denver in November of 1981. Eugene said, "He's over at his horse trailer by the calf chutes." I walked over and there he was with his back to me hanging up some halters. I hollered, "Skeeter Thurston!" He turned around and recognized me instantly. "I'll be go to hell. Kevin Busche!" We shook hands and when his boys were done their trick riding act and the horses were looked after we headed to the beer gardens and did a little catching up on the old days. It's a small world.

JAY FOSCALINA 1
LABOR DAY WEEKEND SHOW

With a 3 day weekend looming I entered four rodeos in California and I thought about the old Jimmy Buffett quote, "Headin up to San Francisco for the labor day weekend show." Two of the rodeos were in Southern California and the other two were up north and as luck would have it the central entry office had drawn me up on Saturday at all 4 of them.

Fortunately, the Yreka California rodeo was a Saturday night performance, but it was way up north near the Oregon border. If I drove I could make it to one rodeo, but if I chartered a plane I could make the two rodeos in northern California, with the day performance being Truckee, California where I had a good Dan Russel bull drawn.

At Yreka I drew a Kish/Growney NFR bull named Kung Fu. So, my traveling partner Tim Viale and I decided to charter a plane and we found a local pilot at a bar in Livermore to fly us around the state and this expensive weekend just got a lot more costly.

Jay Foscalina…Photo credit-dudley@dudleydoright.com

But, that was OK because I had two good bulls drawn, but then the unexpected happened because I got one-jumped at Truckee. So, we jumped in the plane and took off to the night performance at Yreka where I planed to win a nice check. During thunder storms at Yreka I learned that Growney's bull Kung Fu had other plans for me and bucked me off real fast. Come Monday I was hurting financially.

The bad news was, out of the 4 rodeos I entered I didn't last more than two seconds combined and my pilot wasn't too impressed with my bull riding ability. The good news was, I got my nice check the following weekend at Woodland and my pilot finally got to see a first place bull ride on a good young Dan Russell bull #14 Freckles and the next year they changed his name to #14 Pacific Bell. I also learned how to fly a plane because while the weather was nice the pilot let me drive.

BARNEY BREHMER
PENDLETON; COWBOY JUSTICE

In the 70's the ole van headed down the road to the Pendleton Roundup and in it were Twig (John Bland), Mickey Young, Kent Cooper, Brian Claypool, Barney Brehmer and myself. We got there a couple of days early and after checking in at Severe's famous bunkhouse, the Hotel Decowpunch, we loaded up and went down the hill to the pool hall to relax.

When we got there it was already inhabited by the likes of John McBeth, Doug Vold, and a host of other Cowboys. Well, Mickey and I got into some doubles pool games for a buck a stick. We got on a roll and for a while no one could beat us, and no, we weren't that good. The pool room was a small, approximately 36x36 room with a table in the middle, a bar at one end and folding chairs lined the cement block wall. Along the wall were seated the town tuffs, oilfield workers, 3 to be exact.

For some reason they started heckling Mickey and for the longest time they were ignored. We kept on winning and to finish up the game we were far in the lead, Mickey had the 8 ball right ahead of the corner pocket. The heckling got turned up and I could see Mickey's button got pushed. He scratched on the 8 ball, a shot he could make blind folded and he threw his stick on the table and marched over to the oiley sitting in the folding chair.

He politely asked the guy what the problem was and the guy replied, "I don't like your style and I don't like how you shoot." Smack! Mickey bounced his head off the block wall and the guy slumped to the floor. The second guy started to stand up and Mickey smacked him, also. He started to run outside and Mickey followed as the guy was crawling on the floor toward the door, kicking him in the ass all the way out.

We all got out into the middle of the street and the bouncer arrived. The mouthy one got to his feet and hid behind the bouncer. Mickey stood in front of the bouncer with his hands in his pockets, with the mouthy one hiding behind the bouncer. He just kept running his head, but made the mistake of sticking his head around the bouncer's shoulder. Mickey popped him and he went down and the first thing to hit the pavement was the back of his head.

We all laughed and headed back in the bar. We grabbed a beer and Mickey sat at the bar on a stool and had his feet wrapped in the rungs. Myself, Brian Claypool, and John McBeth were visiting at the corner of the pool table between Mickey and the door. I happened to look up and saw the three biggest guys I have seen come through the door. They stopped and spotted Mickey at the bar.

I heard one say, "There he is," and headed towards him. Claypool noticed it too, but the first one had made it past us and took a swing at Mickey. Mickey ducked and grabbed the guy and they went to the floor, barstool and all. Claypool jumped ahead of the second guy, approximately 6'4" or so and 240 lbs. plus. Claypool stepped ahead of the guy and put his right hand on the guy's chest and told him to stay out of it.

Mickey was doing just fine, especially when he got loose of the bar stool. The guy replied to Claypool, "You had better get out of the way or I'm gonna kick your ass." Bad Mistake. He grabbed Brian by the shirt collar and a Puka Shell Turquoise necklace. About that time Brian had to jump to hit the guy and the necklace flew everywhere.

Then, the thug made the mistake of trying to take Brian to the floor. Brian was a four- time Canadian Champion wrestler. Brian went to do a leg take down on the big guy and Brian had on rubber soled running shoes. The shoes stuck to the linoleum floor and you could hear the thug's leg snap. Brian then got him in a headlock and went to work pounding on the guys face and the guy was screaming in pain.

Now, here comes the third guy, just as big and very angry. I certainly didn't want Claypool to get blind sided so I stepped ahead of him and he told me the same thing, "Get out of the way or," as he said that I grabbed a handful of hair on each side of his head and jerked him down to knee him in the face, but I didn't get to. As I pulled him down, Kent Cooper kicked him square on the lips, ripping out hair in both of my hands.

As he staggered up I told him he had better sit in the chair and shut up unless he wanted more. He thought I had hit him and minded like a Border Collie dog. Doug Vold then told me to get Claypool called off and get out of there because the cops were on the way. Exit stage left.

Twig, myself, and Claypool went out and got in the van that was parked at the curb. Claypool was in the back with no shirt and a little scuffed up. They hauled the thug out on a stretcher and his two pals followed on foot. The cops then came over to the van and asked if we had seen what had happened. "Not really," we replied. "Well, if you find the guy that whipped that thug we would like to give him a medal because he put a cop in the hospital a couple of weeks earlier and he's still there."

All was well so Claypool came out of the back and confessed. The cops then explained that we could not get in any trouble in Pendleton and to protect ourselves any way we needed to because the thugs would be back, but nothing ever happened.

A couple of weeks later we flew Claypool's plane in and landed at the airport and headed for the airport café for breakfast. We were seated and eating when two cops walked up to the table and stopped. They said, "Get up and put your hands on the wall." When we looked up it was our cop buddy. He laughed and said, "I heard you guys flew in and I have a friend that would like to meet you.

He had brought the cop that had gotten beat up and had been in the hospital. We shook their hands and invited them to have breakfast with us and they did. Lots of stories were told and they gave us a ride to the Severe Brother's Saddlery and dropped us off. Thanks, Kent Cooper. You should have seen the grin he had on when I looked over at him in the bar.

STEVE SCOTT
FRECKLES BROWN OUTSIDE THE RODEO ARENA

My nephew was in Texas Childrens Hospital. He had Ewings Carcinoma, cancer of the bone. He was six years old. By this time we knew that, there was nothing left but prayer. But, he was pretty chipper, bless his heart. One afternoon we were visiting him when someone knocked on the door. We hollered to come in and when the door opened in walks a guy in a cowboy hat, a hospital shirt, wranglers, a trophy buckle, and boots. It was Freckles Brown.

This was at the time that Freckles was fighting his own cancer and despite that he had come over from the hospital where he was a patient and was going around on his own, talking to all the sick little kids. He said, "I don't mean to bother you folks, but if it's all right I'd like to talk with this cowboy right here."

He went on to say, "Pard. My name's Freckles Brown and I'm an old bull rider." At the same time he gave my nephew a picture of him on Tornado. He had signed it. Then he said, "But what I wanted to talk to you about is my best friend in the world and that is Jesus Christ." He went on to tell my nephew about Jesus and how Jesus had changed his life. When he was done we all bowed our head and Freckles said a prayer for my nephew. Then, he said goodbye and walked out.

We all know him as a great rodeo hand. But, I'll always remember him as a great man who was humble and in the middle of his own problems he took the time to go talk to a six year old little boy about Jesus. I believe that was a lot more important to him than rodeo. It is for me too.

My nephew told his mama that he knew he was going to go be with Jesus, but he wanted to do it at home so they took him home. They got him all fixed up with a hospital bed and medicine to keep him comfortable. A few weeks later he passed away at home. I can still see old Freckles sitting him on his knee and telling him about riding Tornado.

CHARLIE THOMPSON
AN ESCAPE STORY

Back in the 1970's we had a bull get out of the Texas Tech Dub Parks Arena on 4th & Quaker in Lubbock, Texas, and he was headed north on Quaker Blvd. towards Loop 289. Well, we had a truck, trailer, and 2 horses saddled, but no ropes whatsoever.

So, we took off in hot pursuit and the bull gets on Loop 289 and is headed west and by this time we are joined by the Lubbock LPD. There were two cowboys are on either side of the highway outside of the guard rails and two patrol cars behind the bull controlling traffic, but staying right on his butt.

I am in the truck and trailer and have the gates to the trailer tied open. I get around him to try and slow him down, but we are going about 20 mph. All of the sudden I can't see him in the mirrors, but I know he is right behind the trailer so I slammed on the brakes. With the head of steam the bull had built up he can't stop and is skidding on the pavement and hits the trailer.

His momentum flips him into the trailer and a patrol car pulls up and blocks the trailer gate. The cowboys dismounted, secured the gates and I go back to the patrol car expecting a handful of tickets. That cop looks at me and said, "That was the damndest cattle loading I have ever seen. I would like to tell everybody at the station about it, but nobody would believe me and would think I'd been drinking. If it ever happens again give me a call. That was fun."

RICHARD FLECHSIG
JUST A LITTLE HELP

When I was about a year out of high school and rodeoing, I dated a girl that was drop dead gorgeous and to this day. I can't figure out why she always went out with me. We'd go hot and heavy for a month or two and as rodeo cowboys sometimes do, I'd disappear for a few months.

Well, one winter I was home and on Saturday she and I were going to spend some time together. She was learning to be a trick rider and had spent some time at J. W. Stoker's place getting started and was ready to start booking rodeos the next spring.

It was December and colder than a mother-in-laws kiss when I got to her house and she was cleaning out her horse's stall. I was all cleaned up and ready to go and had finished my chores hours before. She kept telling me that with just a little help she'd get done a lot quicker and she could get cleaned up so we could go. I told her I had finished my chores and since it was her horse she really should clean the stall so they could bond while she was working. She kept it up hoping I'd cave in so I finally did.

Now, some of the manure was frozen and I had on a pair of deerskin gloves so I found a nice frozen horse biscuit, as in horse apple, and while she was bent over I deposited it her back pocket.

She was a tad unhappy, but she also was a thinker so she ran to the house and told her dad that she had something in her eye and would he get her hankie out of her back pocket. Being a loving father her dad reached in and guess what, there was no hankie just a big surprise and almost immediately he yelled out my name, knowing I was the culprit.

But, being a good sport he laughed it off and warned me to

watch my back. Funny thing, Barbara never did ask me to help clean out stalls again. Anyway, before long I was back out on the rodeo trail.

DON ENDSLEY
Ft Worth, Texas NFR Announcer Don Endsley Inducted Into To Texas Rodeo Cowboy Hall Of Fame Friday, April 8, 2011

During the 1970's, 80's & 90's Don Endsley's voice was heard at PRCA rodeos from New York to California. A native of Drasco, Arkansas, Don, Sharon and son Tim moved to the Fort Worth area in 1977 where they called home for over 20 years. They have worked and lived in Branson, Missouri producing shows and serving as Master of ceremonies at the RFD-Tv Theatre, and now reside in their Drasco, Arkansas home.

Don Endsley

In 1984 Don was announcer for the NFR's 20th anniversary, the last NFR held in Oklahoma City. After trying his luck as a bull rider in his early years, Don hung up his spurs and picked up the rodeo 'mic' and also worked in television and radio. The rodeo and broadcasting experience was a perfect combination that led to many years as one of the top rodeo announcers and commentators in the sport.

In 1977 Don became the announcer for the famous Tommy Steiner Rodeo Co of Austin, Texas and became the voice of the American Royal Rodeo; Dixie National Rodeo; State Fair of Texas Rodeo; Waco Heart of Texas Rodeo and many others across the country. Over the years Don announced at hundreds of top PRCA rodeos including 5-times Texas Circuit Finals; 6-times Indian National Finals Rodeo; Denver's National Western; Dodge City Round-Up; Belton, TX; Lufkin, TX; Jacksonville Tops N' Texas Rodeo; 20 years as the voice of the Santa Rosa Round-Up; Mesquite Rodeo; New Mexico State Fair; Houston Livestock Show; and Elk City Rodeo of Champions. Don was also called on to lend his voice to the movies 'My Heroes Have Always Been Cowboys" and "8' Seconds'.

I am so glad that I was there during all these special rodeo years and watched some of the greatest and most colorful and exciting rodeo Champions of all time.

In 1996 Don and his family created the award winning 'Great American Wild West Show' which now travels across the country to State Fairs, Festivals, Livestock Expos and Special Events. Don and Sharon have been married for 44 years. Sharon was a cutting horse competitor and was raised in the horse world. Their son Tim is a calf roper and horse trainer.

LEE JONES
SAN ANTONIO HOLIDAY INN

Jim Houston had something about police men. When he saw one he kinda went into another person. One time at San Antonio we were staying on the second floor of the Holiday Inn. I was in one room with Jerry Olson, Jim was in the next room with a bunch of bareback riders, and Senator Clem McSpadden was in the next room.

A real cute little maid was cleaning up the rooms and I knew she was going to have trouble there somewhere. Sure enough a guy next door was in bed with no clothes on and she ran out screaming. He got out of bed, got his clothes on and left. They called the cops and in the meantime Jim came to the room, undressed and got in bed.

The cops got him and he got dressed, but I was trying to tell them they had the wrong guy. When the cop said something to Jim, he exploded and grabbed the cop by the neck and hung him over the rail off the second floor, holding on to his belt. The other cop down stairs had his gun out trying to get a shot at Jim when Jerry Olson grabbed Jim and threw him back in the room.

Senator Clem McSpadden showed up about that time and told them what I had told them was true and that it was not Jim. The cop said, "OK then, but if he'll apologize to me I'll drop it." I got Jim to unlock the door and told him what he had to do. He said, "I ain't apologizing." We finally get him to do it, but gosh he hated to.

Right after the hotel ordeal with Jim, he and I, and Hampton Roberson loaded Hampton's bull doggin' mare in a one horse trailer hooked to a pickup with a small camper and headed to Baton Rouge, Louisiana. Jim got in the camper and we closed the pickup tail gate. Somewhere in Louisiana we were pulled over by three local cops.

The biggest one read us the riot act and said that going through his town with a pickup and trailer the speed limit was thirty-five miles per hour. He also said we were the same to him as an eighteen wheeler. While Hampton was talking to them, Jim called me over to the window of the camper and said, "Lower the tail gate and let me out. I want to talk to them." I said, "No, Jim. Hampton will take care of it." We would still be in a Cajun jail if I had opened that tail gate.

JERRY LA VALLEY
THE TROPHY BUCKLE

Someone could probably write a full size novel about the lure that a trophy buckle (any trophy buckle) has on a competing rodeo cowboy. They don't give buckles away at every rodeo which makes a cowboy want to screw down and try extra hard when he has drawn well and has a chance to win first at a rodeo that has a championship buckle up for grabs. I was fortunate enough to win a few buckles in my day and they each provide a fun memory of a time in life when getting to the rodeo and riding bulls was my first and only focus. This story isn't about any of those buckles.

In September of 1984 I was entered in an International Pro Rodeo Association rodeo in Cherry Valley, Illinois. It was a Sunday afternoon performance and I had drawn the bull fire branded #0, Rodeo Bob. He was about the best one in the pen to have so I was feeling my oats and ready to ride.

Just as I took my wrap and was about to slide up and give a nod, old Rodeo Bob decided to crack a few hard jumps inside the bucking chutes. He threw me forward and into the front slide gate where the first part of me to make contact was my left eyebrow. It didn't knock me out, but gashed me up pretty good with a cut that later took on ten or twelve stitches. I climbed out of the box and one of my traveling partners Bobby Cooper, tied my rope back on the bull while I went to get some first aid from the ambulance medic.

They had probably been working on my eye for only a few minutes or so when Bobby Cooper came over to check on me and the bandage job. He told me that I needed to get back over behind the chutes because they were holding my bull for me up in the front box. There were only two riders left and then it was my "go time." The combination of the cut and swollen the eye, the hot afternoon sun beating down, along with the smell of blood, dust and manure had me feeling pretty weak at that very moment and I told Bobby that I was going to turn him out.

Bobby looked at me and said, "You're kidding me. Have you seen the buckles?" That got my attention, so I asked him a one word question, "Buckles?" Bobby said, "Yeah, they are the small, square Nelson-Silvia buckles. They have a banner that says, "Cherry Valley, Illinois," and they have a tree on them that has emeralds for the leaves and rubies for the cherries." That shed a different light on things and strengthened me back up so I changed my mind, climbed on Rodeo Bob and won the bull riding.

The local fire department was putting on an "after the rodeo" barbecue for the cowboy contestants and that is where my traveling crew went while a lady on the rodeo committee took me to hospital to get stitched up. During the stitching up process I was in a good mood and feeling pretty flush about the trophy buckle that I had just bagged.

After we left the emergency room, the lady took me over the fire station to meet up with my traveling squad. When I went in Bobby Cooper walked up and handed me an envelope with my prize money, but he didn't give me a buckle. I said, "Coop, where is my buckle?" He just looked at me and replied, "Man, they don't give buckles here." He had tricked me. In the flash of a second Bobby had come up with the vision and description of this phantom trophy buckle to make sure that I got on the bull and did my job. I thought about bristling up about it, but when I thought further on the matter I decided how can you get mad at a buddy that tricks you in to winning first?

BILL THORPE
THE BROKE LEG

This story that happened in Beaver, Oklahoma when I drew a Melvin McGarrah bronc called Blue Panic. He bucked me off at the fence and ran over the judge. When I got up I looked the judge in the eye and he looked at me, then we both looked at his leg. His leg was at a 90 degree angle with the bone sticking right through his wranglers. The judge sat up, reached for his boot, pulled the leg off and threw it over the fence, then told his wife to get his crutches. The man finished judging the rodeo on his crutches. Later, I found out that he was Eddie Akridge's brother, a well-known Beaver, Oklahoma cowboy who had lost his leg in a tractor accident.

Back to the practice pen, Melvin's little rodeo arena had his tack room right there with the door opening into the arena. The pot belly stove kept us all warm on the Sunday afternoons when we would take a break from the cold winter wind. The bronc riders would have their saddles in there, the bull ropes were all in there, and the cowboys stood around the fire while others rode.

Melvin had one bull he called Booger Red and he was very mean. He came out of the chute, bucked the cowboy off and chased the clown right into the tack room closely followed by the bull. One bull and nine cowboys come flying out of the tack room's two windows and one door. Booger Red had chased them out of that tack room.

He couldn't get to a cowboy so he took after a bronc saddle and mashed it plumb apart, wiped out the pot belly stove, tore out the walls and broke the windows. Stove pipes and burning embers went everywhere. We used wet gunnysacks to put out the fire in the tack room.

I had read stories about Brother Andy Taylor riding V-61 and he was one of the very few men who accomplished that feat. I want to tell you a story about him riding ole Number 3 of Billy Merritt's string up in Iowa.

In the early 70's Tom Stout and Andy Taylor came to Iowa to rodeo with my friend Billy Hubbard and me. We were at a racetrack/fair/rodeo and Andy drew #3, a big black bull with big black horns and he had a reputation of jumping the fence at the end of the arena. On this particular night Andy rode him across the arena and when they reached the back of the pen the bull jumped the fence and headed for the midway with Andy still riding him.

They got to the first joint on the midway, a trinket tent, and the bull went through the tent and left out the other side with it still attached to his horns. I don't know if that's the night that Brother Andy found the Lord or not, but it might have been.

I was on my way to The American and passed the pens where we used to practice ridin' broncs and bulls at Melvin McGarrahs. We were two miles into Texas and it brought back memories of the Pony Express Ride to Oklahoma.

On Sundays we always gathered at Melvin's house to practice our bronc riding and bull riding. I was living in Liberal, Kansas and my buddy Dick Munsel and I would head down there after church, stop and pick up Bill Newman and be at Melvin's by 1 pm, when the buck out started.

On that particular day Dick Munsel got on a yellow bronc that Melvin had just bought. He rode him to the end of the pen and when they got there the horse jumped the fence and took a hard left and headed up highway 83 to Oklahoma with Dick still on. Dick had some Dash Danner liquid rosin on his glove and he couldn't get loose and Melvin couldn't catch the runaway with his pickup horse.

Two miles later they got to the correction line of the Oklahoma state line and the bronc shot across the street right into the drive-through of Wimp Gilbert's beer joint. Coming out of the bar at the same time was Big Willy and he mugged the horse and took him to the ground. We pulled the riggin' off the bronc with Dick still holdin' on. About that time Melvin showed up on his pickup horse and roped the bronc and led him back to Texas. Every time I pass Bryant's Corner I think about the runaway bronc Pony Express to Oklahoma.

STEVE SCOTT
WORKIN' ON MY CONTEST/CONTRACT CARD

Whoever drew Oscar usually turned him out, but Bob Cook had to buck him because he advertised him. So, Sammy Cope who was one of the hands working for Cook got on him, but he didn't last long. Most didn't.

I bought a mule out of a truck load of killer horses we were hauling and I noticed him because his mane had been roached. I put a hay string in his mouth like an Indian bit and jumped on his back. I laid the string over on his neck and he neck reined. I had some good acts with him, but had to get him cut because he wouldn't act right around the girl horses. And, I couldn't haul him back to Texas when I left California so I gave him to Johnny Hawkins who said he'd make sure he was well taken care of.

I won the bareback riding at the Camp Pendleton All-Services Rodeo. It took my last sixty bucks for the entry fee, but I won over six hundred. I was still in the Marine Corps and had a wife and baby boy and sure needed the money.

Bob Cook put on this rodeo and that's where I met him and Bob Tallman. It was Tallman's first year to announce rodeos for Cook. January of the next year I was supposed to get out of the Corps so they let me go three months early on Project Transition as a Rodeo Clown.

I worked for Bob Cook for free while the Corps paid me for three months and then I got my discharge. Cook also paid me pretty good. By that time I was working on my contest/contract card.

CLINT FORD
ME AND BIG AL

I do recall a night in Stonewall, Louisiana where me and Allan Parrish both got hurt pretty bad. I rode a little bull that bucked like hell for about 5 seconds then run off. As he ran, I started to slide down the left side as usual. The fence was pipe top rail with calf panels welded to pipe posts.

The bull started dragging me down the fence until I was hung up and I only came loose when my free arm went thru one of the holes in the fence. I wound up walking back to the chutes with an arm that wouldn't come below my shoulder. It stuck straight out and was out of socket and I also had an ear barely hanging on.

My concern was for my arm, but everyone else was staring at my ear that was peeled back in the wrong direction. After a little arguing, Allan Parrish or Big Al is what we called him as he was better suited for doggin', but he loved to ride bulls even with his six foot two inches of fun and ugly, came over and yanked my arm back into the socket, fast and hard. As I started to throw up someone slapped duct tape over my ear and that problem was also solved.

Big Al was up next and got his rear end hooked all the way to the catch pen. We duct taped him up and drove back to Bettie, Texas where we had to feed cattle for his granddad Ned Parrish at 5 am. We got back to the ranch and sat across from one another, ate some Butte, put a couple of CCs of Banamine in our beers and watched each other swell up while laughing our asses off.

Old Ned came in to wake us up the next morning and we scared the hell out of him as we really looked bad. He told us to hurry up and not to scare the cattle when we fed. TLC at its finest. Cowboyin' ain't ever been for sissies. Oh, yeah, and I won 60 bucks that night.

RICHARD FLECHSIG
WHAT HAPPENED TO THE DIRT

In the mid nineties, maybe '94 or '95, I judged a rodeo in Jacksonville, Florida. Bob Barnes had the stock and the producer was a man named Sandy Semanik. Sandy really did a good job trying to put on a good rodeo and had a nice hospitality tent for sponsors and cowboys. Howard Klingemann was judging with me, and his wife Mildred, (Sister to the cowboys) was the secretary.

They have a lot of sand in Florida and this indoor arena was deep. It was hard for calf ropers to get the calves up, barrel racing times were off for an indoor pattern and during the bull riding I could hear the bulls grunting while trying to buck in the deep conditions.

After the performance I mentioned to John Barnes that something needed to be done to fix the ground. The next night I got to the arena about 5:30 PM and Howard was waiting for me and I could tell he wasn't real happy so I said, "What's up?"

He said, "Come with me," and we walked into the arena and it was all new dirt. Sandy owned some earth moving equipment and they took all the sandy stuff out and hauled in some nice sand clay that had good footing. This would normally be a good thing, but not at a three performance rodeo where you just changed the conditions.

Of course we had to reset the barrel pattern then we had Mildred call the PRCA office and tell them what happened, then the WPRA was notified. We ended up paying off like three separate rodeos. We divided the added money by three then added the fee's from each night. There was nothing else we could do. We wrote up a judge's report, but never did find out if they were fined.

At St Louis, Missouri, December, 1986 or '87, Jerome Robinson was putting on a three day rodeo and I was judging with Dick Marshall. I got to the arena about 5:30 PM and noticed they are still setting a few panels so I walked walk out to look at the ground. Holy crap. It's mud. I found Jerome and asked what the heck was going on.

He explained that the arena keeps a big pile of dirt way out back for rodeos, Monster Truck Shows, etc. and said they had a real wet fall and the dirt got wet and that it is what it is. I said, "Well, the conditions will surly change over three days as it dries out." He told me to feel the dirt and it was ice cold. The St. Louis Blues HockeyTeam played at the arena and the arena people never took the ice up, they just laid Visqueen (plastic) over it then plywood, then another layer of Visqueen, then the dirt. As cold as it was there was no way it would dry out and it was so wet you couldn't drag it. It was basically a mess.

It wasn't long before here comes the barrel racers and I had to explain the ice and all, many times that evening. I was really concerned for the stock, but the doggers were the ones I worried about as it was going to be next to impossible to slide a steer and if you catch a heel in those holes, pop goes your knee.

Cowboys are not only good athletes and they don't have any back up in them. We got through three performances with no injuries and with very little complaining from the cowboy's however I did turn my ankle over just before the end of the third performance.

DUDE SMITH
MY RODEO STORY

I started out when I was thirteen when my Mom took me to a rodeo and I knew then I wanted to be a rodeo cowboy, but she told me I didn't know how. I told her they didn't know how and they had to learn. I was sixteen when Lucille Richards Mullenhough asked me if I could drive and I told her I could. We were at the McKinney, Texas rodeo and she was going to Topeka, Kansas. My deal was to help her drive and to take care of her trick riding horse and to saddle her saddle bronc. When I got to Topeka in 1946 is when I met Jim Shoulders for the first time.

Neal Gay and I were blood brothers and how we became blood brothers is he got shot in Liberty, Texas in 1950 while trying to save another guy and he was accidentally shot in the stomach. It was very serious and he had to have a transfusion and I was the only one there who had the same type blood.

The other cowboys we started out with were Whiz Whizenhunt, Billy Joe Farmer, and Muscles Foster. Neal and I are the only two left of this bunch. We rodeoed for Larry Sunbrock in the Wild West Show in Texas and Oklahoma and we made a lot of rodeos, one every week. And, we rodeoed at Pleasant Mount before it became Mesquite.

In 1947 Whiz and I were running together and we were at Arlington Downs at the last rodeo that was held there and whiz said if we had enough money to get back to Philadelphia and Detroit then we could go on up to NYC and no telling ho much money we could make. I told Whiz I had just won the bull riding at Tucumcari, NM and I had that money and that I had always wanted a ranch so I had bought me a cow and that I could probably sell her to my Dad.

We got the money together to buy us a plane ticket and we got on the plane in Dallas, Texas, fixing to fly up to Philadelphia. I had my nose against the window looking out and thinking, "How could it ever get any better than this?" I had on a pair of boots that probably had more tape on them than Wal-Mart.

When we got to Philadelphia I won a little over a thousand dollars and about the same amount gambling. We went on to Detroit and I won the bull dogging and some in the riding events too, and won a little over a thousand there and about the same gambling. Whiz was winning along some, too.

Then, we went to New York City and the rodeo there was thirty days with fifty-three performances. I was entered in five events and we got fifteen bare backs, fourteen saddle broncs, fifteen bulls, eleven dogging steers and I mugged fifty-three horses in the wild horse race. What I had won at those three rodeos I didn't think there was that much money in the world. We were going to Boston, but through some complications we didn't go.

Todd Whatley and I loaded his old bull dogging horse T-Bone in the trailer and we fed and watered him in the trailer and never stopped except for gas until we got to Hugo, Oklahoma. I remember when we let him out of the trailer he just ran out there and flopped over on his side and groaned real big.

After I left Hugo I went to work for Paul Long as his arena director, chute boss, hauled the rodeo stock and put up the portable chutes all in Kansas. I worked for George Stittca running his outfit and I worked for Karl Lamar running his outfit.

Later, I was at a rodeo in Memphis, Tennessee and I saw my wife to be, Frances Craine, so I chased her for the next two years I guess and we married in 1950. I was still rodeoing and all along working these jobs. My wife and I rodeoed together. She was a barrel racer and won Ft. Worth, Denver, Houston, Little Rock and many more and made the NFR two times and I won it in 1967.

I always said I wasn't gonna be a rodeo bum, that I was gonna quit when I was still winning and I did. Rodeoing was like a disease and you couldn't just walk away from it without having something to take its place. I was very successful foot racer so I figured, "Why couldn't I train horses, being as I trained myself and made lots of money foot racing and had matched everyone from the east coast to the west coast."

So, I started training horses and it was a successful career for me. I lost my son Mark when he was thirteen and it turned my life around and I almost became a drunk. But, with the help of friends and the good Lord, I got my life back turned the way it ought to be and ended up with sixty-three years of that wonderful cowgirl. Now, I am just Papa Dude living with my grand-daughter Sage and visiting with my family and friends. I've had a most wonderful life.

MARK TRUJILLO
TEXAS VS OKLAHOMA SHOOTOUT

One of my most memorable moments was in 1995. I was invited to the Texas vs. Oklahoma shootout and drew a bull of Sandy Kirby's. I don't remember his brand, but they called him Bumblebee. He was a big ole red bull that would throw everything at you including the kitchen sink and come around to the left.

Well, I got on him at the shootout and only made it a round and a half before he welled me and dislocated my shoulder. Two weeks later I had him drawn at Billy Bob's and at the time he had only been snapped once and I think it was at the PBR, (don't hold me to that).

It's strange because while it was one of, if not the best rides I've ever made, I really can't recall any of it. I remember calling for the gate and then I was making my way out of the arena and the place was going absolutely nuts. It was one of those times when I was totally in the moment and everything was still just a blur.

As I was leaving the arena Sandy met me halfway, grabbed me around the shoulders, gave me a hug and said, "There is no way that just any man could walk thru those doors and ride that bull with the trip he had tonight." It's the only time that I can recall that Skirb ever walked out to meet and congratulate a cowboy before the bull riding was over.

I, unfortunately don't have any pictures or video from that night. All I have is the memory and it's one that will stick with me forever.

JIMMY BLOTZ
GIRLFRIEND'S HORSE

My ex girlfriend Shanna Doores Pollan and I left for a CRA Rodeo in Blue Ridge, Texas in 1983. Shauna was entered in the barrel racing and me in bulls. I drew H.L. Kent's #69 and scored 80 points for 1st. place, but I wasn't going to be paid that night because it was a two day performance.

We were pulling her barrel horse Salty, so we loaded him up and started back to Dallas. We were low on gas and it was late and no stations were open, but we finally found a Shell Station that was closed. We parked at the pumps and let Salty out of the trailer and tied his halter to the trailer. We decided to sleep in the front seat of the truck until the station opened.

The next morning I heard a knock on the window and looked up to see a Gomer Pyle type starring at me. He said, "Who's gonna clean up that horse crap in the water tub they use for checkin' tires?"

Salty must have been a little nervous and had really filled that thing up! He'd also chewed up some of the advertisement posters and Gomer wasn't happy about that either. Anyway, we got gas and away we went.

BOBBY DYKES
OL' PETE

Pete was a big stout chestnut gelding and a good ranch horse as long as you done things kinda on his terms. Just warm him up slow and a strawberry Pop-Tart made him easy to catch and with an occasional treat of Kentucky Twist Tobacco things weren't to bad. Pete started to get in his head that the everyday ranch life wasn't all that it was cracked up to be and wanted to broaden his portfolio.

Now, a guy can put up with a little pitch or hop every now and again as long his mount can still stay on course with its duties, but in a short time Pete seemed to enjoy the art of bucking. The time had come that he was more trouble than help so I called a friend who I worked for and was also a stock contractor. Well, the bright lights and fame of being a rodeo star fit Pete to a tee. He was the saddle bronc horse of the year and also made 4 trips to the IFR. It seemed like my old ranch horse had moved up in the world with no desire to return to the daily grind waiting at the ranch.

The following spring Pete was rank. After the first two rodeos I thought for sure bucking horse of the Finals was going to be his. The next rodeo would play out in the other direction. The first night he locked-up and wouldn't leave the chute and they gave a re-ride on him. The next night we put him under a bareback rigging, but with the same outcome. That night after the rodeo was over I threw a saddle on Pete and around the arena we went without a bobble. The space of a good one had been filled back at the ranch and I was glad to have him back, to be honest.

After bucking for about 5 years I thought he may fill the shoes of one of my pick-up horses in time, but I didn't know that the time would come sooner than later. I got a call to pick up a rodeo in Illinois and Ol' Pete was going to make his debut, ready or not. The short of it was when the pick-up horse is bucking harder and stride for stride with a bucking horse cowboys really don't want to get off on you, which in turn contractors don't want to use you. I tried to make it work for about a month, but it was plain Ol' Pete was not a pickup horse.

That fall I got a call from someone looking for a barrel horse prospect. The horse I had in mind never crossed the mind of that 14 year old girl after she saw Pete. I told her and her dad his story and that he wasn't for them, but she was set on riding him. We sat up the barrels and started looking for a lawyer in my area if things went bad. As luck would have it they got along great and I said good bye to

Ol' Pete. It's kinda funny because he carried that young lady all the way to the High School Finals the next year and after that, I couldn't tell you. I guess he was smarter than I thought. He just figured out a way to get out of work.

TOMMY TARPLEY
A BAD NIGHT IN LOUISANA

Around 1982 or 83 me and my good friend Danny Argenbright made a rodeo in Heflin, Louisiana. I had been rodeoing with Danny for about 3 years. One thing I knew about him was that he had nerves of steel and was a pretty good hand when it came to riding bulls. Run a bad one in the chute and it just fired him up more. We were on a pretty tight budget back then, rodeoing on the weekends, working during the week and trying to support our families. On this trip we planned on sleeping at the arena and driving back in the morning. Well, we were informed we could not stay the night there so we took off looking for a place to sleep. After an hour or two of driving around we found a worn out spot close to an intersection in the road. It looked like a place where people had pulled over to park for whatever reason.

So, we rolled out our sleeping bags and lay down for a few hours of sleep. Danny fell asleep right away, but I could not sleep because of the mosquitoes the size of small turkeys. After an hour or so of slapping myself in the face a car pulled over about a hundred yards down the road. Three guys got out of the car and I could faintly hear some of there conversation which was something to the extent of, "What are those a-- holes doing down there in our spot? We ought to go down there and knock 'em in the head." At this time I thought OK, "Maybe they're just mouthing, trying to scare us off, but I better wake up Danny up just in case." So, I grabbed Danny by the foot and shook it, but he didn't wake up, he just kept sleeping. I shook his foot 3 or 4 different times, but still he would not wake up.

I saw these three Cajuns start walking towards us and everyone of them had a weapon in their hand that resembled a baseball bat. Now, I'm really getting scared. So, my next move was to try and dislocate Danny's ankle. This time he came alive and after a few choice words, asked why in the hell was I trying to break his ankle. I explained the situation to him and his response was, "Well, wake me when they get here," and rolled over and went back to sleep. I wanted to kill him, myself.

Luckily, they were just trying to scare us because they eventually turned around and got in there car and drove up to a house just up the road, where I could still here them. I didn't sleep a wink that night thinking they may come back some time later. Danny got a good cussing all the way home and all he ever said was, "What did you want me to do?" I said, "You could at the least acted a little concerned." After 35 years of having Danny as my friend, I've learned that I probably didn't have anything to worry about. I think with his help we could have taken those three Cajuns.

DALE WOODARD
(1992 NFR Barrel man)
THAT'S ALL I NEED

Back in the day when my clowning career was going strong I was working a hundred plus performances per year. This was one of those rodeos. It was a three performance rodeo in Poway, California. There was a guy who used to come to these rodeos and help on the crew and his name was Josh.

I think Josh drove a water truck during the week, but he loved to come to the rodeos on the week-ends. Josh wore a cowboy hat and western clothes and just fit right in with the rodeo crew. He was a nice guy and always had a smile on his face. I considered him a friend and always spoke to him whenever I saw him around the rodeos. He called me Woody, as many of the crew did.

After the second performance of this particular rodeo the crew was sitting around having a beer. They were just taking a break before having to start their evening chores of feeding the livestock. I had gotten dressed back into my street clothes and was leading my horse past where the crew was resting. As I looked over there and spoke to the crew in general I could see Josh sharpening a knife.

On my way back to my camper I stopped to visit a bit and noticed Josh was sharpening another knife. He looked up at me and asked, "Hey, Woody. Want your knife sharpened?" I said, Sure," and handed him my knife. He handed the knife he was working on back to its owner and started on my knife.

I asked what was up with the knife sharpening and he said that he had just got this knife sharpening kit so he brought it along to the rodeo. I said, "Wow, Josh. That's a great idea. You should charge a dollar to sharpen a knife. Anybody would pay a dollar to have a sharp knife. That way, you could pay for your gas getting to and from these rodeos."

Josh never looked up. He just kept working on my knife and said, "That's all I need, someone else trying to tell me how to run my life." I almost hurt myself laughing at Josh's response. Here was a simple man just leading a simple life that he loved. He had figured out what he enjoyed doing during the week and on week-ends. And now, he had a simple gift that he could give to his friends and it dawned on me that this was a contented man.

To this day whenever someone says to me, "You know what you ought to do?" I think of old Josh and I say to my self, "That's all I need, someone else trying to tell me how to run my life."

RON CHOCKLEY
BARBY RODEO COMPANY

These few stories took place 1974-1977 the second time I had worked for Lloyd. I rodeoed for many years and went to hauling rodeo stock for Lloyd Barby so I could rodeo one last year. Lloyd had worked very hard putting his bucking horse stock together and I felt that he ended up with the best group of bucking horses I had ever seen and there were many other that would probably agree.

On night after getting all the loose ends tied at the arena in Altus, Oklahoma several of the boys, Read Barby, Bill Newman, Guy Payne, and I picked up some supper and spotted a go cart track. We each chose our go cart and the race was on with lots of smack talking and laughing.

We were just getting warmed up when the guy stepped out to flag us for one final lap, so I swerved at him and made him jump back. Well, that started it and every time he tried to get us off the track one of us would aim at him. He was hollering at us to stop, but finally gave up and just let us play. Needless to say when we put the carts up he instructed us to never come back...... words can't even describe how much fun we had.

Lloyd was not a fan of dogs around livestock, but I carried my pit bull Wrangler with me most of the time. I was sure to try and keep him out of the way. Wrangler wore a red bandana and became pretty popular at the rodeos. At the Protection, Kansas rodeo there weren't enough pens at the arena so we kept the bulls at Jay Christenson's place just outside of town.

Lloyd and I went to get the bulls for the evening performance and had them all sorted up and ready to load. It didn't take much to load the bulls because they would pretty much load themselves. Lloyd and I were walking behind them down the alley way as they headed up the ramp to load. One by one up they went up the ramp and loaded at a slant in a perfect line every time.

It was all I could do to keep Wrangler from helping and I had been calling him off several times. As the last bull, #75, a small Hereford bull started up the ramp Wrangler was behind Lloyd and I and he just couldn't contain himself. At a dead run he ran between us all we saw was a brown blur he ran up the ramp and latched on to #75 all the while I'm running behind him screaming for him to stop.

Old #75 let out a beller and went straight to the front of the trailer. By the time I got to there Wrangler appeared out from under all the bulls covered with crap. I slowly walked back down thinking Lloyd was going to fire me because we just didn't handle the stock that way. But, what I found was Lloyd almost on the ground laughing. He said, "That dog is welcome anywhere we go. If he can make it out from under all those bulls feet the whole length of the trailer, he's a keeper."

JAN BARBY PAYNE
ALBUQUERQUE

We were pulling into headquarters one night after leaving a rodeo and driving early into the morning. We had been gone for a while and everyone was tired. We had a pot with bulls, calves and steers, a 40 ft. trailer with bucking horses, not packed really tight, but there wasn't much room to spare, and a pickup and gooseneck with pickup horses then Daddy and Mother brought up the rear with a pickup and all the gear. Daddy always was the last one in the caravan because if someone broke down because he wanted to be right there and not too far ahead.

Albuquerque was a bareback horse Daddy and Jiggs or Elra Beutler had done some kind of a trade to get. Albuquerque had been to the NFR in '57 or '58 when it was in California. This horse was old and had been hauled all over the country, but was still a steady and good draw when Daddy got him.

We had just gone across the cattle guard into the lane of

headquarters where a few feet past, the fence opened into an open area. Low and behold Albuquerque JUMPED OUT OF THE MOVING TRAILER! Jake Parker and his wife Audrey were in the pickup and gooseneck trailer right behind.

Jake laughed and said, "Audrey leaned forward and started holding her arms cradled out like she was going to catch him when he hit the ground." Albuquerque landed on all fours and trotted on around the corner where the first rig (the pot) had stopped to turn on the light at the loading dock and there stood Albuquerque. I guess he had had his fill of traveling and wanted to be home just like the rest of us.

MICKEY YOUNG
RODEO DAYS

I was sitting in the lobby of the Mayflower Hotel in Cheyenne, Wyoming one summer day in July with the first half Winston Tour check winners. We were a few minutes early for the main ceremonies so we had gotten a cold drink and were sitting at a table telling wild west stories of rodeo and bucking horses.

I don't recall who was sitting at that particular table, but I do recall there being about eight or ten guys circled around the large round table. As is generally the case when you have a gathering of like minded dare devils in the same location the first liar doesn't have a chance. As we sat around the table telling stories the conversation migrated to the subject of rank horses and of course you can't tell rank horse stories without mentioning Three Bars of Reg Keslers.

Three Bars was notorious for bucking off the top bareback riders and most of the time hurting them in the process. I had not yet had the opportunity or misfortune of having been on her at that time in my career so I was quite interested in hearing the stories just in case I ever did draw her. As the stories began to pick up steam and I heard how she had bucked off Joe Alexander multiple times and that Royce Smith wouldn't get back on her again and how Gary Tucker had been bucked off, and couple that with my own stories of her bucking off Sandy Kirby and hurting his shoulder, I remembered her bucking off Ike Sankey at the NFR in about three seconds.

About this time Gary Logan who was sitting next to me piped up and said, "Shoot, she ain't so bad." Now, Gary was a tremendously talented bareback and bull rider from Canada and had rodeoed around Keslers a lot. I figured I would get the story from someone who at least had a good attitude about her so I turned to Gary and inquired if he had been on her.

He said, "Five times." I thought to myself, all right here is where I want to learn a little something about Three Bars so I pressed on, "Have you won quite a bit on her?" He said, "No, she bucked me off all five times," to which the cowboys at the table roared with laughter.

I pressed further. "Did she ever hurt you?" His response floored me and made us all roll on the floor with laughter. He said, "I don't know. She knocked me out all five times." Needless to say, he had said nothing to advance my game plan in case I ever drew Three Bars, which incidentally I did do twice in the coming years. I was able to twist her both times I got on her which is something that not a lot of people could boast about, but hey, that was then and who can prove me wrong now, right?

One early Spring I had flown to Cloverdale, British Columbia. I was excited about being able to fly because I had spent all week the week before in a van with some other guys and had logged quite a few miles on the ground. We had been from Colorado to Texas and back to Las Vegas where I had spent the day with my new bride at her mother's home.

One of the guys who I had been with on the Texas run was Mick Whitely a very talented bull rider from Oregon. Mick was headed to Inglewood, California to ride in the rodeo at the Forum, but I hadn't drawn very good there so I had sent my entry fees with him and I had gone on the northern run. When I got to the Vancouver, B.C. airport I took a taxi to the rodeo grounds in Cloverdale. I was about two hours early so I was just hanging around at the rodeo grounds. It was raining lightly so I found an awning by the rodeo office to just wait until time to pay my fees and start thinking about my riding game plan.

While I was sitting under this awning passing the time a young bronc rider joined me and threw his duffle bag down on the ground and greeted me. I introduced myself and he introduced himself as Lee Coleman, the younger brother to Mel Coleman whom I knew quite well. We talked for about an hour before the secretary came and we were able to get inside and pay our fees and go about our preparations to ride. I had a flight out of Vancouver that afternoon and when I saw how they had the rodeo schedule set up with two sections of bareback riding I knew I had to be in the first section to make it to my flight in time so I went to Greg Kesler and asked him if he would switch me to the first section so I could catch my flight and he told me if I could find someone to switch with me he would make it happen.

I went back behind the chutes and ran into Gary Logan and asked him if he knew anybody that would trade with me so I could make it to the airport in time and he said I might ask Calvin Bunny. He pointed him out to me and told me he was a really good kid and that he had won the Canadian Rookie of the Year the year before and he thought he would trade with me. I went to Calvin and introduced myself to him and told him my dilemma and he said he'd be glad to help me out. I thanked him and went to get ready to ride.

I asked Gary to give me a hand getting on my horse and turning his face out of the chute and he said he would. He asked me why I was going through all the trouble to catch a flight because Brian Claypool was going to fly to Las Vegas the next day right after rodeo and they were going to be in Las Vegas by about five or six o'clock.

He said that there was one seat open and I could get in with him, Brian, Calvin Bunny and Lee Coleman if I wanted to. I told him I had a new wife in Vegas and the family was going to throw us a reception party and I wanted to get back there, but I appreciated the invite. I told him to bring me my check if I won one and he said he would.

I had a good horse by the name of Winchester and was winning first after the first performance, but was to be moved to second in the next and final performance. I flew back to Las Vegas and met with my wife and spent the night. In those days they used to hold the Helldorado Days Rodeo at the Las Vegas Convention Center.

The next evening when I went to get on my horse at the rodeo is when I got the news that would rock my world. As I walked into the convention center I saw Ivan Daines who was a bronc rider from Canada. He asked me if I had heard about Mick Whitely and I said I had not. He said he was killed at the Forum last night. He said a bull had stepped on his chest and had killed him.

Holy smokes, I couldn't believe it. I was just with him all the week before. You know how your mind works and fast tracks back through all the things he had done and I was trying to digest that information when round two came. "Oh, and Claypool's plane is missing."

At that point I didn't internalize that bit of information as good as I normally would have because of what I had heard about Mick. When a couple of days went by and they still hadn't found the plane with the rodeo cowboys on it I began to worry. An all out search began as soon as the weather would permit as it was quite foggy and the icing conditions were very high so it took a few days to get the search kicked into high gear, but once it got started it was attacked with the same gusto with which most involved were used to doing things, all out and all hands on deck.

Countless hours were spent by pilot friends and the CAP trying to locate the airplane and the rodeo talent on board, but all search efforts were frustrated. They were suspected having gone down somewhere around Medford, Oregon. There had been bad weather in that area and it was there that they had lost radar contact, but all efforts turned up no airplane.

Some of the cowboys who had their own airplanes like Dale Trotter and Bill Kornell flew for months looking for their friends. Then, in about November some deer hunters in Northern California found the wreckage. It was determined that the plane had iced up and had gone straight down. All on board were killed instantly,. Brian Claypool, Gary Logan, Lee Coleman, and Calvin Bunny all killed and add to that, Mick Whitely, and I will say that was one of the darkest days in my rodeo career.

I am glad to have known each of them and will attest that they were all good folks as well as talented at what they did. Not all things that happen are good or bad, but the mix of both is what makes each of us who and what we are when we grow old. I'm glad for the adversity, but pills like this are pretty sour when you get one.

JOE LATONA
THAT'S BULLRIDIN'

Me and Brad Young were ready to work our way back up north as we'd spent the winter in Davie, Florida and were kinda out of money. So, we decided to go to the blood bank and sell some blood to have entry fees for an Indian rodeo in Hollywood, Florida. Well, we won a little money and started our way home and since Bob Corley was heading north for the summer we invited him to ride with us.

We stopped at a River Ranch rodeo in Florida and I won the bull riding and Brad and Bob won the bare back riding. We entered an ARA rodeo in Tennessee and on the way up there Brad was sleeping in the back of the van so we stopped on the Florida Turnpike late at night for some gas and a bite to eat and got back on the road.

About two hours into the drive I told Bob, "Crawl back in the back of the van and get your guitar out and play us a few tunes." When he crawled back there to get his guitar he said, "Brad's not back here." We had forgotten him at the rest area and had to turn around and go back a hundred miles and there he was, standing in the parking lot with no boots on and mad. So, back on the road and we got to Tennessee one hour before the rodeo started.

It was a Diamond ARA Rodeo and we all kicked butts. I won the bull riding, Brad placed in the bare back and the bulls, and Bob won his first ARA rodeo, his first of many. We all had money now, so off to Pennsylvania we headed and rodeoed hard all year.

I made the Finals and almost won the average that year, but fell off my last bull for the win on a bull I'd already won on before. But, that's bull ridin'.

BRUCE FORD
BARE BACKIN' A BULL

When I was about 19 years old I rode a bull with a bareback riggin. There was a man named Larry Arnold who had an arena in Henderson, Colorado and he used to have jackpot buck outs and practices twice a week on bare backs and bulls. I had become pretty handy at my bare back riding skills by this time so Larry said he had a bull that he would like to see if I could ride him with a bare back riggin. This bull was an old bull that was known for not bucking real hard.

I marked him out like a bare back horse and was spurring him well, but he turned back and drove my head in the dirt. Everyone there thought it was hilarious, especially Larry. Later on that summer Walt Alsbaugh leased that same bull for the Greeley, Colorado Forth of July Rodeo. A young cowboy by the name of Monty Penny from Mesquite, Texas drew him and was very successful on him winning first place, or at least a big part of it at the largest Forth of July Rodeo in the United States. I don't remember what that bull went on to do.

The day Lane was killed I had talked to him after the bare back riding which I had won. Lane asked me how many times I had won Cheyenne and I told him four times to the day. He said, "To the day," and I said, "Well, maybe not exactly this exact day, but last year."

I saw Lane get hurt and watched as they took him out of the arena. Lane kind of motioned to the guys to come and get him and said, "Help me, boys." Later on, Chuck Logue asked me if I'd heard about Lane and I said, "Yes. I saw him get hurt." Chuck said, "No. He died." I was floored. Lane's parents Clyde and Elsie Frost were the nicest people.

WAYNE WHITEHEAD
OLD MURPHY AND ME

In the early 70's in what was then the RCA I had bought my permit and started entering the bull riding at some rodeos. I was working a full time job and stayed relatively close to home. I lived in Mesquite, Texas, which was a good thing for someone that had to work and also wanted to rodeo. Neal Gay produced the Mesquite Championship Rodeo in Mesquite and it was held every Friday and Saturday night from April through September. This gave you somewhere to go every weekend without a lot of traveling. I would also enter any other rodeo that was close enough to get to on the weekends.

Neal was producing the rodeo at Leesville, Louisiana, too. I could get there in about 3 hours so I entered Mesquite for Friday night, and Leesville for Saturday night. I had an uncle in the Army who was stationed at Fort Polk which is also in Leesville. He wanted me to enter so he and his family could come to the rodeo to see me ride. Being from Mesquite I generally knew most of the bulls that Neal had. When I called back to see what

I had drawn I did not recognize the name or number of the bull I had drawn. Neal added new bulls all the time so it was not a big deal. I figured I would find out what I'd drawn when I got there.

Three friends of mine also entered for Saturday night and we all traveled together and split the gas. We left so that we would arrive in Leesville in the early afternoon. My uncle told me that he and his family would come early and we could visit a while before the rodeo. They were to meet me at the rodeo arena.

We all went to the bull pens to see the bulls we had drawn. Mine was a big Brindle with big horns. This was not unusual for a Neal Gay rodeo and anyone that has ever been to one of Neal's rodeos knows that Neal just thought it was a bonus if the bull hooked a little, too. When Donnie Gay arrived he asked me which bull I had drawn and I told him so he gave me the story on the bull.

It turned out that a soldier from Fort Polk had entered with his military ID and drew the bull on Friday night. The bull's horns were so long that he had to turn his head sideways to get in the chutes. When the bull got loaded into the chute the horns hung outside both sides of the chute. The bull also fought the chute pretty bad and while the soldier was getting ready to ride he lifted the chute gate off of the hinges and began bucking across the arena with the chute gate on his horns. He bucked the soldier off between his horns and the chute gate and mauled him pretty bad.

Donnie said the bull was pretty snorty so they had also used him as the money bull. For those that may not know, they tied a string tight around the bull's horns and after he had been bucked they let guys who were bold enough to try and get the string off of his horns come into the arena and give it a try. The winner would win a hundred dollars. There was no winner. I looked for my uncle and his family until time to start getting ready for the bull riding, but had not found them.

When the bulls were loaded in the chutes Donnie tied the chute gate to a post to try to keep my bull from getting it off the hinges as had done the night before. As I began to get on him he started slinging his head and was about to get the gate off the hinges. Donnie got on top of the gate and held on to the post hoping the weight would hold it on until I called for the bull. Just as I got my wrap, every light on the rodeo grounds went off. Everyone was hollering at me to get off because in the dark they could not see me, but I had already gotten off and was standing behind the chute.

After 15 or 20 minutes they got the lights back on and we started over. Donnie told me that I needed to make the whistle and pick a good spot to get off as this bull would really hook. I got out on him this time and made the whistle. I really wanted to make a good get off and get to the fence and safety. Thinking about the escape I forgot about keeping my feet in the bull and they whipped behind me. This stood me on my head right on the top of the bull's head in the center of those big horns.

Fortunately, I flipped forward and landed on my feet about a foot in front of the bull and he was in hot pursuit. The fence was six feet to my right. I made a quick cut to the right and beat him there by about a foot. One of the light poles was right against the fence and I stood on the top of the fence holding the pole as the bull thrashed the fence. As I looked down into the bleachers there was my uncle and his family in the third row. I jumped down and sat with them in the bleachers.

Now was the time they were letting people get into the arena for the money bull. One of the guys that climbed into the arena was a long haired hippy. When they told them to go he began to run directly at the bull and the bull ran directly at him. Neither one weakened and a head on collision occurred and the bull won. The hippy gets up and tries the same tactic once more with the same results. The hippy had to be helped to the fence and this time he elected to leave the arena.

The next day as we were all preparing to leave Donnie asked me if I would ride back to Mesquite since he was driving by himself and the three guys I had ridden with could go on. I told him I would. Donnie at that time drove about a 1964 model Ford Fairlane. It was a six cylinder and it was called Maytag. I think that may have been because riding in it you thought it might be in the spin cycle. It was hot and we had the AC running. We had made it back into Texas and were on IH 20. An 18 wheeler got right on our bumper and was honking his horn to try and make Donnie drive faster. What he did not know was that we were maxed out then.

It was quite irritating and Donnie made a hand gesture that in his opinion meant for the guy to either slow down or go around. The trucker did not appreciate the gesture and began closing in on Maytag's bumper. Donnie turned off the AC and we gained enough speed to outrun the truck and we were successful in getting back to Mesquite.

I know you may be wondering about old Murphy and not know who he is so I will tell you. He is the one that wrote that law, "Whatever can go wrong, will". Murphy and I seem to have been inseparable for most of my life.

DANNY O'HACO
FLYIN' TO SAN FRANCISCO

In 1983 I left the Calgary Stampede on my way to Paso Robles, California with stops in Great Falls and San Francisco. We landed in Great Falls to pick up some new passengers and then on to our final destination of San Francisco. Shortly after take off from Great Falls we reached cruising altitude and the seat belt sign went off.

I got up and was going to the rest room at the back of the plane, but while in there something terrible happened to the engine just out side of the restroom wall. It sounded like metal grinding together then silence. The engine was out of commission.

I exited the restroom to see the flight attendant a pale white and her eyes were big as saucers. I headed back to my seat and put on my seat belt. The cabin lights had gone off and the air conditioning wasn't working. It was dark in the plane and it was starting to warm up in the cabin.

I asked the cowboy next to me if he had heard the engine noise and he said that something had woke him up, but he didn't feel anything. The cabin was so quiet you could hear a pin drop and no word from the Captain if there was a problem. I just sat in silence praying. The unknown is the worst fear of all. I did understand that there was a mechanical problem, but not the extent of the damage.

Finally, after twenty minutes the Captain comes on over the loud speaker and said, "We are going to have to make an emergency landing in Boise, Idaho." Now, we sit there not knowing what the problem was for another twenty minutes, the longest twenty minutes of my life. We landed with out a problem and as we exited the plane the fire trucks and airport personnel had surrounded the plane.

I could see that part of the engine panel was gone and black soot was all over the side of the plane. They thought a bird had flown into the engine and it started a fire. They shut it down and sprayed foam on the flames to put it out. The system is built to do just that. Those planes are designed to fly on two engines if one goes out. We were lucky that day that it didn't escalate into something far worse.

Once in the airport the counter found another connection to San Francisco and we loaded up again and were off on our way. I made it to San Francisco in time to make my connection to Paso Robles and everything worked out in spite of my almost nervous breakdown on the flight out of Great Falls.

ROY DELL
YOGI BEAR

Chimp, been trying to figure out what story I could send you, and then after the reunion I put on last week I figured the story of Yogi Bear riding a bull was it since it was the most requested story I was asked to repeat.

Back in the summer of '85 there was a nightly rodeo in Branson, Missouri. Me and my traveling partner Donnie Osburn made our first trip over there not knowing what to expect. Soon as we arrived I saw a couple of old family friends that I had not seen in a few years, these being Greek Ellick Sr. and Greek Jr., also known as Big Greek and Little Greek. Lil Greek was fighting bulls and Big Greek, well, if you knew him, he was just having fun.

We stood around the bucking chutes catching up and up walks a kid and proudly announce that he was from the Jellystone National Park and he would be riding a bull that night dressed as Yogi Bear. We asked the kid how old he was, where he was from, and had he ever been on a bull. Well, he said 18 and that he was from New York and this was his first trip ever to a rodeo. He had come to Branson to work for the summer and the park had sent him over to hand out coupons to the park. I'm still not sure if we understood what we were in store for that night, but to this day it is still burned into my memory.

As the fans started arriving to the rodeo I saw Yogi Bear for the first time. He was mingling with the crowd handing out coupons and proudly announcing that he would be riding a bull that night. Now, if you have never seen Yogi Bear, this is a full costume with feet and hands that look like bear paws and a head as big as a beach ball. Please remember this description later because the head was so big he looked out of the mouth to see.

So, there were two sections of bull riding, one as the first event and the second as the last. During the first section rodeo announcer Billy Don Cash happily announced to the crowd that Yogi would be riding a bull. Well, after the first section and one minor wreck, Yogi decided this might not be a good idea after all so next thing I see is Big Greek explaining to the young man that all will be fine.

Well, for the next hour or so I see Yogi several times remove his beach ball head to have a little liquid courage and Big Greek telling him he would be fine and the bull he was getting on has pillows for feet and is sweeter than and ole milk cow. Well, they run the bulls in and there is a Longhorn bull that looks like a bucker and they explain that he turns back in the gate to the left and is the best bull in the pen. Some young kid had him drawn, but decided his rope was not big enough that night and turned him out.

Well, ole Billy Don kept asking the crowd if they were ready to see Yogi ride a bull and they are getting louder and louder. The next thing I know Yogi is being lead into the arena by Big Greek. I turned and looked down the chutes for this bull with pillows on his feet and sweet as a milk cow and the only bull in the chutes was the Longhorn. Now remember, he supposed to be the bad cat of the herd and he's been standing in the chute for at least 30 minutes.

So, Big Greek helped Yogi get on this bull, pulled his rope and not only takes a wrap, but also a finger tuck. Before anyone could object Big Greek hits that big head and yells, "He's noddin', boys." Now, let's remember that the head is as big a beach ball and the kid has to look out of the mouth to see. Well, sure enough, this Longhorn is a bad cat and cracks in the gate to the left.

The next thing I see is Yogi Bear parallel to the world and that big head has now shifted back and all you can see is the big eyes and smile. Now, the noise coming from Yogi is not anything I had ever heard up that point in my life and still to this day I cannot describe it. Everyone is in shock and I'm sure what I witnessed only took a few seconds, but in extremely slow motion.

Lil Greek is fighting bulls and is going in for the save and the next thing I see is a paw flying through the air. Now, this kid must of somehow buckled that big ole head to the body of that suit because it is not coming off and it probably saved his life. Now, the head has turned a quarter or more to the right and is missing an eye and the fur from the side of it.

Then, two more paws are seen flying through the air and finally Lil Greek is able to get past that big head and get him loose. The crowd is in silence after the carnage as Yogi Bear somehow gets to his feet and you can see his socks. He has no paws left and only the glove that he borrowed from Big Greek. He was lead out of the arena and the head is still turned sideways, missing an eye and the fur.

Well I hate to admit, but me and Donnie Osburn were laughing so hard people were starting to stare at us. I felt bad for about a second, but how many times do you get to see Yogi Bear attempt to ride a bull and loose paws and eyes and then walk out of the arena. Yeah, I laughed. We never saw that kid for the rest of the summer and got word from another person that worked with him that he went back east shortly after that. There are pictures of this incident and the two guys on the back of the chute laughing are me and Donnie.

JAN BARBY PAYNE
MANGUM, OKLAHOMA

We were at Mangum Mounties Rodeo and Terry Funk had entered in the steer wrestling. Terry Funk was an American professional wrestler and had done some acting as well. He was known for his hardcore wrestling style and was branded the "bad guy" in the wrestling ring. Terry was just as successful in the rodeo arena as he was in the wrestling arena; however, his demeanor was completely different. (Sorry Terry if I have exposed something I wasn't)

He was the nicest, most polite guy when he would come to

our rodeos. He was respectful to me when he paid his fees, was never one to get in the pens and shake up the steers when looking for his draw, just all around good cowboy that we appreciated entering our shows.

So, at this particular performance Terry's steer did a dog fall. He didn't ever get all four legs out for a flag. Bill Newman was flagging and he just rode away from the steer and pulled up in his usual spot to wait for the next contestant, just never gave us in the stand a no time flag. Curt Donley was announcing and asked Bill over the loud speaker as Terry was walking up the middle of the arena if we were going to get a no time or what. Bill shouted, "You can decide, I'm not!" Curt chuckled and about that time, Mother, said, "Terry, Honey, no time!" He looked just up at her and waived.

Daddy had a bareback horse that would always stall in the chute, but once he got past the gate he would really buck. Daddy didn't want to haul anything would be prone to get a cowboy in a bind intentionally and not leaving the chute the right way could certainly fall under that category. This horse would just stick his nose down in the inside front of the chute and stay there a much longer time than necessary.

One evening Daddy and Uncle Chalk, Mother's brother, decided they should try to fix this horse from doing this every time the gate cracked so Daddy put a coffee can (back when they weren't plastic) full of gasoline in that very corner where the horse put his head down. When the chute gate opened the horse did that same little trick except they threw a match in that coffee can. Well, guess what? The horse was cured of that bad habit.

Daddy shared that story with several other stock contractors and one year at the NFR in OKC, Daddy and Mother always spent the entire week down there and had box seats just up from the bucking chutes. One night a bareback horse did that same trick and Jim Shoulders yelled up at Daddy, "Barby, get the coffee can!"

RED DOYAL
COWBOY HAZARDS

When we were traveling in the 60's it was pretty customary on the long runs for each driver to buy one tank of gas and then wake up the next driver, buy a new take of gas and drive until tank was empty. One year we left Colorado headed to California and on the way we filled up with gas in Wells, Nevada, changed drivers and drove out that tank full of gas and for some reason when the driver pulled into the truck stop he circled around and headed back east before he filled up. We woke up the next driver and he filled up the car and drove out his tank. When the next driver put gas in we realized we were back in Wells, Nevada.

Heading back west for the second time to burn out another tank of gas, we were all mad as hell because money was tight in those days and we were not happy campers to say the least. But, cowboys have and always will be a close net bunch and we got over being so out and down with the driver of that long ride back across Nevada for the second time that night. But, after all the extra miles we still made it in time for the rodeo and that's all that concerned us anyway.

Ken Henry told me this story as he was traveling to a rodeo in Del Rio, Texas. A group of cowboys were traveling over night for an afternoon performance the next day. This is a part of Texas where towns are few and far between and the generator on the car stopped working, causing lights to get dimmer and dimmer. One cowboy came up with the idea that the next car that passed them that they would turn off their lights and just follow the vehicle that had lights.

A fellow blew by them in a huge hurry so they fell in behind him with no lights and just kept following the tail lights in front of them. This well lit vehicle in front had the pedal to the medal and the tail lights seemed to get smaller and smaller. All went well until we ran off the road and hit a mailbox so one can only imagine we damaged a lot of property including this very nice mailbox. Luckily they were able to limp on into Del Rio after all the excitement that particular night. Needless to say these cowboys still remember that night and have shared this story to many friends over the years.

One year five of us left the Albuquerque Rodeo night performance and headed to Omaha, Nebraska for another rodeo performance the next day. We were traveling in my Ford station wagon and I drove to the edge of Kansas where we needed a tank of gas. It was about 6 AM and nothing was open.

I found a policeman who knew the owner of a gasoline station and he contacted the owner who came to meet us at the gas station. None of us had any cash on us so I finally ask the gentleman if he would accept a check if my banker back in Texas would assure him that all is OK. After he talked to my banker back in Texas, he accepted the check and we were on our way to Omaha. All seemed to be happy after all this, but not sure how happy my banker was at 6 AM. I hope I didn't disturb a good night's sleep.

Having driven for a while I asked Bo Ashorn if he would drive. The only place for me to sleep was on the top of the suitcases and rigging sacks in the back of the station wagon. When I awoke up the station wagon was doing donuts in the middle of the highway and suitcases and rigging sacks were flying everywhere. All I heard was Bo saying, "Move over on this side. I don't have any driver's license." The car was still spinning as the passenger switched with Bo.

An older man working for a grain company had run a stop sign and hit the wagon behind the rear wheel, causing us to spin. He had no driver license and was scared to death. We borrowed a crow bar from the old fellow, bent the fender off the rear tire, said goodbye to our new friend and went on to Omaha.

One summer I was making a run with my son, Royd. He was going to a couple of rodeos in Colorado and I thought I'd see some of my old friends. Royd drove all night and I started driving in

New Mexico. When I stopped at Clayton, New Mexico to fill up with gas, Royd was asleep in the back seat.

I filled the tank, paid the attendant, got back in and hit the road for Raton. When I asked if he wanted to stop and get something to eat I realized he wasn't there. He had gotten out to go to the restroom while I was paying for the gas. Heck, he had the Highway Patrol guys after me. It's a long backtrack from Raton to Clayton and we missed a performance he was up in Durango, Colorado. Royd never asked me to go with him again.

JOHNNY RIVERA
TOUGH AS THEY COME

One time I was at work and Mike White calls me to tell me he was coming to trim a horse for me. I told him not to bother because he was too hard to catch. He said, "I'm coming, anyway," and hung up on me. At the time I lived with another bull rider who traded horses. We had three or four head plus a mule or two. Mike showed up and had to round up all these horses and mules into a round pen to catch my sorrel.

He finally got the sorrel cut out and was trying to put a halter on him when another guy from Oklahoma showed up. He climbed up on the fence and asked Mike what he was doing and Mike turned to him and explained he was going to trim my horse. This guy tells Mike he's going about it all wrong. Mike, being upset from trying to catch the horse and halter him, said, "Why is that?" The guy said, "Because, that ain't Johnny's horse. It's a flippin' Mustang." So, Mike had to gather them all up again and this time he lost his shoe in our leach bed, but finally got the right horse.

When I got home Mike had three feet done and was working on the fourth. I was holding the lead rope for him when the horse tipped over the stand and stepped thru it. It hung on his foot and he went to trying to kick it off and he got Mike's knee. I saw Mike running away from the horse on the opposite side that I was on, his eyes were rolled back and he hit the ground.

I thought he got kicked in the head so I ran over to him and asked if it was his head. He said, "No, it's my knee." I knew it was bad because his head was as hard as they come and his knee wasn't. He rolled around the ground for a bit then got up and finished trimming the horse.

He asked me for a towel to sit on because he was driving his wife's new car. When I went in the house to get one my buddy's little dog ran out the door and went to barking at Mike while he was checking his knee out. The dog jumped into his car and Mike was yelling at the dog trying to get him out. I told him that I'd get the dog out if he would pull his pants up.

He was winning the world in the PBR at that time and was supposed to be flying to Billings, Montana, in two days. He ended up with a broken knee and not winning the world that year. But, true to form he told me everything happens for a reason. He truly is a champion in and out of the arena.

JAN BARBY PAYNE
R. j. PRESTON

I was cranking my hand in my rigging on Stevens at the Watonga, Oklahoma rodeo when Jan hollered down from the announcer's stand at me and said, "R,J. you forgot to pay your fees. I looked up at her and hollered back, "Take them out of my check." I got under my rigging and called for him and ended up winning second place.

Jan's brother Read Barby picked me up and dropped me off right in front of the bucking chutes because it was really muddy that night. Their dad Lloyd Barby leaned way over the bucking chute and said, "Good ride, R. j." Then, in a low voice said, "Don't be making a habit of that," and winked. Getting to go to the Lloyd Barby family rodeos was a high point of my life that I'll always cherish and never forget.

© Roger Langford

Part IV

1. Andy Taylor: Branson To Cherokee-The Longest Night I Ever Spentb
2. Skeebo Norris: Some Stories Are Just Worth Repeating
3. Marie Ellen Foltz : X I T Cowboy Reunion Queen
4. Red Doyal: The Great Cowboy Boycott
5. Dennis Luton: My Little Bovine Buddy
6. Kevin Marshall: Fourth Of July Run
7. Jeana Day: The Year I Won The World
8. Barney Brehmer: San Antonio; A Kid With All His Heroes
9. Steve Scott: Gene And Bobby Clark
10. Chimp Robertson: Trophy Buckles
11. Richard Flechsig: Stay Awake, Damn It
12. Don Endsley: A Rodeo Story
13. Lee Jones: Traveling Stories
14. Jesse "Cr" Hall: Cowboy From Harlem
15. Bill Thorpe: Kokomo, The Horse Mother Prayed For
16. Steve Scott: Why Didn't You Grab The Wheel
17. Curt Brown: Montgomery, Alabama
18. Richard Murray: Julio's Bulls
19. Dude Smith: Old Time Rodeo Legend
20. Mark Whitaker: Our Pal, Monkey
21. Jimmy Blotz: Roanoke To Lone Oak
22. Brad Besancon: Starting Off A Little Over My Head
23. Tim Sample: Five And A Bug
24. Dale Woodard: The Wild Ride
25. Ronn Warr: A Week I'll Never Forget
26. Jan Barby Payne: Arkansas City, Kansas
27. Monty Penny: Yellow Jacket
28. Joe Liles: Just Another Day On The Road
29. Bubby Boyd: God Bless Muscles Boyd

30. Virgil Ingram: Rodeo Has Always Been In My Blood
31. Darryl Chestnut: One Jumped
32. Scott Fletcher: Me And Kirk Allmon
33. Jan Barby Payne: Ramblings
34. Red Doyal: Denver, First Time Around
35. John Vic: 1984
36. Dennis Merrell: Kowbell

ANDY TAYLOR
BRANSON TO CHEROKEE-THE LONGEST NIGHT I EVER SPENT

The year was 1979. The rodeo season was in full swing. Denny Flynn and I were traveling together and we were both having a successful season so far. We were to ride in Branson, Missouri and leave immediately to head for Cherokee, Iowa where we'd ride the next afternoon.

As soon as we arrived in Branson I saw my good friend Roy Carter. The first thing out of his mouth was the devastating news that our friend Mick Whitely from Halfway, Oregon had been killed the night before in Inglewood, California. A bull had stepped in his chest with both feet and he died before he got to the hospital. Mick was a close friend. Just a few weeks earlier, he, Wacey Cathey, and myself, had spent nearly a week in the same hotel room in Edmonton, Alberta. How was I to know it would be the last time I'd see Mick?

But, that wasn't the end of the bad news in Branson that night. Brian Claypool, Gary Logan, Calvin Bunney, and Lee Coleman, all Canadians, had left Cloverdale, BC, in Brian's private plane on their way to Las Vegas. After clearing customs in Salem, Oregon they were never heard from again. After an all-out intensive search no evidence of the guys or the plane was found. In fact, it was later in the year during hunting season that hunters happened on to the wreckage.

I didn't know Bunney or Coleman. They were young and just starting their professional rodeo careers, but Brian Claypool was a great friend. We'd become friends soon after I cracked out in '72. He was a great bull and bronc rider, one of the best, and the 'fittest' guy I ever knew. Gary Logan, or Moon as we all called him was also a good friend and great bareback rider. Just two weeks before there were two carloads of us staying at our ranch in Allison, Texas. The last day before we all left and went different ways Gary and I were working on a new pair of spurs of mine. Looking back it was a great day, always lots of laughs with *Moon*. It would be the last time I'd ever see him.

There's an incredible camaraderie in the rodeo world, more like a brotherhood. It wasn't just that we'd lost some friends, we'd lost family. Denny and I headed out for Cherokee. I'm not ashamed to say I shed a lot of tears that night. We stopped at a truck stop somewhere and I called Julie just to hear her voice. I called my dad hoping that he'd say something to make me feel better. *I didn't want to go to Cherokee and I didn't care anything about riding bulls. I just wanted to go home. But, we were already committed.* I guess in a lot of ways I grew up some that night.

My traveling partner and best friend Denny Flynn and I *talked a lot about the guys and a lot about life that night.* We both had our turn at driving, but I don't think either one of us slept a wink. We rolled into Cherokee not very fresh and not thinking much about bull riding. It was the longest night I ever spent.

SKEEBO NORRIS
SOME STORIES ARE JUST WORTH REPEATING

I was rodeoing for New Mexico State University in the southwest Region and let me tell you it's a long damn way from Las Curces, New Mexico to Stephenville, Texas, home of Tarleton State University and make it back for classes. (That's back when you had to go to class.)

But, this little epoisode was at Amarillo, Texas and the host college was West Texas A & M in the Range Riders huge old outdoor arena. My traveling buddy Frank Hayes and I headed out, and I'm up on Friday night slack. We arrive in plenty of time to watch the whole performance and get geared up for the slack.

But, if you've ever been to Amarillo you know the wind blows and it can be 110 degrees or 40 below zero and this night it was the latter, 40 below. The stock contractor was Campbell and Cordell (as in Freddy Cordell) from Childress, Texas and I drew a little black bull that was supposed to turn back into my hand. Good news. I've got a picture somewhere of me in a down-filled coat with my NMSU vest over the top.

Cold, cold, and more cold, but I got lucky and made the ride and was sure a happy camper. So, we loaded up and headed to the room to get cleaned up to hit the town. I can't remember the establishment's name, but they served adult beverages and had a huge dance floor. My kind of deal and a large time was had by all, packed to the wall with college rodeo guys and gals.

So, they are trying to shut the place down as its closing time and lo and behold we walk outside and it's snowing a little. Not too bad, but pretty dang cold and most everyone had imbibed a few beverages.

Everyone had seen the big fiberglass Quarter Horses that are generally on top of feed stories and western wear stores and there just happened to be one of those stationary steeds about two doors down on the canopy of a store. The wheels are turning and I turned to Bob Wilfong from TSU and said, "Hey, Bob. Betcha' can't mark that horse out."

He looked at me with that little sheepish grin and said, "Bet's on." So, we proceeded to climb up on the canopy with assistance, of course, and he slides up on that wet, slick, critter and begins to spur the crap out of it. So, it's now my turn and I did a decent job, but not like Wilfong.

By this time we had a pretty good audience of college folks down below and we also drew the attention of one of Amarillo's finest. Yep, we were busted. However, the cop had a little compassion for poor college cowboys and just asked us to move on and go home or to our room. Whew, close call.

We woke up the next morning, opened the motel room door

and there was about 12-13 inches of snow. We made it out to the arena for the 9 AM slack for my traveling partner, but they couldn't clear the snow enough to think it was safe and that's the only rodeo I've ever been to that was cancelled.

So, we struck out toward the west, back to school, but that trip took 16 ½ hours and we spun out twice on the slick roads between Hereford, Texas and Clovis, New Mexico, but of course, back then we were ten foot tall and bullet proof. Such good times and made and a friend for life in, Bob Wilfong.

MARIE ELLEN FOLTZ
X I T COWBOY REUNION QUEEN

Marie Ellen Foltz–First XIT Queen.

In 1937, Marie Ellen Foltz was chosen the first XIT Cowboy Reunion Queen in Dalhart, Texas. The following year as she was retiring her reign the cowboy reunion committee had invited Gene Autry to judge the queen contest.

His choice for queen was Marie Ellen who was not eligible, as the rules stated that the queen could not succeed herself. Gene Autry was insistent on his choice saying that she was the best looking woman he had ever seen.

The committee finally convinced him that he had to make a different choice which he reluctantly did. Many years later she was jokingly why she passed up fame and fortune by marrying a local cowboy instead of the famous cowboy movie star.

She simply stated, "Because, Gene Autry was too short." Nonetheless, this memory never failed to bring a smile to her face.

RED DOYAL
THE GREAT COWBOY BOYCOTT

When I was traveling the rodeos, Albuquerque and Omaha overlapped quiet a few performances. For some reason Omaha decided not to give the cowboys any trade-outs. This didn't bother bull riders very much because we were just getting one or two bulls, but in the other bucking events the cowboys were getting three or four head.

So, it was almost impossible for them to work the two rodeos. The cowboys had a meeting about boycotting Omaha which many decided to do. During the meeting someone came in and said that it appeared that Omaha was going to get a horse at every performance.

I had noticed Freckles Brown leaving the meeting early and when we got to Omaha, Freckles was there and had entered all three bucking events. He got on a saddle bronc and a bareback horse each performance, plus the three bulls everyone else was getting in the bull riding. After the last performance I asked

Freckles what was going on and he said, "Red, this is the greatest I have been to in years. It was just like going to Madison Square Garden in the old days."

I don't know how much trouble rodeo has with the animal humane society today, but in the 60's this organization was very active, checking spurs and equipment at rodeos. I remember one year at San Diego before the rodeo began they were behind the chutes checking all the spurs and equipment of the cowboys. When at the same time they were presenting the trophies for the parade they had that morning downtown.

Into the arena rode a guy dressed up in fancy western clothes on a big black and white Paint horse. He had all of the fancy trimmings, silver bridle, silver saddle, and large Mexican silver spurs. The poor Paint horse had bloody spots from his front legs to near his black legs. I don't know if they even saw him or would have said anything if they had noticed him at all. That is just one of those things that has stuck in my mind all these years.

DENNIS LUTON
MY LITTLE BOVINE BUDDY

I was needing some money and also some points for the year-title and I was hoping to draw something that I could win it all on. Well, it didn't work out that way. When they gave my draw I was expecting to go out to the pen to see a big-horned Brindle that was breathing fire out of his nostrils. Instead, it was a scrawny little black-baldy muley with a rail for a back---ha ha! Needless to say, I was not a happy camper.

When I asked if anyone knew him all I got was smart remarks like, "I don't know, but he looks like a bad cat that will get in your back pocket," or "Watch him, he looks like a real terror." He was so small that I had to adjust the loop on my rope up to steer size and when they ran him in he just sat in the chute like he was waiting in line for the school bus.

They un-latched the chute gate and he nonchalantly stepped out and started his lope down the arena with about the same difficulty as riding a merry-go-round horse. I was pretty upset at this sorry-excuse-for-a-bull and even while I was riding I was wondering why any stock contractor would haul such trash.

So, after he passed the clown barrel I went to thrashing him with both feet in the neck like a bareback horse. But, it was all for naught because I still got a super-low score, but at least I'd made my statement to the stock contractor about how I felt about is sweet little pet.

The next morning when I showed up for slack all my bull riding friends were holding their hats over their hearts with sad faces. I asked them what was up and they said that when they had showed up earlier they discovered that my little bull-friend was found dead in the pen. He was already stiff so he must have died not too long after I got off him.

What? They all kept their faces straight saying, "Yes, you spurred him so hard you broke his heart and he just lay down in the pen and died." Well, after a quick scan of the pens I found my little bovine buddy munching on some hay. And of course, the laughing and hoorah-ing kept a-going for a few minutes while I was threatening to whip the entire cowboy crew. Bunch of smart alecks......ha!

KEVIN MARSHALL
FOURTH OF JULY RUN

I knew at a young age that I wanted to be a cowboy and I thought any kind of cowboy would suit me fine. Me and my brother would ride anything we could catch which was usually our dad's or our neighbor Mr. Frank Powell's stock. Let me tell you that made both of those men pretty mad. Mr. Frank took it better than dad did and we receive many a strapping because of it.

Next thing we knew dad bought us some horses and said, "If

you got to ride, it better be those horses." Dang it, they were broke to ride and we wanted something that would buck. So, we started looking around to find us some place we could get on anything that would buck, but that we wouldn't get in trouble for getting on them. We found the auction barn.

Why shoot, they would even pay us a couple of bucks to work in the back pushing and penning the stock and we tried riding everything except those big bulls because they would get on you. My brother's name was Dennis Mark Marshall, but I just called him Bubba, the best brother and best friend I ever had. Ole Bubba and I were on the fence looking at the biggest meanest looking bull we had ever seen and Bubba said, "I dare you to get on him."

Well, when we were kids a dare wasn't taken lightly, but I thought about it for a few seconds and said to myself, "Now, how am I going to get out of this without looking like a coward?" That old mean bull had drew a crowd and one the men must have heard what Bubba said, so he's watching us pretty close. I said something like, "Why, he'll tear up that pen if I jump on him." Bubba said, "You can't be crazy enough to get on that bull." So I said, "I better not we'll get fired."

The man who had been watching said, "Son, if you really want to get on a bull I'm putting on a open rodeo Saturday night and if your not all talk I will see you there. Now, get down off that fence because that bull will kill you. I'm selling that bull because he keeps hurting my other bulls. See you Saturday night 7:00. Be there if you're not all talk"

So, to me that was a dare and I always wanted to be a cowboy so I caught up with the man and said, "Where, mister?" and he said, "At the Rodeo arena in Newton, Texas. Are you going to be there?" I said, "Yes sir," so the man said, "Son, you ever been on a bull before?" I said, "No, sir, but I want to be a cowboy." The man said, "I got just the bull for you. See you Saturday."

Ok, so this is Wednesday so I got a few days to think on this and more than once I thought I might be rushing this cowboy thing and I wondered what the man mean when he said, "I got just the bull for you." Something else to worry about, did he not like me? What did he mean by that?

So, Saturday rolls around and we went to the rodeo grounds and we are early, but not too early as the stock was already there and the cowboys, too. A lot of guys standing around the back pens looking at the bulls so I joined them. Now, these are grown men and I'm just a 13 or 14 years old boy. They were nice enough, but I got a few sideways looks.

Looking back on it now, those old boys probably had a good laugh at my expense. Not being from a rodeo or ranchers family I know I was a sight in my old run down boots and throw away hat that I had found somewhere, but I didn't know that then. I didn't know anything about it. I didn't even know you need a bull rope and spurs.

I'm sitting up there on the fence with the rest of the guys looking at the bulls and I'm seeing all the humps and horns and thinking, "What have I got myself into and maybe I should get out of here before the man sees me."

While I'm climbing down off the fence the man had walked behind me and said, "I see you made it here." I said, "Yes, sir." He said, "You still want to get on a bull?" and before I can say," Well, I don't know," he said, "I got a special bull for you first timers. He's over here in my horse trailer. Come on, get your bag and I will show him to you."

So, I said, "It's just me and my brother and we don't have no bag." He looks us over, gives a shrug and said, "That's OK, you can borrow my son's stuff. Let's go look at that bull." We went over to his trailer and he's got a little Hereford bull, about a 900 or 1000 pound muley and boy was I relieved. Long and short of it was, that little muley jumped and kicked in big circle and I made the whistle and right then and there I was hooked for life.

I was going to be a bull rider or die trying. Now that I was hooked and I'd made up my mind to be a bull rider I had to figure a way to do this without mama finding out. Since we are still working at the sale barn every chance we could I saw some of those cowboys from the rodeo and I asked one of them how to find out where the next rodeo would be?

He said it was easy, to just watch for the posters. I said, "What posters?" and he pointed out that the telephone poles all had posters on them and I had never noticed them. I started checking out those posters and noticed that they had what they call a play day every Saturday night. So, we start working on the old man to let us go to the play day at the rodeo arena in Kirbyville on Saturday nights.

He probably took us just so we would leave him alone about it. What I didn't know was a play day was for timed events, not bucking events. Worse yet, everything cost money for entry fees. But, as luck would have it some man came pulling up in an old run down truck and trailer with 4 bulls in the trailer and he was looking for someone to get on them.

Some boys about my age ran over to watch the bulls get unloaded into the holding pens and these guys were dressed like cowboys and they were there get on the bulls. The man that owned the bulls said, "Everybody to get ready. It's time to buck the bulls," and these guys go back behind the chutes and start pulling on their ropes and putting on their spurs.

I started talking to them and I still don't have any equipment, but one guy said I can use his stuff if I really want to get on a bull. His name was Mike Kent and he's bigger and older than me and he looks like a real cowboy. He was a nice guy and after this little impromptu buck out he is nice enough to tell me I need to get my own equipment if I really want to be a bull rider. And, he tells me where there's a boot and leather shop that sells Donnie Gay rodeo equipment. He said I could get a job hauling hay for Mister Powell and that he paid 10 cents a bail and that's how I could make enough to buy my first set of equipment.

I started hanging out with these guys and going to the practice pen with them. This was in the mid 70's, like '74, '75, & '76. I went to high school rodeos and then on to the SSS Rodeo Company owned by brothers, Johnnie and Icky Shroader and they had some good bulls.

I never had much luck at the high school rodeos and in fact after that first little muley the only place I could get one rode was at the practice pen. After about 3 years of being added money I started riding everything I got on and decided it was time to see if I could make it at some bigger rodeos.

There was a winter indoor rodeo series in Orange, Texas at a place called Tin Top Rodeo. I met a lot of great people there and the most important one was Mr. Jim Hancock because he started giving me rides to the rodeo and encouraged me every way he could. He introduced me to guys who traveled to rodeos every weekend and he introduced me to John Stormy Gloor, one of my first rodeo heroes.

During the winter series there I met Big Joe Hillman, Little Dicky Richards, Custer Coleman, Kurt Richards, Dicky's, Jimmy Ray Sullivan, Kirby Gillifillan, Alan Ace Craigen and Rodney Hot Rod Dishman. These guys were planning a fourth of July run, making 7 rodeos in 4 days and I was invited to go. To make 7 rodeos in 4 days we would have to be entered just right. So, Joe's daughters and I worked the phones and we managed to get up sorta the way we wanted.

We started out with a day show at Beaumont and the S.S.S. Rodeo. I had always had trouble getting to the whistle at their rodeos, but this time would be different. I drew #1, a big black droop horn bull who had thrown me off 3 times already, but this time I ride him easy and I was winning 1st place when we left to go to the next rodeo which was a night show.

We were up at Livingston, a Flying J rodeo and there I had another black bull #312, Payday. He took one jump and turned back to the left and I spurred him and left there winning second.

Rodeo Stories II

I should be telling you about the other guys, but for the life of me I can only remember what I got on and how I did.

So, we left for Rock Springs to a Tommy Preio rodeo, a day performance and slack afterward. We took turns driving and got there sometime in the middle of the night. I woke up and went to look for something to eat. Then I checked out the bulls and the whole rodeo grounds is coming to life. There are cowboys and cowgirls climbing out of trailers, campers, trucks, cars, and some had even made themselves beds on the ground just like ranch cowboys out on the range.

Most of the Cowboys were gathering over by the holding pens and so were the guys in our van. Now, Mister Preio had a pen full of some big humps and horns, some rank looking bulls. Only two blacks muleys in the pen and the odds were I wouldn't get one of them. It was getting close to the time to start so we headed over to pay our entry fees. We waited our turn in line to pay our fees and they told me I had #37 Helicopter, another black muley. Damn if I wasn't happy about that, but Kirby has #107, the biggest and the ugliest bull in the pen.

We didn't know those bull so off we go to find Larry "Wolf" Turner since he knew all the bulls and he would give the book on what we'd drawn. He tells Kirby that he didn't draw that well, but me, I had one of the best bulls there, a real bucker that turns back to the left as soon as he can. Old # 37 turned back to the left soon as the gate opened and I'm right where I wanted to be, spurring him every jump.

Everybody was hollering and that was when I got the idea that it was easy that I'd just waive at Big Joe on the back of the chutes. When I picked my hand up to waive, that's all that bull needed, just for me to make one mistake and he threw me back into the chute. I'm hurting as Big Joe reaches down and lifts me out of the bucking chute looks me right in the eye and told me that I just threw first place away by showing off and that I should wait until after the whistle to pull that kind stuff. That hurt worse than what that old bull did to me. Kirby was out next on that giant bull he'd drawn and when he nods his head, that big old bull leaped out toward the middle of the pen and after about 4 of those big jumps he jerked Kirby down. He was hung up and that hind foot came down on Kirbys neck and scrapes every stitch of clothing and hide off his back. That old bull was dragging Kirby closer to the Grandstands with every jump and right in front of the Grandstand, Kirby came loose and stood up, all but naked.

This was the 4th of July day performance and everyone for miles around was there and the place was packed. Poor ole Kirby couldn't even take a step he was hurting so bad and the crowd had no mercy for him and they razzed him something terrible. I knew this is not supposed to be funny, but I couldn't stop laughing and I wasn't the only one. Big Joe went to his rescue and helped carry him out to the van, and that crowd never let up on him one bit.

Next stop was Wimberly, Texas to a George Haines rodeo. They took every bull rider that entered, 256 or 286, depending on who you believe. I felt like I'd embarrassed the guys and I wanted a chance to make up it. The last time I was at a George Haines rodeo he had 3 or 4 bulls that had never been ridden before and they were mean rank bulls.

We went to pay our fees to find out what the luck of the draw had for us and the one I wanted was branded #6, but I saw that Fred Yancy had him so I went down the list to find what bull my name next to and it was what looked like GRR. I didn't know him and couldn't find anybody who did so I went Mr. Haines and he told me that there was no GRR there and to go back and check the list again

When I get back over to the list Rusty Bradberry was there and I told my situation. He looked at my name and said, "I think that is #6 in, the re-ride," and told me to go ask the Secretary. When I found her, she confirmed that there was no GRR in the bull herd and that it was in fact #6 and that the RR meant re-ride.

Now, I was happy as I could be, but I didn't want to get carried away because I still have to get him rode.

Ok, so I got him in the slack so I went to get a good seat. Those open rodeos drag on and on and when it's finally time for the bull riding I'm right there. When they opened the gate #6 came around right there, but he's too close and hits his head hard enough to come to a full stop. They hit him with the hot shot and he starts spinning, but his heart isn't in it and Fred rode him easy for 73 points.

Fred rode him first, but #6 didn't have his day by any means. I wanted to be the first one to ride him because I always liked being the man to ride a bull that had a reputation for having never been ridden. My turn didn't come until 2:00am in the morning and when I put rope on #6 I knew I was going to ride him. This time he kicked out of the box and turned back to the left and bucked as good or better than anything I had been on up until then and I spurred him up all the way to the whistle.

As I carried my rope out of the arena Mr. George Haines walked out to meet me and told me what a great ride I'd made. Then, Robert Chambers and everyone else was telling me, but I needed to hear it from Big Joe. As I walked out the arena gate Big Joe was right there with the biggest smile on his face and that did it for me. 79 points held up to win first place and paid $1,885.75 the most I'd ever one at an open rodeo and also the most I'd ever heard of an open rodeo paying in 1979. We went to three rodeos that weekend and I had three more blac bulls and they all turned back to the left and I rode all three of them, a great weekend with many more to come.

JEANA DAY
THE YEAR I WON THE WORLD

One story in particular happened in 1974 the year I won the world. I was married at the time and we were making the Fourth of July run in Montana and Wyoming. We had not received our International health papers to get our horses into Canada so I stayed in Livingston, Montana to await the papers while Arnold flew on to Calgary. We had a thirty some foot long gooseneck trailer with living quarters.

I was only nineteen years old and even though I had traveled all over the USA I didn't have experience driving in the mountains. I looked at a map and picked the shortest route to Calgary from Livingston. Unbeknownst to me, I should have gone the Interstate route.

We had a four speed pickup and I was in the low gear to get up the mountain and I was so thrilled I geared it on up to start down the other side. However, I soon realized that I was going too fast and tried to gear down and all it would do was grind. I worked the brakes, but I just kept going faster around the curves and pretty soon my brakes were on fire.

A family in an International pickup pulled up beside me and wanted me to roll the window down, but it was broken and wouldn't roll. They were screaming for me to slow down and I was crying and signaling that I couldn't so they pulled in front of me and let me run into them and got me stopped. It was a miracle.

The man put dirt on my brakes and got the fires out and I was just sitting on the side of the mountain sobbing. He offered to drive me the rest of the way down the mountain. He explained that the pickup had disc brakes and that once they were cool they would hold. I swear they were sent by God.

He told me that one or two more curves would have been it for me and the horses. Being young and scared to death I did not get the people's names and I have regretted that so much because I owe them my life. I made it to Calgary and we sold the trailer. It was just too big for the pickup we had and I learned a valuable lesson about driving in the mountains. Always go down a gear lower going down hill than you go up.

I had another trip that was exciting. It would have been the year that Phil Lyon won his first All-Around Championship and for the book, in my opinion he is the true All-Around Champion because he competed in timed events and rough stock. He was a great cowboy and a good friend.

We were in Albuquerque and we were both trying to get to as many rodeos as we could. My dad and I decided I could make Albuquerque, Memphis, and Omaha if I would fly from Albuquerque to Memphis. My sister Barbara would be in Memphis and I could ride her horse Sis, then fly on to Albuquerque and Dad would have driven from Albuquerque to Omaha. If anything could go wrong, everything did.

Phil Lyon and I decided to fly together to Memphis. We could get a better flight out of Amarillo and I had a jockey friend that was riding at the State Fair there so he would drive us to Amarillo. Things were going great until we got to Amarillo, but we took a wrong turn and ended up on the backside of the airport just as the alternator went out of the car.

It was the middle of the night and we were in a warehouse district. We finally found a night security guard that gave Phil and I a ride around to the terminal. Phil had called the airlines so when we came running into the terminal with all Phil's rodeo equipment they said they were holding the plane for us and we made it on the flight. That wouldn't happen now in the times we live in.

There were 3 performances at Memphis and I was up in two of them that day and then up at the night performance at Omaha. I made my first run on Barb's mare Sis at Memphis and then a horrible storm hit and flooded the streets. It delayed the second performance and I had to turn out my run to catch my flight to Omaha where there were five runs if I remember correctly.

All that time I'm in my colorful barrel racing clothes because I had gone straight from my run in Albuquerque to the airport. I was a little muddy by the time I left Memphis because even though it was an indoor arena the alley way was outside and it was muddy. I was probably about 15 years old.

Chimp Robertson

I got to Omaha and took my first cab ride ever. I told him I needed to get to the rodeo fast because I was running out of time and the driver was awesome. But, because I was just a country girl from Oklahoma I did not know about tipping cab drivers and I was so proud I had the right change to pay him and I've felt guilty about it ever since.

I ran into the building and June Ivory was the secretary so she called me to the office and told me Dad had broken down somewhere in the middle of Kansas with my horse. Now mind you, the barrel race was about to begin and if I didn't make a run I'd lose the rest of my runs there. Kay Vamvorus loaned me a green, a very green colt, to lope around the barrels that night. Dad came dragging in after the rodeo was over with only 3 tires on the trailer. He was exhausted and so was I. Neither of us had gotten any rest for those 2 days and nights and my trip was pretty much a bust. I honestly don't remember how it worked out for Phil, but I hoped it was better than mine.

The next year or two after that I decided I could make all of the rodeos driving. My sister Barbara was working for Cervi and had to work at Omaha so we decided to take a car and trailer so we could make better time. We finished at Albuquerque and left that night with a couple of rough stock cowboys hitching a ride with us and headed to Omaha. I drove all the way and it's a long trip. It was the night that Jim Croce's plane crashed and I'll never forget hearing about that on the radio.

We got to Omaha in time for Barbara to work and compete and me to make my run. I was up at Memphis the next day and Monty Henson and someone else rode with me, but they slept and snored all the way there. I drove another all-nighter to Memphis and I can't remember if I had 2 or 3 runs there. I know I ran that afternoon when we got there and I think I ran that night and also the next day, but can't remember for sure.

I was so tired I was kind of out of it. I was in the alleyway getting ready to run so I took Chick Elms hat. Normally, you walk your horse into the Memphis arena a little to the left because the gate was on the right side of the end of the arena and it was a small arena. I told them to open the gate and ran my good horse Excuse from the alley. I said if he didn't know where the first barrel was by then he never would and I won the go-round by a full second.

I did get some sleep that night in the back seat of my Grandpa's car and made my last run and drove back to Omaha. I finished my run there and headed to Oklahoma City to the State Fair. I believe it was Steve Hyatt that rode with me from Omaha to Oklahoma City. I met Dad at Oklahoma City and he took a look at me and told me I looked like hell. I felt even worse.

I won a lot more money that trip driving than I had the year I flew, but it was certainly tough on the body. My horse Excuse was awesome. The more we hauled, the harder he ran. It was like he thrived on it. Dad always said, "If we had loaded him in the trailer at the National Finals Rodeos and just drove around all day then unloaded and ran him you would have had much better Finals."

The rodeo world was a lot different back in those days. We certainly did it for the love of the sport because the money wasn't there. I am very proud to have served on the Board of Directors that stood for equal money for the barrel racers. I have been asked if I had ever taken the results from the National Finals I ran in and checked what I would have won now, but I haven't because I don't want to feel sick. I'm glad they are finally winning good money.

But, I was never for the Finals moving to Vegas. I attended a reunion there about 5 years ago and went to a performance. It's not a rodeo anymore it's a circus. It's so loud you can't hear yourself think. And, it goes so fast that you can't even go to the bathroom. It's not what rodeo is about, but unfortunately no one else can seem to compete with the Vegas money. Also, with the money the rodeo brings into Vegas they should build a new building that would be more fair to the timed events. There, I got that off my chest.

BARNEY BREHMER
SAN ANTONIO; A KID WITH ALL HIS HEROES

1972, I was working the labor list, opening the out gate and mounting out horses and bulls every performance for $10.00 a head. The reason being, I was broke because my suitcase had been stolen in El Paso with my credit card, money, and checks. Dumb rookie mistake to leave all that in my suitcase in a motel room.

I placed in the first round on a Kessler bull and won third and was looking at the draw for the second round with Pete Gay. As I scrolled down the list I found my name and across from it was #11 Batman. I turned and asked Pete, "What bull that was," and he replied, "You call yourself a bull rider and don't know Batman?" He just turned and walked off

"Must be a good one," I thought. Well, after asking a few others I found out that he had only been ridden once by Sandy Kirby in about a three year or so span. He belonged to Jim Shoulders. Yep, one of my heroes and when I arrived to get on, there was the Shoulder's brand, a J-Lazy-S on the bull's flank.

I had stayed at his home with Marvin Paul and he was a friend, but without mercy. Old school. He knew what I had drawn and asked if I was sick or scared because I sure was pale. I looked at him and asked, "Do you think you could make him turn back?" He grinned and said, "Tell me about it when you're laying on your back looking up at him."

A kind of cowboy respect. A little pushing and shoving, and his way to get my motor running as if it wasn't going pretty fast anyway. As I slid up I heard Jim say, "Try a little." I did and Batman went round and round, kicked, rolled and the whole deal. When the whistle blew and I was still aboard and Jim Shoulders was the first one in the arena with an extended hand. I wondered if life could get any better.

Well, during the last performance Butch Kirby and I were sitting in the arena along the fence and Butch said, "If we beat several top hands tonight you are going to be the champion and I'll be reserve."

First out was Freckles Brown and he bucked off. Next was Myrtis Dightman, but he didn't score enough points. Next out was Larry Mahan and he also bucked off. Next was Johnny Quintana, but he didn't get enough points, either. Then Ronnie Bowman, but he also didn't get enough points and it was over.

I had just won San Antonio with a lot of my heroes entered and I was just a kid. Life was good. One of those things you remember for a life time just like what it paid, $2131.25. I had won third in the first round, won the second round and won the average. Maybe, I was good enough to compete with the best.

STEVE SCOTT
GENE AND BOBBY CLARK

I was lucky enough to get hired on to work the California College Rodeo State Finals at Cal Poly, San Luis Obispo. I think it was about 1973. Rusty Walls and I would be working with Gene and Bobby Clark. Rusty's father had been in the Navy with Gene, and Rusty and I were still in the Marine Corps and rodeoing on the weekends when we could.

Well, when we got to Cal Polly, Gene and Bobby introduced us to Ronnie their pet Chimp. I had no idea how strong a Chimpanzee was. Ronnie and I were rolling around, scuffling on the mattress in the back of my pickup when Ronnie reached up and grabbed me with one arm and threw me out of the pickup bed like I was a rag doll.

He would sit around and drink a beer with us and he'd kind of wrap those lips around the whole top of the can and just kind of suck the beer out of it. Sometimes, they'd let him smoke a cigarette which he really didn't smoke, but I'd light one and give it to him and he'd take a drag on it, but wouldn't inhale.

I guess he'd probably already met Bill Clinton who taught him that trick. Anyway, he'd run those lips out there and roll them back and blow that smoke out like he was just one of the boys. Anyhow, Gene and Bobby would take it away from him and tell him that it was gonna stunt his growth.

They had another little Chimp named Ahab and he was cute as a bug. He was learning how to do the tricks from Ronnie, but Ronnie was the cutter. They also had two Queensland Heelers to get the bulls out of the arena.

We went to Gene's sister in law's house in Morro Bay and while we were there she cooked a beautiful dinner for us. It was lasagna. Well, Ronnie the Chimp sat at the table with us and ate lasagna with a fork and spoon. He had better table manners than Rusty and I. When he wanted something he'd point to it and they would put some more on his plate.

Well, one evening we were sitting behind their horse trailer visiting and I had a beer or three and would drink a few swallows, then Ronnie would drink the rest. We went through a couple or three more like that and Ronnie got to feeling rough, so Gene told him to go get in his house.

His house was a two horse, round nose, double axle, bumper pull trailer which had two expanded metal doors on the round nose so the two Chimps each had a cubbyhole to ride in when they hauled them. They also hauled a pony that the Chimps rode on during their acts.

The pony rode on one side of the trailer and their props for their acts were on the other side of the divider. The side where they hauled the props had a hole in the floor which was put there on purpose. It was so they could step in there and relieve themselves, if you get my drift. Anyhow, Ronnie had had enough so Gene told him to go get in his house.

Ronnie went straight to his cubbyhole, opened the door, and

Rodeo Stories II

sat down in there and looked and acted like a grumpy old man. Well, I went in there to relieve myself and was standing right in front of him. At the same time I started giving Ronnie a hard time.

I was saying things like, "Yeah, you can't hang can you old man? So, you just go on and go to bed. The rest of us are going to cowboy up and drink some more beer. But, you just be a good old man and go on to bed like you was told. You hear?"

Gene and Bobby told me not to pick on him like that because it would make him mad. I said, "Aw, he can't understand what I'm saying. Besides, he's tight as a fiddle." They said, "OK, but you better leave him alone because if he gets mad he might hurt you."

I was being pretty stupid because I was a little tight myself and said, "You ain't gonna hurt nobody, are you, Ronnie?" I had a new Bailey straw hat on my head and I was sure proud of that new hat. Well, old Ronnie had had enough and quick as lightening he snatched that hat off my head.

I yelled, "Hey, he got my hat. Gimme back that hat." Gene and Bobby hollered out, "Don't try to take it away from him or he'll hurt you." Gene stuck his head in the trailer and said, "Ronnie, I'll get the BB gun." I stood there like a kid waiting for his little brother to do what daddy had told him to do.

I said, "He ain't kidding, he's gonna get the BB gun." I felt pretty sure that I'd said just the right thing. Well, it backfired because all of a sudden Ronnie just squashed my hat and wrung it out like you'd wring out a wet wash rag. Then, he took it and stuffed it behind his butt and just set back on it and folded his arms across his chest and I swear he was grinning at me.

I said, "He tore up my hat," and Gene said, "Well, I told you not to mess with him." Gene and Bobby and Rusty were all laughing and rolling around holding their bellies, laughing 'till they hurt. I turned around and started to gripe at Ronnie, but he reached out and pulled the cage door shut and just folded his arms and sat there on my hat like a big old Budda or something.

Some time later I was at the San Diego Sports Arena sitting on the ground out behind the chutes and Gene came walking down the ramp holding Ronnie's hand. I hollered out, "Hey, Ronnie," and Ronnie pulled loose and ran and jumped in my lap, pulled a pack of cigarettes out of my pocket, got one out, then threw the rest of the pack on the ground. He remembered me.

Gene and Bobby Clark were some really great guys and they were a blast to be around. They helped a lot of young rodeo clowns. That's what rodeo is all about and that's why I loved it. You just couldn't find any better people in the world than a bunch of cowboys. Still can't.

CHIMP ROBERTSON
TROPHY BUCKLES

I guess it's always been that way where some cowboys ride for the trophy buckle and some ride for the money. And of course, some ride for both. But, there are certain rodeos that give a trophy buckle that is sure desired by the cowboys. But, rather than me saying which buckles were more desired, I asked a few cowboys what buckle they'd won that they liked best and also what buckle did they wish they'd won during their rodeo career and here's what they had to say on the subject.

Dickey Cox; I won Cheyenne in 1974 and it was such a great win because I think every cowboy wants to win Cheyenne, The Daddy of Them All and especially that buckle with the diamond in it.

Randy Majers; The National Finals buckle would be my pick and the Cow Palace buckle would be next.

Don Mellgren; The prettiest ones in my day were the Salinas buckles. I wish I could have won one of those. I gave a lot of buckles away to friends and grandkids. I kind of wish I wouldn't have.

Ronnie Van Winkle; I won buckles while participating in youth rodeos, college, and in the Pros, but the one I have worn since I won it is the Texas A&M College Rodeo buckle. I guess everyone would like to have won the World Championship and the buckle that goes along with that.

Johnny E. Roberts; The Western Region buckle which I won twice, in 1975 and 1976. Some of the proudest rides were big wins that didn't give up buckles.

Abe Morris; Salinas and Dodge City. After I retired San Antonio started presenting some very nice buckles. The nicest one I won was from the Circuit Finals and it's the one I wear to all of the biggest occasions. It still catches everyone's attention.

Brent Clark; The XIT Rodeo in Dalhart, Texas because they gave the best looking buckles.

Bill Putnam; The Jess Evans Memorial buckle, but I missed it by one point and it was a beautiful buckle.

Andy L. Adams; I won the ARA Finals average buckle and I wished it had been the NFR and the Double M Rodeo buckles.

Casey McGlaun; I guess the most coveted buckles that I won would be the Texas Circuit All Around Rookie of the Year and the Texas Circuit Bull riding Rookie of the Year. The most desired would have to be Salinas and Albuquerque where I won 2nd at both.

Barney Brehmer; I won Pendleton, but at that time they never gave buckles. And of course, the PRCA World Champion buckle.

Charlie Cook; I made three trips to Salinas and nothing. I would have let them keep all the money to have had that buckle. I placed twice at Pecos and that was another buckle I would liked to have had.

Monty Penny; My pick would have been the Salinas buckle, besides the NFR buckle.

Don Schmid; The one you crave of course is to have the World Championship buckle hanging on your belt. I always felt the most pride of the Senior Finals buckles, more from the idea of winning it at an advanced age when most are hobbling around and complaining.

Wes Ward; Other than the World Championship I would have

liked to won the Salinas, Cheyenne, and Pendleton buckles. But, I wear the Dodge City Roundup buckle because it was my biggest win. I also love my West of the Pecos buckle.

Ken Rigler; My favorite is the last one I won from the PRCA California Golden Bear Rodeo in 1994 at Huntington Beach.

Joe Latona; The one I craved was the AFR average buckle. I had it won until the last bull and rodeo him for seven seconds.

Randy Taylor; I won the Pendleton Roundup buckle and wished I'd have won the Daddy, as I won 1st. in the 1st. go round and 2nd. in the 2nd. go round, but spurred over my horse's neck in the short go round and only won 4th. I sure wanted that Cheyenne buckle. I also wanted the Oklahoma High School Rodeo Association buckle and the Prairie Circuit Finals buckle, but got screwed out of it, literally. The Lord has provided me with humility. We all have different fates.

Rod Sinclair; Well, I suppose it would have been a Canadian Championship buckle or at least a Canadian Finals Average hampionship buckle. That's what I really wanted.

Gary Williams; I won the Circuit Finals in 1983 and 1984 and won the Vinita, Oklahoma Coors buckle, but the one I craved was the NFR buckle as I ended up 17th one year rodeoing with Joe Spearman and Rick Carpenter.

Red Doyal; Growing up in the panhandle area and wanting to be a cowboy you hear about the Old Settlers Reunion rodeo at Roaring Springs, Texas. I worked it many times, but only won it one time and that was the buckle I wore most if the time. I had three buckles I won in a row at Hardin-Simmons University and my three girls wear them today.

Dave Sampsel; Salinas, California, 2007 is my favorite. I'd won the PBR twice there and always did well there. I wish I could have won Ft. Worth, but I placed second, third, fifth, and sixth, but never was able to win it. Cheyenne was also a dream buckle that eluded me. Another would have been any NFR average buckle. I still hold the arena record at Salinas with 184 points, a 93 and a 91.

Jay Foscalina; In my neck of the woods Salinas had the finest buckles. I never won it. My brother Joe won the CHSRA State buckle and I came close to winning it two years later.

When I received Jerry LaValley's story, "THE TROPHY BUCKLE,' my thoughts drifted back to a rodeo at Dumas, Texas where Morris Stevens had the stock. This was back when we could stand around in the arena. I had already ridden my bull and was standing out in front of the chutes with several other cowboys.

Two guys standing next to me were talking about where they were going next. One guy said, "Are you going to Dalhart or Pampa?" His buddy answered, "I'm going to Dalhart." The cowboy who asked the question said, "Well, the bulls are tougher at Dalhart," and his buddy said, "Yeah, but they give better buckles at Dalhart."

RICHARD FLECHSIG
STAY AWAKE, DAMN IT

Back in about 1963, myself, Whitey Tapley, and Jack Wolf were driving to a rodeo in Peoria, Illinois where Jim Shoulders had the stock. We are driving along in the middle of farm country with not much scenery and Jack was sound asleep in the back seat.

I told Whitey we needed to wake Jack up and told him I was going to slam on the brakes (no cars were behind us) and when I do you slap the dash board and yell, "Cover your face. We're going through the windshield."

At the correct time I hit the brakes and Whitey yells, "We're going through the windshield," as he slapped the dash board and Jack came out of the backseat like a cat shot in the rear with a tack.

Needless to say he was awake the rest of the trip. This method beats running off on the rumble strips all too heck.

DON ENDSLEY
A RODEO STORY

I've wanted to be in the rodeo world since I was a kid, as a bull rider in high school and into several years after that until the mid seventies, when I decided I wanted to be a rodeo announcer. After working my way through small time rodeos for a few years taking a job with anyone who would hire me for the experience, I took the jump and got my PRCA card in 1976 and announced all year for Bob Barnes Rodeo Company and then got hired by Tommy Steiner Rodeo in 1977.

I was in the right place at the right time and also worked for other top producers. One of my most exciting times was when Steiner hired me to announce the big American Royal Rodeo in Kansas City because as a kid of about 5 or 6 years old, my parents were living in Kansas City and they took me to the American Royal. It was my first time to see the cowboys, horses, and all the fun in the old Royal Stadium Arena.

This was in the 50's and twenty five years later as I stood in the announcer's box looking out into the audience and I could remember it like yesterday and could see that little kid sitting in those seats with his eyes big as silver dollars. It had come full circle.

In 1977 or 1878, me and another fella were driving to Winston/Salem to do the advance promotion on a big rodeo that Winston/RJ Reynolds was having, as Winston was a big sponsor at the time and this was in their home town and it was a big deal.

It was 2:am and I was driving with the other cowboy sleeping in the back seat and he was snoring very, very loud, because his nose had been broken so many times. Turning the radio up didn't really help much. It gave me time to think of just what I was a part of at that moment.

A young, green fella from an Arkansas farm now getting to

work and travel and be friends with people I had looked up to all my life, people who were my heroes...and one of them was asleep in my back seat. A man I had idolized since I was a kid. It was the greatest cowboy Champion of all time, Jim Shoulders. I had to pinch myself and smile.

LEE JONES
TRAVELING STORIES

I won't name the four steer wrestlers who left Oklahoma headed to the Cow Palace. Two of them were in the front and the other two were sleeping in the camper. When they got to Las Vegas they traded places. The new drivers pulled out and turned the wrong way and drove all night back toward Oklahoma.

Donnie Bowles and I left one night to go to San Angelo, Texas. When we stopped and filled up with gas we asked the attendant how far it was to San Angelo and he said 110 miles. I drove that tank of gas out and when I filled up the next time I asked the attendant how far it was to San Angelo and he said 150 miles. The road had forked at the first station and I got on the wrong one, ending up in Fredericksburg.

One time Donnie and I were coming home from the Big Springs, Texas rodeo and about two in the morning we started running out of gas just as we came into Snyder, Texas. We rocked and coasted about a mile down a long hill and came to a stop down town. We had passed a lot of stations on our way in so I thought we could drain the gas hoses at those stations and get some gas that way.

So, when we got our gas can out Donnie stuck his pistol in his boot. We walked and walked, draining gas hoses and hiding from a cop car that kept driving by. We didn't get 3 ounces total and finally ran out of gas stations. There was a motel right by the last station so I cut the dinger hose that lay across the driveway and ciphered my can full.

When we got back to the pickup there was a cop waiting. I told him we'd ran out of gas and that we had gone all the way to the last station draining their hoses. The cop said, "Yeah, well, I've been looking for you boys. I have a 5 gallon can of gas to give you." We had hid from him 4 or 5 times because Donnie had his shooting iron in his boot.

One year I made the finals at the Houston Rodeo in the bull dogging and Clyde Vamvoras had made it in the bare backs so he rode down there with me and my wife Jackie. Jackie had a Coke in a bottle and Clyde, with a full lip full of snuff, reached over and took her Coke and took a big swig then handed it back to her. She was horrified and insisted that Clyde keep the Coke as she had all she wanted.

I had also entered the calf roping there to qualify for the All-Around honors so I asked Clyde why he hadn't entered the bull riding since I knew at one time he rode them pretty good. He gave me the best description of bull riding I'd ever heard when he said, "Them big bastards have drug their rear end across my face for the last time."

JESSE "CR" HALL
COWBOY FROM HARLEM

I'm one of many, one of 8 children raised in Harlem, New York by a single mom. Of course most everyone knows how rough the city ghetto life could be by just reading, going to the movies or watching TV. I was always unusual with the group I hung out with. My mother was very strict and tough so I was afraid of going against the grain. There was trouble all around me, but I knew how to dodge it because of repercussion from mom.

When I graduated from high school in New York a bunch of us went to Bear Mountain which was an area in upstate New York where they had a lot of activities such as a zoo, a park, boating, and horseback riding. Someone suggested we go riding so we all went for the first time ever and I loved it.

Back in the Bronx they had several riding academies which I rode at every weekend. I became very knowledgeable because of several Pro Cowboys at that academy such as Gene Lorenzo, Jack Meli, and Charlie Parks, all PRCA Cowboys and good ones, too.

I started going to the Cowtown Rodeo every Saturday Night and Memorial Weekend until the season ended on Labor Day. I had a permit in 1965 and paid the rookie price in learning to ride bareback and in the steer wrestling and won my card in 1967 and was an up and coming so I started going to more rodeos.

June, 1st, 1968, I bucked off a bareback horse at the Cowtown Rodeo in New Jersey and broke three vertebras in my neck. Before the operation which was the only chance of living or being paralyzed, I was given the last rights by the pastor and my family was summoned.

My third, forth, and fifth vertebras were fused together and of course I had a long recovery period. In 1971 I renewed my PRCA card and started rodeoing again. I went to several Larry Mahan Rodeo Schools to sharpen my skills and headed down the road to Denver, Odessa, Lawton, Durant, the Cow Palace, Fort Worth and several more. I wasn't winning much, but was knocking on the door and the only compliment I got from any one was from Larry Mahan at the Cow Palace when he said, "Charlie Reno," which is the name I used at that time, "They don't know you yet, but keep coming."

In 1972, I was on the rodeo road and broke my riding wrist at Tulsa, Oklahoma during the steer wrestling and had to turn a steer out at Fort Worth so I headed back home to New York. I met my wife Marie during that time, got a job, and started raising a family.

Rodeo wasn't in the picture, but it was still in my heart so in 1979 I started to rodeo again in the APRA Association which covered the east, mid-south, and north region of the country and was made up of PRCA, IPRA and various other associations throughout the country and there were no gimmes.

During the 1979 season I was leading in the barebacks and the All-Around when a bareback horse fell on my foot and broke it. About two months were left of the season before our Finals and the runner-up cowboy passed me for the Bareback and All-Around Title.

In 1980 all my hard work, denial from some people of being totally fair and my positive attitude and faith, finally came through and I fulfilled my dream by winning the APRA All-Around and Bareback Championship, the one and only since in that Association. Not bad for an African American from the ghetto of New York City.

BILL THORPE
KOKOMO, THE HORSE MOTHER PRAYED FOR

In the winter of '82 when I clowned and worked a rodeo for the Lone Star Rodeo Company at Shelbyville, Tennessee I found a Tennessee Walking Mule that I just thought I HAD to have. After dealing on this animal for a week I was $800 short on money. So, I called my mother and said, "Mom! Loan me $800 so I can buy a walking mule." She said, "I don't know, Billy. We'll have to pray on it." Then, I knew I was not going to get $800 to buy any Tennessee Walking Mule.

That Monday night I didn't pray, but Momma must have because the next morning Randy Sullivan knocked on my door and asked me if I wanted a horse. I said, "Randy, I don't have any money to buy a horse." He said, "I don't wanna sell you a horse, I wanna GIVE you a horse."

So, I took the gift horse and took him to the corral. I didn't have a feed pan to feed him in so I put his feed in a Frizbee. The next morning when I go out to feed, this little pony picks up his Frizbee and brings it to me to put his feed in. I didn't pray, but Momma did. By the middle of the morning I could throw a frizbee as far as I could toss it and that little horse would bring it back to get his bite of grain.

Bill Thorpe

That afternoon I watched him stand on his hind legs as tall as he could in order to eat the Spanish Moss from the oak trees. So, with the help of a broom and a wad of Spanish Moss I taught this horse to walk on his hind feet. Two tricks in one day. He had a rope burn on his flanks so I found out I could doctor him and say, "Don't kick," and he would almost kick my head off and kick as hard as he could. With the help of a bite of grain, he got that cue. Three tricks in one day.

On Friday I used him in a rodeo act at Green Cove Springs, Florida and I had taught him to lie down, walk on hind legs, to rear, to say 'yes' and 'no', to kick on command, to catch a frizbee and to 'smile' when I took off the hackamore. I know this was Divine Intervention that I was blessed with this small Cracker Pony and Me and ole Kokomo toured the rodeo circuit for 20 some years.

Everyone should have Cotton Candy at a rodeo. My friend Jan Barbie Payne asked for stories about her dad and their Lloyd Barby Rodeo Company. He had a great set of bucking bulls. I remember Pete, Repeat, Cut Across Shorty, and State Trooper, all great bulls, but none of them was as great as Cotton Candy.

Cotton Candy had to be the first 'tame' rodeo bull I was ever around. I saw kids ride him around, then pet him and rub all over him. But, I'll never forget the night in Dumas, Texas when Tommy Carr tried to ride him. He spun like a top. He was a 'rodeo'-looking bull with big horns and a huge hump and he bucked Tommy down underneath him.

Cotton Candy stopped dead still in his tracks with the cowboy underneath. I think Cotton Candy might be the only bull in rodeo history who raised his foot in order for the cowboy to crawl out from under him. I will never forget that bull and Tommy Carr in Dumas.

STEVE SCOTT
WHY DIDN'T YOU GRAB THE WHEEL

I was living on the Fame Farm in Clements, California. It was the headquarters for Rodeo Stock Contractors Inc. Bob Cook let me live there because I was clowning all of his rodeos and when Bob didn't have a rodeo I'd work for Cotton Rosser and the Christensen Brothers. I worked a lot with Jerry Mariluch. He was about as crazy as anybody I'd ever been around and we had a lots of fun.

Jerry had a Volkswagen and we liked to get some girls in it and play a trick on them. Jerry would be driving with his girl in the front passenger seat and I'd sit behind her in the back seat with my girlfriend on the driver side of the back seat. We'd be going down the road and Jerry would pull the latch on his seat back and lay it almost all the way back and crawl backwards over the seat into the back between me and my girl. At the same time he'd yell, "We're gonna crash!"

Immediately, I'd jump from the back seat over the top of him and into the driver's seat and take over the driving. It would scare the girls, or whoever we had in there to death. Usually, there'd be lots of screaming and cussing and we just thought that was as funny as it could be and would get a real good laugh out of it.

We decided to go see my girlfriend in Lodi one night, and she had a girlfriend for Jerry. We were going to drive around on the back roads out in the country and drink some wine so we stopped on the way and got four bottles of Boone's Farm Strawberry Hill. We only drank the good stuff. We finished off the four bottles of wine so we stopped back at my girlfriend's house and she stole some of her daddy's whiskey.

Driving around the back roads we passed around the fifth of whiskey and we pulled the seat swapping trick on the girls. My girlfriend had already seen it, but it scared the pee out of the other girl. She said, "I think I peed on myself a little bit." We all laughed so hard we had to stop and get out in the road and staggered around laughing till it hurt.

By this time we were getting pretty drunk and it was getting late. We took them back to my girlfriend's house and dropped them off so we could go back to the ranch. My girlfriend ran in and took a couple of beers out of the fridge and me and Jerry drank them on the way back to the Farm.

The bunk house was about three hundred yards or so off

the county road. It was a long driveway. He dropped me off and decided that he was going to go to another old gal's house. As he turned around I leaned up against an old tallow tree and was watching his tail lights go back up the driveway.

He turned out on the county road and was going through the gears when all of a sudden the car swerved off the road and jumped the ditch and hit the fence, but luckily it didn't do much damage to the fence. I took off half running, half staggering, stumbling and staggering to go see what the heck was going on. It took me a while, but I finally got to the blacktop and had to sit down because I was really getting sick.

Finally, I got up and staggered on down to where he was and grabbed the passenger door, pulled it open and looked in. The driver's seat was laid almost all the way back and Mariluch was lying halfway in the back seat and halfway in the floorboard. He was moaning and groaning.

I said, "What the hell are you doing?" He looked over at me and said, "Why didn't you grab the wheel?" I said, "You dropped me off back yonder at the ranch!" He started laughing, and I started laughing and we laughed so hard I could hardly catch my breath. We staggered back to the bunkhouse and went and got his car the next day.

CURT BROWN
MONTGOMERY, ALABAMA

My brother Lyle and I left Michigan heading to a rodeo in Montgomery Alabama. We met our brothers Ronnie, Dallas, and Barry at a hotel and later we went to the restaurant just down the road from the coliseum. We were discussing our ordeal with the cop at the gate a year earlier and how we were going to have to drive past him like we had in the previous year with him in pursuit.

While they were discussing the incident I drew a cowboy

hat on a white place mat then cut it out with a scissors I borrowed from the waitress. It looked almost identical to the window decal we got the previous year. However, instead of it reading Southeastern Livestock Exposition and Rodeo I printed the words, Let Me in Free Pass.

Everyone thought I did a good job with my art work so we headed to the rodeo to pay our entry fees. Barry was driving and had the special decal I had made stuck to the windshield of his 59 Oldsmobile. As we approached the cop at the gate he saw the decal and motioned us to come on in.

Barry drove by the cop very slowly and pointed to the decal making sure the cop read it and then we sped on through the gate. We were laughing as the cop just stood there watching us drive off. There were five of us Brown brothers in that rodeo that night. After the rodeo was over Lyle and I drove back to Michigan. It was about 1:00 AM when Lyle pulled his car into our sister and brother-in- law, Gloria and Bernie's driveway and said, "I'm going to throw an M-80 under their bed."

Now, just the mention of an M-80 reminds me of the time me and my brothers Lyle and Barry went to Toledo Ohio to buy some fireworks because they were not legal in Michigan. Once we arrived at the fireworks store the man who worked there showed us some fireworks that were new on the market. He told us we had to buy some M-80's because they were much more powerful than the Cherry Bomb which was the most powerful firecracker of that time.

We were headed back home to Michigan and Barry was driving his 1959 Oldsmobile. I was sitting in the back seat alone when Lyle rolled down his window and lit the fuse to an M-80 because we were anxious to see how bad it would sound. Lyle gave it a toss, but it blew back inside the car and landed right beside me on the back seat.

I let out a yell and jumped as far away from it as I could, hugging the door as Lyle hollered, "Plug your ears!" Barry was driving the car with his elbows and his fingers stuck in both ears. In an instant the car was filled with smoke so bad Barry had to roll down his window and stick his head out to be able to see the road. Once the smoke cleared I looked to the middle of the seat where the explosion took place and there was a hole in the seat the size of a softball and just as deep.

Anyway, we quietly entered Gloria and Bernie's house through the back door and as we were walking down the hallway to their bedroom I noticed the thermostat on the wall so I turned it up to the maximum heat. I think it was around 90 degrees.

We walked quietly down the hall and to the bedroom and the door being open made it easy. Lyle held the big fire cracker as I lit it and he tossed it under the bed. We took off running out of the house and as we were running down the driveway we heard a loud boom and we were cracking up as we drove off.

We saw Gloria and Bernie a couple of days later and they had a pretty good idea where that fire cracker came from. Gloria said, "We were finally able to go back to bed, but it wasn't long before we both woke up sweating and wondering why it was so hot in the house."

RICHARD MURRAY
JULIO'S BULLS

Shawn McNair, Jimmy Miller, and myself, were entered at the Crows Landing, California rodeo with Jimmy and I, in the bull riding and Shawn, fighting bulls. We figured with a bull fighter in the car with us we had a check for sure, but the odds were favored.

Sure enough when the Flying U got the show on the way I was first one out in the bull riding and my bull fouled me so I declared. Well Tony, I don't remember his last name, was running the bulls and flanking for the show and he got so upset when I was rewarded a re-ride he yelled out, "I got a bull for him."

It was either J-22 or 26, I'm not sure, but he was a big,

Rodeo Stories II

painted bull with horns. That was all I knew. I could hear the guy talking smack and making comments and it was getting to me. All I could think about was that bull for the next three sections plus a section of women's bareback riding and I was pacing behind the chutes like a bird dog wanting to get at that duck. Man, I was hungry and hot.

I could catch a word here and there, but my focus was tunnel. When they ran the bull in the chute and I was getting on I heard a bet taking place with the announcer. "I bet I throw this guy off hard." That was it for me so I slid up and called for the gate. The bull turned back both ways and I remember looking down at McNair and seeing him turn him back under me.

When the whistle blew I jumped off and as I passed that flank man, McNair grabbed me and said, "Hey, Man, get your money." I was like, "What?" McNair said, "Yeah, man, he bet against you." So, I went to get the money and he had to borrow twenty bucks to cover the hundred I was taking off his hands. Boy, talk about humiliation.

One Wednesday evening out in Lincoln, California I went out to the flying U ranch to get on practice bulls where Julio bucked them for us guys. He generally bucked the bulls he was talking to the next weekend performance and that was nice because I got to see what was what in case I drew anything I knew.

But, that evening when I showed up the bulls were already loaded and no one was really in a hurry that I could see. So, I set my bag down and walked around to see what I could get on. Jeff Sheer was in the arena and when saw me he began to tease me and make comments at me, but I ignored him and kept going about my business.

I got my stuff out and hung my rope, etc, and again Jeff started ragging me, something about, "Never seeing me really ride," and things like that. I thought to myself, "What's his problem, anyway," but, he wouldn't quit. My blood was boiling and I was getting hot, but I wasn't letting him see it. I just went ahead and warmed up my rope and got focused.

When I climbed up to the top of bucking chutes with my rope I eyed a few bulls and spotted a juicy little Brindle. So, I asked if any one had had him and the only reply was, "No, but if you think you can ride him, go for it."

So, I got my rope on the Brindle, pulled on my glove and proceeded to mount up and hammer down. When Jeff saw me getting on with no boots or spurs, only my tennis shoes, he said, "You're not riding that bull like that, Murray." I just remember I kept on with my business. I was hot and I wanted to shut him up so I slid up to my rope called for the gate and away we went.

That little Brindle cracked it back both ways right in the latch and my only mind set was to ride the hair off this booger. I snapped him as I got off on my feet and right after that it was quiet. "Ha. Take that," I thought. I just snapped him maybe just for a moment, but I got respect and Jeff said that was the best bull he had seen me ride. I thought to myself, "Maybe this guy was just pushing me to be better. After all, he had been to the NFR and he knew what it took." Just for that day anyway I was walking tall and I felt a little respect. And, even though it was short lived it felt great.

DUDE SMITH
OLD TIME RODEO LEGEND

In 1953, at Grady, New Mexico, the Pettigrews had a bull dogging contest with the top twenty-five doggers in the world. John Dalton won it and I won second and in 1966, I ended up sixteenth in the world. Bull dogging had been a good event for me in my rodeo career and I worked both ends of the arena.

In 1966 we were in Shreveport, Louisiana, in the Joe Dean bar. There were three of us, Roy Duvall, Donnie Johnson, and myself. We were talking about bull dogging, drinking whiskey, chasing it with beer, and we were odd man out for five bucks and the other two paid.

We worked up a match and there was a little misfit steer in the bunch and Roy had him first and won the first go round on him. I had him in the second go-round and I was 3 on him, and won that go round. Other than that little steer the others were very un-even and the sorriest steers we ever bull dogged. I don't think there was a steer other than that little one that was thrown under seven seconds.

We go to talking and Roy and I matched a bull dogging for five hundred dollars. Donnie Johnson bet me another hundred that I'd made a bad bet. Tommy Steiner had the stock and he told us we could pick out the steers we wanted after the steers had been picked out for the last performance.

We picked out the toughest ones left in that bunch and we each dogged each other's steers. I dogged his four and he dogged my four. The steer I had missed Roy almost let get away. We had a two minute time limit if you missed one. By throwing that steer I'd missed, he beat me. A lot of money was bet on that match.

I was awful hot that year. I had won money at Ft. Worth, San Antonio, Montgomery, Alabama, and San Angelo. At that time I was right in there for the lead for the year, but obligations at home kept me from continuing and I ended up sixteenth for the year.

MARK WHITAKER
OUR PAL, MONKEY

About 1978 my buddy Andy Pollock and me were out at a rodeo in Pierson, Florida and we had dragged our buddy, Monkey Sellars, along for the ride. At this point Monkey failed to inform us that his wife was 9 months pregnant and due any day, but more on that later.

After we rode our bulls and was leaving the arena we saw two girls that we knew that were broke down on the side of the road in a little MG car. We stopped and tried to get the car to run, but mechanics we ain't so we hooked up a pull strap and pulled that little car all the way to Cocoa, Fla.

We had to stop for gas and somehow at 3:00 in the morning Monkey wound up with three cases of beer. Now, back in those days you couldn't by beer after midnight on Saturday so I'm not even gonna try to explain how he got the beer. Needless to say, by the time we got the girls to their house we were slightly toasted. We said goodbye and started for home.

Andy was driving his truck, but soon realized he didn't know his inebriated way home. I did, so I was elected to drive. As we were heading down I-4 the sun was coming up. Monkey was in the middle, Andy on the door, and me behind the wheel, all passed out. I was in the medium strip asleep at the wheel running about 60 MPH when the bouncing around stirred Andy awake.

Mark Whitaker, Photo credit, Mike Rastelli.

He just looked over at me and yelled, "Hey, Whit! Wanna get this thing back on the road?" As I opened my eyes, we were about 500 feet from an overpass pylon. I just grabbed the stick, dropped into 3rd gear and mashed the gas and pulled back onto the interstate. I don't think I blinked twice all the rest of the way home.

Now, to finish up with what happened when we took Monkey home about 7:00 that morning. As we pulled up to his mobile home Andy stepped out of the truck to let Monkey out and it was at this point that I saw the door of the trailer open and the barrel of a gun sticking out.

Then, his wife was screaming something about a female dog and other choice words and it was at that point that I yelled for Andy to get the hell back in the truck. He grabbed Monkey by the shirt and jerked him out of the truck and we jumped in and got the hell out of there. We never heard from Monkey for several months, but he never got shot and to this day he still refuses to talk about what really happened.

JIMMY BLOTZ
ROANOKE TO LONE OAK

Me and a few buddies were entered at a rodeo in Roanoke, Texas, that my girlfriend had called in for us and it was a Saturday performance that started at 8:00 that evening. I always went to rodeos a little early to make sure there was plenty of time to get ready so we started for Roanoke which was about fifty miles west of Irving.

We showed up at the arena where we had ridden before and felt sure this was the right place. As we drove up to the rodeo it was about 6:00 PM and there was nobody in sight. We thought at least the stock contractor would be there. We waited a few minutes and decided to go up to the Dairy Queen and get a bite to eat. When we got there we asked around and nobody knew anything about a rodeo.

We started to just wait, but something told me to call my girlfriend. We found a payphone and I called her and said, "Are you sure you entered us up on Saturday night in Roanoke?" and she said, in a shocking voice, "ROANOKE"? She then said, "You're not entered at Roanoke. You're entered in Lone Oak." I said, "Holy Crap," and just hung up.

I told the guys and the race was on. It was 2 hours east of us and we drove like madmen to get there on time and we put on our spurs and chaps and rosined our ropes going down the highway. Now, this was a sight because there were 4 of us and we were driving my mom's 4 door Monte Carlo.

We drove 90 to 100 mph all the way there and when we showed up my bull was in the chute and my buddies were in the 2nd performance. I jumped out of the car carrying my bull rope when a buddy of mine ran up to me and said, "You have #8, one of the best in the stock." I threw my rope on him and started to climb on when I noticed one of my rowels was missing off my spur. I'd forgotten to fix it from the last rodeo.

The big, black Angus took one jump and turned back to the left away from my hand and I had a good hold of him, but my right spur was worthless so I just started letting him have it with the bare shank. I won the bull riding and didn't get to stretch or loosen up at all. I just did what came second nature to me and it all worked out.

BRAD BESANCON
STARTING OFF A LITTLE OVER MY HEAD

I started riding bulls in the fall of 1979 my senior year of high school. I remember as a little boy watching a rodeo on the television and knowing right then that I wanted to be a bull rider.

That first year was pretty rough as I did not have a clue what I was doing and really didn't get much help from experienced bull riders. My summer of bull riding in 1980 was cut short when my appendix ruptured and I had to stop for the rest of the summer and still green as a gourd when it came to riding. I did win my first check that fall at a rodeo in Jonesboro, Arkansas, fifty three dollars and eighty cents and I thought I was on my way to the NFR.

In the spring of 1981, after some promising practice pen sessions, I entered a 3 rodeo series that Jerald Smith was putting on in Hot Springs, Arkansas. I had only been on 20 or so bulls, but I thought I was on the right track. Little did I know there was a huge difference in the practice bulls and the killers that Jerald hauled.

I remember looking out over the back pens at a sea of Brindle hides, horns like baseball bats, and big, I bet they averaged 1700 lbs. It was pretty intimidating for a guy who was just starting out, but I still did not know the level I had jumped to.

I had drawn #111 Shotgun Sam and there was no need to ask if he bucked as I was told by everyone that they all bucked in this pen and hooked. I got down on ole Sam, pulled my string tight and nodded my head and it all went south from there.

He started around to the left and I went in there after him sitting pretty good, but he turned back so quick that he nearly hit the chutes then changed back to the right so fast I did not have the experience to react. Yep, I was on the outside of a Brindle tornado and hung up tight.

Now, this was my first hang up so all I knew was to get my arm over his neck if I could and try to stay on my feet. No dice here as I was whirling around like a helicopter blade totally unable to get my feet under me.

A round or so later I guess he saw me out of the corner of his eye and turned back on me and hooked me upside the head hard enough to black my vision out, but I could still hear just fine. He then started back to the right and by now I was under him and he was stomping my legs every time he came down on me. It felt like someone was working me over with sledge hammers.

Well, I was hung up FOREVER. I could hear the crowd screaming and the bull fighters cussing and trying to get in on me and feel the hoofs hammering me and every so often he would sling his head around and hit me in the head or ribs for good measure. I thought to myself, "This is it. I'm going to die bull riding and haven't even gotten started good yet."

All of a sudden I felt my hand move a little bit in the handhold. Hmmm, maybe its not over yet. Over the next several jumps it got looser and looser until my hand popped out and rocketed me into the fence and I thought, "Well, looks like I ain't gonna die after all."

As I held onto the fence some jackass with foul whisky soaked breath was hollering me from the crowd side of the fence, telling me that he really got his money's worth that evening. If I could have seen him I would have knocked his head off, but I was still seeing black. I actually thought I may have been blinded. Over the course of the next several minutes a pinpoint of light got bigger and bigger until I could finally see again.

As I looked out over the arena I saw scraps of clothes everywhere. I looked down and saw that the bull had stomped my boots off and I had used dog collars to keep them on. My socks were stretched out where he has stomped my feet after the boots were gone, my chaps were in pieces and my pants were split from the crotch to the knees. My shirt was in shreds and I had no idea where my hat and rope were.

As I hobbled around the arena picking up my tattered belongings I figured maybe I had bitten off a little more than I could chew with this caliber of bulls. Hell, it's a wonder I didn't get a ticket for littering the rodeo grounds with that stellar crowd pleasing performance.

I started going to some lower lever amateur shows and did learn to ride at an above average skill level and won my share later on down the road. I will tell you this though, "Do not start out on a killer pen of big Brindles hauled by Jerald Smith. It is not good for your wardrobe or your pride."

TIM SAMPLE
FIVE AND A BUG

This is just some fun memories from the early days back in the mid 80's when me and my four hauling partners traveled to jackpots and rodeos in my 1973 Volkswagen Bug. Usually, on Sunday afternoons after coming back from a rodeo somewhere that weekend we'd go to a jackpot to win a little money so we could rodeo the next weekend. We'd pool our money so at least one of us could get on and win some more gas money.

We would go to the Cold River Cattle Company on Sunday after the jackpot and play pool for money to get our entry fees and we'd usually win just enough to get to the next rodeo.

One time the five of us were all crammed into the Bug and were headin' to a rodeo at Leesville, Louisana and we probably looked crazy to other travelers on the road because about all they could see were five big hats jammed close together and a bunch of feet hanging out the windows.

A State Trooper stopped us and said he just had to see what the heck was going on with this VW. The five riggin' bags in front were so heavy it was loaded down and he said it was the funniest thing he'd ever seen in his life. Thank God he didn't give us a ticket for having our feet and legs sticking out of the windows because we barely had enough cash for our entry fees.

By the time we'd get to a rodeo we would be so sore and cramped up from being in that little car that we'd hate to get back in it. So, we'd go to a bar or pool hall and sometimes we'd win and sometimes we'd lose, but we always made it one way or another.

If you can picture all of us traveling to rodeos in a VW and hardly able to get out of the car and barely able to stand up straight or walk for an hour or so after we got there and we did this for a year or so and loved every minute of it.

DALE WOODARD
(1992 NFR Barrel man)
THE WILD RIDE

One of the rodeos that I always enjoyed working was at Sonora, California. This rodeo is held every year in May on Mother's Day weekend. The town of Sonora sits in a beautiful mountainous setting. One of the unique events at this rodeo is the Wild Ride where the contestants ride saddle broncs and dress up in wild costumes.

Some are dressed like big-busted women wearing dresses and wigs and the more outlandish the costume the better. It is a judged event with the winner taking the cash prize that is put up by the rodeo committee.

An act that I used for years was called the Bubble Gum Box and in this act I used two mean roosters. The gist of the act was that this was supposed to be a box of bubble gum that I had found. Before I gave the gum away I tested it and to my surprise the gum turned out to be chicken manure.

Once these roosters were out of the box one of them somehow ended up going down the front of my baggie pants. When I finally got him fished out of my pants I would say to the announcer that I thought he had untied my belly button. Then, the announcer would say, "Well, I've always heard that the early bird gets the worm." Then, I would look at him with sad eyes and say, "Please don't say that."

Anyway, back to the Wild Ride. David Bothum was a good bronc rider during this time and I'm sure he made the NFR several times. On this day he came to me and asked if he could use one of my roosters in the Wild Ride so I said he could and the deal was on.

David was the third rider out and he wore wooly chaps with lots of baby powder sprinkled on them and a big old, long, yellow rain slicker. Once he got sat down on the bronc I handed him my rooster and he tucked it under his free arm with his hand holding the rooster's body. When he nodded for the gate the bronc reared out and started bucking and David was spurring that bronc just like he did during the regular bronc riding contest, but when the horse go to the top of the third jump David threw the rooster in the air.

Between the height of the jump and the distance of the throw the rooster fluttered down from about twenty-five feet in the air. I hustled over and caught my rooster and as I walked past the Judge on the left side I hard him say, "I've got my winner," and sure enough when the contest was concluded David was proclaimed the winner.

Twenty years later I was in Las Vegas watching the National Finals Rodeo and as I walked through the South Point Hotel and Casino there was a bunch of bronc riders visiting and telling rerun stories. David Bothum stepped out and called my name and when I walked over to them David said, "This is the guy who loaned me the rooster so I could win the Wild Ride I was telling you about." David thanked me again for the use of the rooster and offered to buy me a drink. I turned down the drink, but I thanked him for remembering me and my rooster.

RONN WARR
A WEEK I'LL NEVER FORGET

I am very honored that you would ask me to send you a rodeo story for your next book. Thank you. Just a little background about me I started riding bareback broncs and bulls when I was 16, and saddle broncs at 17 in Little Britches Rodeos in Colorado back in 1959. I did pretty good, winning really good in the bareback and saddle bronc, but not so much in the bull riding.

Once I turned 18 I couldn't ride the junior rodeos anymore so I thought I was good enough to ride in the RCA (now PRCA). I got my permit and was gonna, "Go down the road and make my mark." That's another story in itself. I did ride for 20 years before I retired at age 36 for the first time. I wasn't the best bronc rider in the bunch, but I did win a few bareback and bronc ridings along the way. The story that might make a good one for your next book (actual account of the way it happened).

At the California Cowboy's Professional Association's (CCPRA) year end awards banquet in Red Bluff, California (around '76 or '77) I can't remember for sure, a number of our

Nevada cowboy friends invited us to a sanctioned rodeo in Tonopah, Nevada in the middle of November. It was a 2 day rodeo.

You never know for sure what the weather will be at the time, but the forecast was to be only overcast cloudy skies. My wife and I dropped our very young daughter off at Lake Tahoe with her parents and headed for Tonopah. As predicted the weather was cool and cloudy.

The rodeo started about 1 p.m. and the bareback riding had started, but the weather was getting colder and it began to snow. By the time the saddle bronc riding started it was snowing hard. Why they didn't stop it then was a mystery, but they didn't. You could hardly see across the arena.

I got on my bronc and rode him till the 7 second mark and was in the air at the tooter. The judges could hardly see me because it was snowing so hard. They did mark me, but I know I had already lost a stirrup and was in the air. After he bucked me off, somehow he got out of the arena and headed out for parts unknown with my bronc saddle, rein, and halter. The pickup men gave chase, but lost him in the storm.

Needless to say, at that time they cancelled the rest of the performance. Who knew if I would ever see my gear again. That night in town we went to one of the local restaurants for dinner where all the cowboys were and everyone in the place knew who I was when I walked in. They knew I was the bronc rider who lost his saddle in the storm so they all bought my wife and I drinks and dinner and started to take up a collection so I could buy a new saddle.

The next morning the storm had passed and we went to the rodeo grounds to see what was going to happen. They told me they had bad news and good news. The bad was, they saw the bronc, but he was way up on one of the hills above Tonopah. The good news was, my saddle was still on him, but was under his belly. I could just imagine what kind of shape it would be in.

We had to head back to California that morning and one

of my bull riding friends said if they could catch the horse he would bring my saddle back to me when he came to see his sister at Thanksgiving as she just lived about 15 miles from me. John called me and said they got the horse and my saddle back and surprisingly it was in good shape, but muddy. My halter was ok, too, but my rein was about 2 feet shorter. It sure was good to get everything back. That was quite a weekend. One, I'll never forget.

JAN BARBY PAYNE
ARKANSAS CITY, KANSAS

During the VEE outbreak, we were putting on a rodeo in Arkansas City, Kansas. We had just come about 18 miles north of the Oklahoma border from putting on a rodeo in Newkirk, Oklahoma. Timed event entries were low because many contestants were stuck in other states. Most contractors have a certain following and usually we were not light in any event and Daddy was able to run a pretty even show.

However, this weekend was going to be a challenge. Blackie Williams, our dear friend who drove a truck for Daddy as well as served as pickup man, decided that the Barby Rodeo crew could fill in the empty spots. Blackie was a brother in law to Eddie Akridge and JR Akridge and had hauled with them as well as with Casey Tibbs. That should tell you he wasn't a timed event man, but he thought he could at least run a steer in the steer wrestling and he said he just wouldn't get down on him. If you knew Blackie you knew his size would have crushed the steer and probably torn Blackie's knees as well

Anyway, his wife Ruby was taking entries so he entered a few of our hands up in the team roping and he entered in the bull doggin'. The barrel racing was where it was the shortest. I did have a barrel horse and did enter most of daddy's rodeos so Blackie entered me with my barrel horse, but he also entered me under several other names with the great idea that the guys would have different horses ready for me and I could change horses.

The horses were the pickup horses. I never worried about this because if Daddy and Blackie thought it would work, I would do it....take one for the team type deal. All was going great until they started loading the bulls and the last time I went around the pattern I was on a big horse we called Mocho. We got through the first barrel fine, actually the best first barrel of even my trained barrel horse. We got to the second barrel and Mocho saw those bulls and stopped right in his "usual" place and started prancing side to side.

I couldn't get him to even look at the barrels no matter what I tried. I was getting pretty embarrassed I will have to admit. I just wanted to die because I was about 15 or 16 probably, the age where everything embarrasses you. The announcer did a great job of trying to cover up, but really what can you say? Anyway, Mocho did not budge and I had to get off of that old scutter and lead him through the out gate and Blackie put his saddle back on him and back out into the arena for the bull riding.

MONTY PENNY
YELLOW JACKET

At Fort Worth, Texas in 1972, as I was walking in front of the bucking chutes Reg Kesler hollers out, "Anybody want to get on a bull?" I looked up at him and said, "Yeah, I would." He looked at me and said, "Damn, son. You ain't got any spurs on." I said, "I don't need any spurs." So, I got me a gate rope and climbed up on the chute. He said, "Son, do you know what this bull is?" I said, "Yeah. It's Yellow Jacket." He said, "Yeah, and he bucked off Randy Magers just two performances ago."

Me, being the cocky little prick that I was, said, "He don't ride as good as I do. Can I borrow one of your gloves?" As he was peeling off his leather work glove, he said, "Hell, yeah. I gotta see this." He didn't buck me off and I rode him about 7 seconds and just stepped off on the ground. When I walked back to Reg, I thanked him for the use of his glove and handed it back to him. He said, "Boy, you're gonna be somebody." I said, "That would be what I got in mind," and just turned and walked off.

JOE LILES
JUST ANOTHER DAY ON THE ROAD

Gordon Stone and I were in the middle of a rodeo run in Colorado, Kansas, and Nebraska. We got to the next rodeo which was at the fair grounds where the arena was inside the race track and was mostly a big grass covered area. We were sleeping in the camper in the middle of the night when we were woke up by gunfire all around us and yelling and car lights going everywhere.

We could hear a voice saying, "There he is—get him!" and more gun shots. Gordon said, "Joe, go out there and see what's happening," and I said, "I'm not going out there." So, we crawled under the bed and finally the noise stopped and we went back to sleep.

The next morning we got u and climbed out of the camper and there were dead rabbits everywhere. Those drunk cowboys had been shooting rabbits. Just another day on the road.

Many years ago I dropped in Mr. Kelly's bar for a beer and the place was empty, but the owner was sitting at the bar reading a small book. A friend had sent him the original Turtle Association rule book that was published around 1945.

He was reading a section of the book titles, "Inactive members due to military service. On that list were some of the most famous rodeo cowboys in the sport. Yes, cowboys were quick to answer the call. Always have been, always will be.

If you don't like your draw just wait as fate may step in and give you a break. At the Springerville rodeo in 1977 I drew a no-good, lungin', duckin', divin', arm jerker and was waiting in the morning slack to get on him. The horses were lined up in a long alley to be loaded in the chute when my draw started fighting and throwing a fit and finally jumped out of the alley and ran off.

I reported it to the stock contractor and after looking at what horses were in the alley, he said, "Go ahead and get on that Paint and he pointed him out to me. I asked him what the horse was and he said, "He's the Navajo Nation Association bareback horse of the year. Well, I ended up splitting first on him and left with a big grin on my face. What had started out as a bad day turned into a pretty damned good one.

Shortly after I soloed I started flying to rodeos and logging it as "touch and go," practice. On Monday mornings when I met my flight instructor she would check my log book and say, "So, you're telling me you practiced touch and go for three hours?" Then, she would grin and said, "Did you win…?"

BUBBY BOYD
GOD BLESS MUSCLES BOYD

My name is Bubba Boyd and yes, I am the son of Robert "Muscles" Boyd, the 1999 Texas Rodeo Cowboy Hall of fame inductee. I myself rode bulls competitively for over 20 years and have tons of rodeo stories that could be told. I'm sure I could narrow it down to one and some pretty good times could be relived. There is one common factor that stands out in almost all of my memories; this factor of course is my dad, Muscles.

From the time I was just a young boy riding steers every single chance I got all the way up to my adult years, he was there. He and I went to a ton of youth rodeos together; really we went to all of the ones that were close enough of a drive. We became more than father and son, we became traveling partners. Amongst numerous life lessons, he told me lots of rodeo stories; stories about him and all kinds of cowboys. His old traveling partner Carl Satterfield was a regular guest in the stories he told.

One of my favorite stories was listening to him recount the time he traveled with the Steiner family as he worked the barrel for Buck Steiner for numerous years. Sometimes when my dad would break out the whiskey he would sing old cowboy songs along our journey to each destination. He was quite the character and there was darn sure never a dull moment. He was my best friend and he never allowed me not to always try my best. When he felt like I wasn't putting forth enough effort he was never shy about letting me know it. He always said, "That's what good traveling partners do."

He was very supportive to me and extremely supportive to many cowboys including Roger Davis, Bo Davis, Brent Thurman, Jim Bob Stoebner, Spot Stoebner, Larry Godwin, Ricky Levy, Larry Turner, and Mel Kimbro- just to name a few. My dad always made sure a guy had his entry fees and he expected half the winnings of course, but a cowboy always had a chance if my dad was there.

On numerous occasions several of them might travel with us from Texas to Oklahoma. If Muscles wasn't there to go with me, which was rare, he always made sure that I was in good hands. He liked for me to be around the cowboys who were winning money so I was able to rodeo with some of the best cowboys Texas has to offer. I went to the smallest of jackpots in Texas to the biggest events in the country. I enjoyed riding bulls and I loved making my dad proud.

When I was 17 years old, a junior in high school, I rode in the Super Bull and was invited to return again the next year. I was awarded a rodeo scholarship to attend Hill College, all thanks to Brian Herman who vouched for me to the rodeo coach at the college. I lived with and learned from the best including Brent Thurman and Andy Carey and I was given an opportunity to do what I loved.

Some guys make it big in the rodeo business and some of us just go to a bunch of them. Never the less, I wouldn't trade a second of every experience I had for a 'gold buckle'. My dream was like every bull rider's dream, to be a World Champion and for me that day just never came. One day in my later years of riding I was going from Fort Worth to a rodeo in Vivian, Louisiana. It was one heck of a drive and Muscles loaded up with me like he always did. On our drive we got to talking and I asked him why he was still willing to continue to go with me, especially since I wasn't winning that much.

He thought about it for a minute and then he said, "Well I'll tell ya why son. Sometimes when we go and you got one drawn that everyone there, including me, knows there's no way you can ride him- you do the impossible and get the job done. I don't want to miss that, ever. That's why I go."

There ain't a gold buckle in the world that could ever replace the feeling of hearing those words and what they meant to me. So, no, I never reached the ultimate goal of World Champion, but I darn sure got to fulfill my dream; the dream of being a rodeo cowboy just like my dad. God bless Muscles Boyd.

VIRGIL INGRAM
RODEO HAS ALWAYS BEEN IN MY BLOOD

I started riding bulls in 1980. Rodeo has always been in my blood. I grew up around it and I'm a third generation cowboy. I have uncles and great uncles who competed when I was growing up. One of my late great uncles James Ford roped calves. Joe Ford could do every event, but I never got to see him compete because he died before I was born.

Billy Ford was chute boss for more than thirty years at Kowbell Indoor Rodeo, Mansfield Texas. He also was as a good calf roper and he passed those skills on to his son Billy Jr. better known as Bud Ford. Bud qualified for the NFR in 1995 and ended up sixth in the world. And there is also B.F. Ford who lives out in Kemp, Texas and he was a pick up man for many years. He worked for the Lightning C Rodeo Company.

My Uncles Rookie and Timmy Brooks were the two who were tough to beat. They won everything you can imagine in high school and afterwards Rookie was a bull rider and bullfighter. He retired around 2010. Timmy roped calves and bull dogged and he still competes at the age of 57.

As a kid I hung around them a lot and wanted to do what they did. My bullriding career lasted 12 years and I rode in the high school associations an a few AJRA Rodeos, but unlike my uncles I wasn't a natural at it and in my high school years I wasn't that good. I'd win every now and then, but not enough to make it to any Finals. It wasn't until after high school that I was finally starting to figure it out.

I attended two of Gary Leffew's bull riding schools in 1987. I was riding 80 percent of my bulls and folks would ask me why I didn't get my permit and buy a card and my answer was because I got hurt to often, which was true. I was hurt 40 percent of my career, dislocating my shoulder 23 times, reconstructive surgery on my cheek bone, broken ankle, and a horn in my leg and one under my arm and I had stitches from my head to my feet. So, I chose to rodeo close to home, riding bulls in Texas and Oklahoma.

In the summer of 1991 my uncle Rookie asked me to go on a summer run with him. He didn't travel with just anyone. You had to be a rider. I've seen guys draw out of the bull riding because he was entered, and some stock contractors even hated to see him show up. So, we hit the road that summer following Terry Walls, Freddy Cordell, and Mitt Lloyd and we were having a great time. He was winning and I was winning and every thing was great, but after about three months of just going and going it started to wear me down.

We were entered in Azle, Texas, and when we showed up and paid our fees and were walking back to the car to get our rigging bags I just stopped in my tracks and said, "Rookie, man, I'm tired of this and after tonight, I'm done."

He said, "You're crazy. You're riding too good to quit now" I said, "I know, but it has gotten boring." That night he won first and I won third and when we got home I tossed my bag in the closest and didn't look at for a long time. Back then I had a job making ropes for Johnny Emmons Rope Company at Mansfield, Texas ,and that was the coolest job ever because all the employees either rodeoed or had at one time or another and you set your own hours.

It had been almost a year since I had been on a bull and I was missing it a little bit and one day a co-worker Mickey Lewallen from Grand Prairie,Texas who was a good bull rider said to me, "Vern, they got this new bull at the dome and you should go get on. Dome is what we called the Kowbell Rodeo because of its shape and I said, "No, I'm good."

But, he kept after me for about la month and I finally did and it was sweet. It was a nice little bull. He took two jumps out and went into a spin to the right into my hand. About the third round I opened up on him and he was all mine for the long haul. After I got off some cowboy that I never met came up to me and was so impressed that he offered to pay my fees in the jackpot that night. I said, "No, thanks, but that's not why I'm here."

Well, needless to say he pressured me into it and paid my fees and told me who he was and how much he liked my ride. Little did he know I wasn't listening to a word he said as I was so caught up in the moment of riding that last one. I drew a bull named Mission Impossible, so I ask my uncle Billy what he was and he said, "He ain't been rode." I said, "Well, OK, I guess I'll be the first," so I went back to the back pens and found him. He was a little red short horned bull that weighed about 1500 lbs. and from what I gathered he would kick out of the chute real hard and fade to the left and then spin to the right ninety to nothing.

After all the preparation he was in chute two and it was my

turn. I crawled over on him, went through the procedures, slid up and nodded. When they opened the gate he and did just what they said he would and kicked outta there hard. Well, the gate men didn't open the gate wide enough so my toe hung in the slate as I was coming out and that was a foul but I was still in good shape so I kept riding instead of declaring myself and about 7 seconds into the ride he took my rope and bucked me off.

But, that night I got the fever again and was rearing to go. The following weekend I went back to the dome and enter the jackpot and won it, so I'm thinking, "Hell yeah, here I go again." I entered the dome the next Saturday night and ran into Johnny Uselton, a well known bull rider and stock producer. He asked me what I'd drawn and I said, "Honker."

I was the first one to get on this bull when they had brought him there 4 years earlier when he belonged to Mickey Shirley He fouled me on the gate, but they wouldn't give me a re-ride. Well, this time it would be different. I had been looking forward to this re-match and I'd been studying him all these years and he hadn't gotten any bigger or stronger, but had been bucking off a lot of good hands.

I crawled on him and Johnny pulled my rope and my heart was racing as fast as a jack rabbit. When I took my wrap and slid up Johnny slapped me on my back real hard and said, "Bare down and ride this SOB, Vern," and that's exactly what I did and it was the best ride I'd ever made. After about 5 seconds or so he took my rope to the tips of fingers and I remember saying to myself, "Don't open your hand." When the whistle blew it felt like I had just won the world even before my feet hit the ground. I rode him and won the bullriding.

After it was over Johnny comes to me and says, "Vern, you wanna go on a summer run?" So, here we go again, Johnny, his son, Jay, and myself took off for a few rodeos and followed the Roland Reid and Torti Rodeo Company. We were all riding good, but we weren't winning any money. We entered the Forth of July

Rodeo at Denton, Texas and I drew the bull they were winning it on from the night before. I'm thinking, "Hell, yeah. That's just right. I need to win some money."

He was #10, a light colored Brindle muley cross and belonged to Torti Rodeo Company. He went out there about three jumps, really getting some air then started spinning to the left. I rode him and thought it was at least an 81 or 82 point bull ride. They were winning the riding on this bull with an 84, but they gave me a 72. Unbelievable, but without raising any hell we just packed up our gear and headed home again with no money.

On the way home I ask Johnny where we were going next and he said, "I'm going to take the next weekend off." I told him I was going somewhere because although I hadn't won any money I hadn't bucked off either, so I called a couple guys to see what they had going for the following weekend and they were all booked up. I thought, "When all else fails, go to Kowbell." When I entered they told me I'd drawn "Wolf-Wolf." I had always wanted to draw him and had watched him for about two years.

I crawled on him, went through the procedure and nodded my head. Wolf-Wolf jumped out like he was shot out of a rocket, but I had a good seat up until the 7th or 8th jump when I felt my free arm pop out of socket. When that happened there was nothing I could do and he jerked me down and I hung to him and he made a mess out of me. I finally got free and was helped out the arena. I'm standing there in pain so I asked John Teague and Cory Turnbow if either of them would drive me to the ER? They said, "Hell no. We're goin to the bar." Well, some guy I didn't even know drove me in my car and his girlfriend follow us in his car. He dropped me off handed me my keys and said, "Hope your OK, Dude." What's so funny about that is me and that guy, Colby Colburn, became good friends and became co–workers shortly after that.

Well, that happened July 11, 1992 and that night I hung up my rope for 23 years. After my bull riding career ended I started fighting bulls and that lasted for 9 years. I really loved fighting bulls. I was good at it and I believe it was because I rode them and that gave me good bull sense. I knew what was gonna happen before it happened, so I was always at the right place at the right time.

Well, it was on July 1st 1995 when my bullfighting career came to a halt. I was working a rodeo in Jackson, Mississippi when a rider got hung up. I was working with Jason Gibbs, an outstanding bullfighter who now fights in the PBR. I got the flank and he got the rider free and just as I was stepping out of the storm the bull just so happened to be turning the same way and I was sitting on his head and when he bucked again and in the kick he threw his head up and launched me about 20 feet into the air. I landed flat on my back and dislocated my shoulder again and fractured my pelvic.

So, again, I'm done. I go and watch a few bull ridings, but I still wasn't interested in competing again until I went to watch a Senior Pro Bull Riding around 2010. I saw guys that I hadn't seen in several years and I was in awe that they were still competing. At this time I was 45 yrs old and I started going to a few of those shows just watching Johnny Uselton, the last guy I traveled with before I retired and a few other guys I'd rodeod with.

Well, now it's 2014 and I've been watching these guys and they keep putting pressure on me. One night my phone rang and it was Troy Moseley, a good friend and reserve World Champion and also President of the WSPBRA. He said, "Hey, Virg. You want to go the WSPBRA Finals with me?" I agreed and that was all it took to get that fire burning inside of me again.

As I was getting ready for my bull, last year's World Champion Robert Mimms came over to me and asked how long has it been since I'd competed and I told him twenty-three years. He asked if I was ready for this and I said, "I'll let you know in a few minutes." A couple of bulls bucked, then the next guy out was Robert Mimms. His bull was nasty and threw everything but the kitchen sink at him, but he managed to win that fight and that gave me a little bit of fire.

Now, it's my turn so I crawled down on him and everything was just right. He wasn't too big or too small and he stood nicely in chute. I stuck my hand in my rope and nodded and he blew out of the chute one jump, two jumps and my left foot came up behind me and that's all I recall. The next thing I remember was standing in front of my rigging bag and all my stuff was still inside.

I said, "They're not gonna let me ride?" Troy was standing behind me and he said, "Dude, you already rode. You got knocked out, hung up, and stepped on." I had seven broken ribs and a punctured lung. One of the EMTs heard the conversation walked over to me and asked me if I felt OK. I told her I did and she said, "Do you know where you are?" I said, "Yeah, I'm in Arkansas." The EMT said, "No, but you're close." From then on when I show up at a bull riding I'm known as Little Rock. But, I made history by coming out retirement and going back into it faster than anyone in the history of bull riding.

DARRYL CHESTNUT
ONE JUMPED

Back in the late 80's I traveled around with some boys around Salina, Kansas and we usually all hung out at a country bar in Salina called Rangers. I had met a girl in there one night and of course she fell in love. I didn't have time for that kind of nonsense so she kinda became a stalker of sorts.

We were all up at Burlingame, Kansas that weekend so we always took a van to the rodeos and from time to time some of the guys would take their true loves along. This girl begged and begged to go along and I put her off time and time again. I knew a lot of people in this bar I mentioned and she tried like hell asking everyone if they were going and could she go.

Many knew this girl was hard to lose and she wasn't having

much luck finding a ride. We went on to the rodeo and I never even thought about it again. I was in the bareback riding and most the guys I was with were in the bullriding. So, I was getting ready and the other boys were messing around and while I was putting my rigging on my horse, Dennis walked up and told me while he was getting a pop he talked to a girl from Salina that was friends with this girl and she told him that she was going to be here.

I never gave it a second thought and was getting ready to ride when I heard a small plane and it sounded like it landed somewhere real close. This girl worked at an airport fuel stop and had many friends with planes. Anyhow, I was in the chute and started to hear a lot of laughing behind the chutes from the guys I came there with I looked over and there was that girl standing on a fence behind the sorting pens. I got one jumped and never lived it down about that lil gal flying to a small rodeo just to see me.

SCOTT FLETCHER
ME AND KIRK ALLMON

Me and Kirk Allmon were entered at Mineral Wells, Texas and had left Durant with plenty of time to get there. The sky seemed to be getting darker with each mile we traveled and it began to rain on us. Not normal rain, I'm talkin torrential. It was really dark now and the wind was blowing hard. As we past a rest area not far from town we saw a motor home that had flipped over onto the boat it was pulling. What the heck!

When we pulled into the rodeo arena someone told us there had been a tornado and that the Friday performance had been moved to Sunday afternoon so we headed back, but not to Durant. We were gonna stay in Dallas at Bobby Delveccio's and Mike Hudson's apartment. It was still raining terribly.

At that time I owned a1977 Lincoln Continental, one of those really square ones if you remember the model. Anyway, we were between Ft. Worth and Dallas when we ran into a whole lot of water in the road and began to hydroplane and kinda drifted into the other lane. Running beside us was an 18 wheeler pulling a lowboy flatbed. Yep, we hit him and that's when the wild ride started. There was a guard rail there to keep us out of the median, but when I tagged that trailer it put us into a spin between the big rig and the rail. It all happened pretty fast, but at the same time it was all in slow motion.

Kirk said that I was giving him a blow by blow of the exchanges made between us, the trailer, and the guard rail, as we went spinning down the highway. I finally got that 'ol Lincoln back in control and eased it off on the shoulder. I look over at Kirk and he was a little pale to say the least.

Praise God, the only thing that happened was Kirk hit the rear view mirror and left a clump of his blonde hair where he cracked it. The truck driver stopped to check on us and he kept telling me what a good job I had done handling that car, but I think he was just trying to make me feel better.

His passenger was a young woman singer who had just recorded a record. She gave me a copy of it, an 8 track tape, where she signed her name and personalized it with,"To Scott. A hit." They left and me and Kirk was just standing there lookin' at my car, a car that once had nice, sharp, square features that now looked more like an egg, but it still ran.

So, we took off and spent a couple of days in Dallas and went back to Mineral Wells Sunday afternoon. I won some money on Steiner's Bad Scene and went back to Durant. Lookin' back, I see where God has had His hand on me and Kirk too all our lives. Something that could have ended so tragically is now one of our funniest stories.

JAN BARBY PAYNE
Lloyd Barby Rodeo
RAMBLINGS

Daddy had this little muley Hereford bull he called #75. He was tiny, but certainly had little man syndrome if I ever saw it. He was just so cute, but when he left the chute he would buck and if he had the chance he would maul around on his rider. He wouldn't hurt anyone, but just had to get that mauling in Daddy and Jim Shoulders were quite good friends and Jim was contracted to do the Boy Scouts Rodeo in Amarillo, Texas for many years.

Actually, they just used Jim's name to get an attendance so we would pick Jim up at the airport and Daddy would provide the stock. Jim always wanted to make sure Daddy was bringing #75 and he would always try to buy him. I think there were several that just liked his little character. We got so attached to our bulls and horses and they provided for us a lifestyle and friends that wouldn't have been possible otherwise.

Rodeo was something Daddy always loved, but never was a competitor. I think that is the amazing part of what a great contractor he was and what a good rodeo he ran especially from not ever being a contestant. San Antonio was another bucking horse that was special to us. She was just a solid mare, one Daddy could depend on and you can't say that for lots of those mares.

State Trooper was a big Brahmer bull that wasn't one the rankest ones we had, but he would usually buck hard enough to get them on the ground before the eight seconds. Kenny Wilcox said he'd seen this picture in a newspaper back east of our youngest daughter Abby feeding State Trooper. She'd stand up in the back of the pickup and call his name and State Trooper would leave the herd and walk over to her and she'd feed him by hand. He told us Bobby Del Vecchio said, "I saw that little girl feed that bull at a college rodeo and it gave me chills because I'd seen him buck the night before."

**Abby and her pet.
Lloyd Barby Rodeo bull, State Trooper**

Daddy and his brother Stanley built an arena east of the house. It had a roping chute for Uncle Stanley who became quite a contender in the calf roping as well as team roping. Daddy put in three bucking chutes. Before we started really going down the road providing stock Daddy would put on a, "Buck out at the Barbys," as it was known around Beaver, Oklahoma every Tuesday night.

Daddy's sister Bonita and her husband L.W. owned the local Tastee Freez and they also had a little mobile concession stand. They would bring that out, plug it in and sell concessions. People would park all around the arena for an evening of a little roping, some bareback riding (which at that time were the saddle horses) and some bull riding (which were our cows). Daddy even had some calf riding for the young kids. It was the summer entertainment.

Daddy was co-owner of the Livestock Sale and the sales were on Wednesday. If we had a Thursday, Friday and Saturday rodeo, many times the guys that had worked at the sale the day before, those that had CDL's, would more than likely haul cattle to as far as away as Dalhart or Wellington, Texas and then come home and start loading stock to head off for the rodeo as soon as they all got home.

Daddy and Mother were strong Christians and tee teetotlers. Daddy served as elder in the First Christian Church and Mother was a deaconess for many years and they were faithful servants until their deaths. With that being said, it didn't take long for those that respected them to abstain at least until they got away from them. Most of the boys didn't drink around them. Many cowboys have also told me of times that Daddy had gotten on to them for their foul mouths. Those have shared that were a testimony to Daddy and Mother. It makes my heart swell with pride.

RED DOYAL
DENVER, FIRST TIME AROUND

Two young, hot shot bareback riders were going to the rodeo in Denver for the first time. They were pretty proud of themselves that they had made it to the Pros. and being part of such an historical event. After getting all settled in at the Mayflower Hotel and having a few beers the two of them decided to go check out the college life that was going on in downtown Denver.

Having a couple of altercations which they took care of very easily, they returned to the Mayflower Hotel. After a few more beers they once again decided to make it three in a row as being victorious so they made the decision to invite an individual out to the side street to accomplish their mission.

Now, coming into the picture was a gentleman by the name of Darrel Herman. Darrel was six foot tall and had an eyebrow that was half white and half black. I had known Darrel from going to rodeos in New Mexico and Arizona and everyone knew not to mess with Darrel Herman. However, obviously Clyde and Paul did not know him.

Soon after the fight started Darrel knocked Clyde over backwards right into a big snow bank, covering him with snow. Paul rushed to his side and assisted him in getting back on his feet and giving Clyde some encouragement by telling him, "You can take him, Clyde."

A short time later Clyde was back in the snow bank, face down. Paul rubbed snow on his face and once again told him, "Get up Clyde, you can handle him." Clyde just lay there almost freezing to death and quietly tried to convince Paul to just leave him alone. "I'm not getting back up," he said, and ended the story with, "WELCOME TO DENVER and HELLO, DARREL HERMAN."

JOHN VIC
1984

It was 106 degrees and I was at the Georgetown, Texas, rodeo when I was volunteered to do a clown act where I would get into the barrel and be turned into a young girl in a bikini. So, I stuffed myself into the barrel where a girl was hiding and a top was placed over the hole. It was so hot in there that my makeup melted off onto the only place I had room to put my face and when she popped out of the barrel people started laughing, not at the act, but at the imprint of my face on her bosom. I was the hero of the day.

My good pal, said, "Good story, Jon, 106 degrees? It doesn't sound like you were having a bad day. Are you sure your makeup melted or did it rub off?" I told him, "I have a wife. It melted off. It really did. It had to be around 112 degrees in that barrel and at the time I thought I was going to pass out. It was the hottest rodeo I ever worked. All the people sat on the shady side of the bleachers. It was more like a sauna steam bath and I really did come close to passing out…but, it was all in fun."

In 1984 I was fighting bulls and would often team up with Lange Spence. Lange and I had a deep trust that no words can hold and we would go out of our ways to work the same rodeos. At Rockdale, Texas on a Friday night we had about fifty bull riders up and had a few bumps and hooks, but no big deals. We hung around till about one thirty the next morning and packed the barrel and gear, setting out for home.

Lange and I both lived in Round Rock, Texas at this time. Lange had a bad habit of nodding off behind the wheel, but I would gently reach over keep us on the rode and give him a nudge, everything normal.

We passed through Thorndale and somewhere between Thorndale and Taylor, Lange and I saw a fire. Lange said, "I think a house is on fire." When we came closer to view, sure enough an old white farmhouse was on fire. Lange found the dirt road entrance and at high speed we headed towards the house. I said not a word.

We reached the house to find two volunteers from Thorndale with a pump truck and an old couple standing around watching as the fire at the rear of the house began to spread. The volunteers said the Taylor Fire Department was in route, but Lange was not going to wait so he took charge.

With me and a volunteer on one hose and Lange and a volunteer on the other, we started fighting the blaze. At some point Lange said, "Let's move to the front of the house and push the fire out the rear so we did. That move seemed to work as we were actually pushing the fire back.

The Taylor Fire Department arrived at about this point and we were more than happy to turn the job over to the Pro's and they had the fire out within an hour and a half. The back of the house was lost, but the front was saved. As we climbed into the truck no one even asked who we were so we headed for home.

Somewhere out of Round Rock, Lange nodded off and again I gently gave him a nudge to keep us on the road. We arrived at my house about three forty in the morning and Lange said, "See ya, tomorrow." I never gave the incident another thought, but how many can say they fought 50 bulls and a house fire all in the same night. It's just another day in the life of a rodeo bull fighter.

DENNIS MERRELL
KOWBELL

One Friday night I was heading to Kowbell and saw a dead snake in the road at Cedar Hill. I stopped and put it in the back of my pickup and when I got to Kowbell I propped the snake's mouth open with a toothpick. Then I tied a fishing line around its neck and curled him up at front of truck bed and ran string to the rear of truck.

Later, when we all got to gathering around my truck and was talking and such, Shotgun Brooks wandered over to get in on the conversation. I waited until he noticed the snake and then I jerked the string making the snake jump at him with its open mouth and things got pretty exciting.

ABOUT THE AUTHOR

Chimp Robertson has been a rodeo contestant, rancher, private pilot, auctioneer, song writer (songs recorded by Chris LeDoux), Texas and Oklahoma Real Estate Salesman/Broker, skydiver, and U.S. Army Veteran.

Chimp has had articles, poems, and stories published in various publications including the Western Horseman, Horse Lover's, Hoofs and Horns, Cattleman, Yamaha World, Farm Journal, Paint Horse, and Horseman magazines. His other books include:

- **Killin' Time** (A Collection of Short Stories)
- **POW/MIA: America's Missing Men** (The Men We Left Behind in Vietnam)
- **Mortal Secrets** (A Mystery Novel)
- **I'll Be Seeing You** (A Battle with Cancer)
- **Tall Tales and Short Stories** (A Family Legacy)
- **Rodeo Stories** (A Collection of True Cowboy Tales)

Raised in Dalhart, Texas he is retired and currently living in Hooker, Oklahoma where he is pumping wells, driving combines, working at a feedlot and team roping.

Contact: www.chimprobertson.com
or chimp.robertson@hotmail.com

www.ingramcontent.com/pod-product-compliance
Lightning Source LLC
Chambersburg PA
CBHW071137160426
43196CB00011B/1921